The England No One Cares About

Sonics Series

Atau Tanaka, editor

Sonic Agency: Sound and Emergent Forms of Resistance, Brandon LaBelle

Meta Gesture Music: Embodied Interaction, New Instruments and Sonic Experience, Various Artists (CD and online)

Inflamed Invisible: Collected Writings on Art and Sound, 1976–2018, David Toop

Teklife / Ghettoville / Eski: The Sonic Ecologies of Black Music in the Early 21st Century, Dhanveer Singh Brar

Dissonant Waves: Ernst Schoen and Experimental Sound in the 20th Century, Sam Dolbear and Esther Leslie

New for 2024

Take This Hammer: Work, Song, Crisis, Paul Rekret

Ruins and Resilience: The Longevity of Experimental Film, Karel Doing

Building a Voice: Sound, Surface, Skin, Zeynep Bulut

Goldsmiths Press's Sonics series considers sounds as media and as material – as physical phenomenon, social vector, or source of musical affect. The series maps the diversity of thinking across the sonic landscape, from sound studies to musical performance, from sound art to the sociology of music, from historical soundscapes to digital musicology. Its publications encompass books and extensions to traditional formats that might include audio, digital, online and interactive formats. We seek to publish leading figures as well as emerging voices, by commission or by proposal.

The England No One Cares About

Lyrics from Suburbia

George Musgrave

Goldsmiths Press

Copyright © 2024 Goldsmiths Press
First published in 2024 by Goldsmiths Press
Goldsmiths, University of London, New Cross
London SE14 6NW

Printed and bound by Short Run Press Limited, UK
Distribution by the MIT Press
Cambridge, Massachusetts, USA and London, England

Text copyright © 2024 George Musgrave

The right of George Musgrave to be identified as the author of this work has been asserted by him in accordance with sections 77 and 78 in the Copyright, Designs and Patents Act 1988.

Every effort has been made to trace copyright holders and to obtain their permission for the use of copyright material. The publisher apologises for any errors or omissions and would be grateful if notified of any corrections that should be incorporated in future reprints or editions of this book.

All Rights Reserved. No part of this publication may be reproduced, distributed or transmitted in any form or by any means whatsoever without prior written permission of the publisher, except in the case of brief quotations in critical articles and review and certain non-commercial uses permitted by copyright law.

A CIP record for this book is available from the British Library

ISBN 978-1-913380-66-3 (hbk)
ISBN 978-1-913380-65-6 (ebk)

www.gold.ac.uk/goldsmiths-press

Goldsmiths
UNIVERSITY OF LONDON

Contents

1	**Finding England**	1
	English Spatial Imaginings	1
	Where Are the Suburbs? What Is Suburbia?	5
	Knowing by Doing	17
	Goals	25
2	**Who Do We Think We Are? 'Context' in Context**	30
	George & Edith	31
	George & Victoria	35
	George & Charlotte	39
	My Story: Class and Identity	53
3	**What Stories Do, Why Stories Matter**	62
	Stories and Identity	63
	Life Stories as Relational Stories	69
	Rap and Storytelling: Technologies of the Self	77
	Conclusion: The Flames on the Ceiling	80
4	**Lyrics, Truth, and Ethnography**	84
	The Truth, the Whole Truth, and Nothing but the Truth?	85
	The (Lyric) Book of Revelations	90
	Rap as Ethnography?	94
5	**Small Town Lad Sentiments**	105
	Small Town Lad Sentiments	107
	20Something	108
	This Is Us	109
	Long Way from Nowhere	110
	1.4 at 12	111
	I Can't Kickflip Anymore	112
	Stretch	114
	Afghan Letters	115
	Choose Lager	117
	Being 21 Goes	119

6	**Dreaming from the Margins**	122
	Possibility and Ambition	123
	Work and the Future	128
	Masculinity and Violence	137
	Recognition and Remembrance	142
7	**Based on a True Story**	152
	'Represent, Represent'	152
	A Vignette on Peripherality	160
	Writing the Narrative Self	164
	Bibliography	171
	Index	205

*There are moments where it feels like he's
just passing on what really gets talked about.
You can't fake that sort of thing.*

                                    Mike Skinner (The Streets) about Context (Cragg, 2013)

Middle England's Poet Laureate

                                    MistaJam (BBC Radio 1Xtra, 2013) about Context

1

Finding England

English Spatial Imaginings

There are many Englands: all stereotypes, oversimplifications and abstractions, but revealing nonetheless. I know each of these Englands personally. Some of them are close friends I love fondly, some are embarrassing uncles best avoided, and others are the dearly departed, remembered wistfully. There is the bucolic countryside of village greens, pubs which still sell proper pies, and housing split between cottages with thatched roofs and miniature doorways for some and Barrett new-builds with miniature windows for others; of walks through stiles dodging cow pats, 'good mornings' from strangers, cricket on Sundays with cheap cider sold from makeshift bars in the village halls of childhood birthday parties, dry Women's Institute Victoria-sponge cake sales, ploughman's lunches, old Barbour jackets and new Hunter wellies; of smoking borrowed roll-ups of Golden Virginia in village bus stops where buses never come on boring Sundays before you learn to drive and can borrow your Mum's car; of post office gossip, village schools with patchy Ofsted reports where you sing 'Oil in my Lamp' and 'Lord of the Dance' in assemblies sat cross-legged on the floor, and where chip vans come on Wednesdays. As so wonderfully captured by scholar of literature Roger Ebbatson (2005), this is an idealised, occasionally utopian – even fetishised – *Imaginary England*: a pastoral idyll reflected (often with highly problematic implications) in literary and poetic constructions from Wordsworth's 'Daffodils' to Rossetti's 'Lambs of Grasmere'. An England which the poet Philip Larkin (2012) mournfully sees as slipping away in 'Going, Going'.

There is another England too, exemplified in the cosmopolitanism of the inner cities, embraced by some as an example of progressive, multicultural enlightenment and derided by others as the playground of a self-satisfied and self-righteous 'metropolitan elite' (Rundell, 2017). The England of pubs with copy-and-paste chalkboards selling Thai food and fashionable lagers, EU flags, and houses no one under twenty will ever grow up to own without inheritance; of Notting Hill carnival, curry miles, 24-hour off-licences, functioning public transport, and warehouse conversions with exposed bricks and themed coffee in ridiculous vessels; of expensive trainers by unpronounceable brands, pirate radio stations where the advertisements are for raves, and six-figure cars wrapped in Swarovski crystals which visit for the summer; of barber shops open at seemingly inexplicable hours, overpriced butchers, 'farmers markets' which neatly sanitise farming, efficient cocaine delivery services, and foreign languages; of confidence and brashness, towering inequality, aggression, vibrancy, and – as illustrated in work by sociologists Robin Mann and Steve Fenton (2017) – a degree of unease among those who live there about being called, or even thinking of themselves, as English.

More recently, another England has captured the attention of many, from political parties and pundits to demographers and statisticians. This is the England brought into sharp focus by the aperture lens of the Brexit vote and somewhat disparagingly categorised as 'left behind' (Goodwin and Heath, 2016; Sykes, 2018; Watson, 2018); places understood to contain the debris of globalisation and which were both framed and analysed as standing in opposition to the aforementioned England of Islington-dwelling graduates (Maronitis, 2021: 247). This is an England caricatured as broke lads in Ladbrokes where cans of Special Brew and bags of spice are consumed on decrepit benches in '60s-era brutalist shopping promenades with vanishing shopping and negligible promenading; where unemployment is inherited, food banks are banked on, and UKIP posters adorn the windows of 'two-up, two-downs' with their brickwork still blackened from – and perhaps still defined by – the Satanic mills of Blake which stand broodingly on the horizon like cruel memories. I know well or have lived in each of these parodies of England: a village in Lincolnshire when me and my little brother were boys, my first flat in Ladbroke Grove with my wife (and our home today in often-derided North London), and the Barnsley of my grandparents.

But there is another England I have lived in: the suburban England lamented by J.B. Priestley (1934: 405) as 'lacking in character, in zest, gusto, flavour, bite, drive, [and] originality'. This is, in many ways, the England I grew up in, or at least the England I came of age in. The England of driveways with two unexciting cars, housing from all the eras where architects abandoned any sense of flair, and where conversations centre on school catchment areas, the prices of appliances in John Lewis and the state of National Rail; of inconsistent street lamps on cul-de-sacs to nowhere and exaggerated accents; of late night drives to petrol stations on A roads for fags, where fake IDs are tested in Harvesters on roundabouts, and faded tracksuits and over-gelled hair line up in Toby Carverys; of two-litre bottles of White Lightning from Budgens consumed in a kids playground, smoking questionable hash from a 'mate of a mate' while wearing gloves so your Mum won't smell it on your hands. Where everyone, in their own way, is experiencing the quotidian of escape: either dreaming of escaping, or hiding having safely escaped the imagined vulgarities and vicissitudes of the 'other' Englands. The England captured so succinctly by Clive Martin (2013) in his *Vice* article entitled 'A bittersweet love letter to the London suburbs' as being 'semi-detached, semi-affluent, semi-deprived'. Much mocked. Unglamorous. Ordinary. Cultural vacuity and small c conservatism. A compromise. A hodgepodge. An apparently middling, middle-of-the-road middle England of middle-class middle-mindedness. This is the England no one really cares about.

In many ways, each of these depictions is a fantasy, conceptualised by geographer Olivier Sykes (2018: 137) as having been emphasised and emboldened in the United Kingdom's post-Brexit landscape in the nation's 'spatial imaginary and lexicon'. They are an awkward combination of cartoonish fictions, idealisations (Watkins, 2015), and, yes, uncomfortable truths from which we can derive sources of joy and meaning, but which are also weaponised in their manufacturing of otherness and the performance of power over who is, or is not, included or welcomed. They are constructions and stories pieced together from perceptions and interpretations in our collective cultural imagination, encapsulated in the kinds of poems and novels we see included as classics in GCSE or A-level poetry anthologies. The aforementioned work of Ebbatson (2005) contains perhaps the greatest example of these forms of media in constructions of England. However, they are also captured, as excellently explored by MP, academic and Co-Chair of the cross-party Suburban Taskforce Rupa Huq (2013), in more contemporary media representations such as soap operas, novels, TV programmes, films and song lyrics. This book will focus on how the final England above – English suburbia – has been represented in music, and what these representations tell us about the country those of us proud – and less proud – to call ourselves English both love and despise, but also about how we emotionally construct our understandings of the places that mean the most in our lives. I want to bring together both a sociology of English provincialism and a psychology of placemaking to interrogate the relationships between the two; after all, as the French sociologist Pierre Bourdieu (2014: 164) notes, 'sociology is, in fact, a cognitive science'. In other words, simply, I want to see if I can ascertain, or at least clarify in my own mind, what the *psychology of suburbia* is and how this conceptualisation has been represented musically, and what this representation means both in my own life and in wider society too.

To do this, I will be adopting a highly personal analytical prism given that I too have played my own small part in representing this version of England in my music and my lyrics during my career as a rapper where I performed as 'Context'. My depiction, like all depictions, is a specific depiction. It is personal, not scientific; *a* truth, not *the* truth – but a truth nonetheless derived, as subjectivities are, from my class, my upbringing, my race, the parameters of the genre of rap, and, as I will explore here, my family and the stories my family told as I grew up about who we were, who we *thought* we were, and how these stories shaped the way I saw the world. As such, I want to try and accomplish a bringing together of the popular, and my own – somewhat less popular – vision of provincial England and ask what this vision tells us about this wonderful and hugely problematic country. In doing so, I want to examine music's particular, peculiar and special role in how places are articulated, and the power lyrics might have as forms of ethnographic social and cultural representation; that is, lyrics as sources of data and information, and what they can and cannot *do* to help us reach new forms of understanding about particular geographies. Ultimately, though, more than this, this book is an examination of the power of stories. It is about the stories of England, the stories told in music and lyrics, the stories we tell ourselves about who we think we are, the stories which shape our identities, and the methodological importance of understanding stories for the subtlety they have the ability to reveal.

Where Are the Suburbs? What Is Suburbia?

A good place to begin is to ask whether we might move beyond the cognitive constructions of England conceptualised above as 'spatial imaginings', and more explicitly try and define what we mean when we talk about 'the suburbs', and more specifically how the lives of suburban inhabitants have been thought of. In the first instance a suburb refers to a (principally) residential area that is outside of, or on the periphery of, an urban metropolitan centre. Indeed, this concept of being peripheral, or what is sometimes called peripherality, is a theme I want to return to and which will become central in my analysis. A great number of the classic academic texts on where the suburbs are and the nature of suburban life come from the United States, where perhaps the grid-like structure of cities and their surrounding road networks makes the delineation of the urban centre and suburban verges easier to identify and subsequently explore. Here I am thinking of work by the sociologist Mary Baumgartner (1988) on morality and conflict resolution in the wealthy New York suburb of Hampton, the ethnographic insights of John Dorst (1989) on representations of Chadds Ford, Pennsylvania, or more recent texts focusing on the American suburbs such as those by urban historian Jon Teaford (2008), or geographers Becky Nicolaides and Andrew Wiese (2007). I do not wish here to dive too deeply into these texts as my interest is distinctly UK focused, and even more specifically *English* focused: American suburbia has its own dynamics. That being said, these texts highlight my particular areas of interest in a transatlantic context, notably the intersections between geography, perception and cognition. In other words, they highlight how the places we live come to shape not only the ways we behave, but also the ways we see and understand the world – a concept beautifully captured, in a quote often misattributed to Ernest Hemingway, in the description of the American suburbs as being places where inhabitants possess 'wide lawns and narrow minds' (Sindelar, 2016).

The idiosyncrasies of English suburbia too have a rich academic history. As unravelled by sociologist Mike Savage (2011), the development of post-war sociology and anthropology in the United Kingdom in many ways privileged the understanding of small town and suburban 'ordinariness', encapsulated in work such as Stacey Margaret's (1960) early studies of Banbury in Oxfordshire, a tradition which continues to produce impactful scholarship today such as Steve Hanson's (2014) *Small Towns, Austere Times*. However, perhaps the most famous studies of suburbia emanate from London suburbs, such as the 1960 sociological classic *Family and Class in a London Suburb* by Peter Willmott and Michael Young which compares the experiences of those living within the inner London of Bethnal Green and the outer-London suburb of Woodford. Here, differences are richly outlined between the decussation of family life and class, with close familial bonds bounded by geography present amongst working-class Bethnal Green residents contrasted with the more dispersed and fractured family lives of middle-class suburbaners. Here then, as per the other examples above, we see a sense in which the experiences of those growing up and living in suburbia are distinct, in various ways, from those in the inner cities. However, this and other studies of London suburbs such as Southall (Baumann, 1995; Nasser, 2004; Bertolani et al. 2021), Redbridge or Tooting (Watson and Saha, 2013), highlight a degree of ambiguity over the extent to which we can, as per in the United States, cleanly delineate when somewhere is a suburb and when it becomes part of the city. As cities grow and expand, their porous borders morph and subsume areas once considered suburban and amalgamate them into 'the city'. For instance, Jeremy Boulton's academic study of *A London Suburb in the Seventeenth Century* (1987) focuses on Southwark, an area now very much considered inner London, and Jeremy Whitehand's (1975) work on suburban nineteenth-century London focuses on Kensington, defining it as a suburb. However, new developments in travel, primarily railways but road networks too, would bring areas such as Southwark and Kensington into the body of inner London, and indeed today the same is taking place. The recently opened Crossrail train service (known as the Elizabeth Line) means Southall is now twenty-seven minutes away from Paddington. Likewise, the Woodford of Wilmott and Young is only twenty minutes from Bethnal Green, and Ealing – famously known as the 'Queen of the

Suburbs' (Hall, 1996) with its 'leafy avenues of lime and chestnut mix'd' from the poetry of John Betjeman (2005: 163) – is today less than twenty minutes from Bond Street.

Why does this matter? Because these London suburbs do not, I would suggest, experience the same kind of *isolation* and *cultural marginalisation* that the suburbs I grew up in do. Many of them are less than thirty minutes from a global metropolis; they are plugged-in and connected to the heart of a dynamic, diverse, culturally exciting and chaotic capital city with all of the empirically demonstrable cultural advantages that come from that proximity (Oakley et al., 2017; Brook et al., 2022) – albeit with the requisite throat clearing and clarifications that these advantages, like all advantages, are not evenly distributed nor experienced (Mckenzie, 2016, 2017). This is something I will be exploring in more detail in this book, but I find the notion that we can treat the cultural opportunities of those living in suburbs which have tube stations as comparable to *my* suburbs in Nottinghamshire, or Lincolnshire or Norfolk, which are isolated, detached and peripheral on various metrics, something of a silly suggestion. For this reason, I am rather less interested in areas of suburbia which strike me as being part of London. However, as outlined below, the London suburbs feature predictably heavily in both cultural representations of suburbia and the creative output of suburban musicians. Despite this, or indeed perhaps because of it, my music was keen to express suburban life outside of the M25 and engendered my interest in how the suburbs and their inhabitants are *thought of*. In other words, I am not interested in a cartographic delineation of where is and is not suburbia, but am instead concerned with an exploration of how place and psychology intersect alongside other forces (family history, class, etc.) to mould perceptions and perspectives.

Representations of Suburbanites

When thinking about how the suburbs, and more specifically the lives of suburbanites, have been represented in forms of popular media, without question the work of academic and MP Rupa Huq (2013) is something of a gold standard. Her work delineates what she describes as the 'powerful suburban iconography served up through popular culture' (ibid.: 6), including, as per the focus of attention in this book, music. Certainly her study, like many of the other studies of suburbanisation, has a distinct focus on London and London suburbs, but nonetheless they all offer an insightful window into thinking about the themes of my own endeavour. Her work is a magnificently researched compendium of cultural references, dizzying in its pinball-like ricocheting of artistic representations of the suburban experience. The book grapples with the duality of cultural visions of the suburbs which have 'oscillated between a commiseration of suburban drudgery and a celebration of the periphery and its possibilities' (ibid.: 56) to ask of this 'liminal space of inbetween-ness: is it prison or promised land?' (ibid.: 190).

There are certainly those for whom the latter is the case, with famous examples below recently shared by broadcaster Ian Hislop (2022). Suburbia is, for some, as The Kinks sang ironically in their 1969 single, a 'Shangri La' (Pye Records, 1969); a haven of respectability where someone could, as represented in the BBC TV sitcom *Terry and June* (BBC, 1979-1987), live their slice of *The Good Life* (BBC, 1975-1978). The suburbs signified somewhere to escape to, 'from increasing dirt, noise, stench and disease' (Thompson, 1982: 16). From the McCartney family escaping inner-city Liverpool to the relative tranquillity of life on *Penny Lane* (Parlophone, 1967) in the suburb of Mossley Hill (Norman, 2004: 16), to Jewish families leaving behind the smog of the East End for wider North London (Ewence, 2022), many fleeing the decaying, polluted urban metropolis saw the suburbs as places of optimism and aspiration. However, more commonly, the suburbs are represented less favourably; their inhabitants and their assumed perceptions either light-heartedly mocked or angrily despised as places of 'broken hopes and limited horizons' (Harris, 2010). For example, with reference to the example above of the Jewish families who chose to leave areas such as Stepney and Bethnal Green in East London for outer zones like Golders Green, some saw this apparent suburban haven as 'a vapid sanitised alternative' (Ewence, 2022: 7), an abandonment of the heart of Jewish cultural life for the kind of place, described by Simon Blumenfeld in his 1935 work *Jew Boy* (1986: 143), as 'the anaemic narrow-minded dreariness of suburbia'.

This derision and even hatred of the suburbs has a long history; in the Victorian era they were stereotyped as 'vile' places which offered 'nothing but the deadness of the grave' (Bilston, 2013). Indeed, ambition becomes a fascinating and multi-layered concept in understandings and representations of suburbia, and one I will return to throughout this book. The ambitiousness of those who move there has often been comedically derided as a kind of lower-middle-class pomposity. From Hyacinth Bucket in the BBC sitcom *Keeping Up Appearances* (BBC, 1990–1995) who answered the phone from her Royal Doulton-laden suburban home in affected Received Pronunciation as 'the Bouquet residence', to the status-obsessed Charles Pooter in the 1892 comedic diary-novel *The Diary of a Nobody* (Grossmith and Grossmith, 1919), audiences have long poured scorn over, and openly questioned, what it is those in the suburbs are aspiring *to*. Even the title of the Grossmiths' novel is revealing, labelling Charles Pooter – this emblem of suburban pretension – as a 'nobody'. Indeed, we today derive the word 'Pooteresque', indicating self-importance or narrow-mindedness, from this suburban character obsessed by social climbing.

Likewise, it is a proposed kind of suburban outlook which theatre director Jonathan Miller so snobbishly loathed about British Prime Minister Margaret Thatcher when he described her as possessing an 'odious suburban gentility' (Peacock, 1999: 28). In this context, we see the emergence of a perceived lower-middle-class suburban cognition. We see this amongst those whom the Orwell-Prize-winning author and former Conservative speech writer Graeme Archer (2018) – drawing an inference from George Orwell's 1936 novel *Keep the Aspidistra Flying* where the flower stands as a symbol of a specific kind of middle-class value system – rather more flatteringly calls 'the aspidistra class'. This 'class', and the emergence of a suburban discernment many find so unnerving, is treated with disdain by many. It is precisely this 'class' the English poet Stevie Smith (1972) derides when she says: 'There is far too much of the suburban classes, spiritually not geographically speaking. They're asses'. What do representations of suburbia and suburbanites such as these tell us? Perhaps one of the most interesting things they emphasise is that, whilst suburbia of course has a geographic constitution – albeit one which is often hard to be precise about – it interestingly has a *psychological* constitution too: what the place and its residents assume to stand 'for' or 'against'. Reflecting Smith's emphasis of suburbanness being a spirit instead of a place, Huq (2013: 6) notes: 'in some ways suburbia is metaphorical rather than a literal or geographical term, a mindset as opposed to a strict definition'; it is, she notes, 'more than a place on a map' (ibid.: 193). Her suggestion echoes that of

Gail Cunningham (2004: 424) who writes, of late Victorian representations, that 'suburbia should be recognized at least as much by attitude as by location'. This attitude, then, might be characterised as, stereotypically: narrow-mindedness, small c conservativism, ambitiousness (but of the 'wrong' kind and for the 'wrong' kinds of things), insularity, prudishness and predictability – in others words, tropes which are everything the apparently artistically radical and transgressive, anti-authoritarian genres of popular music reject.

The frequent loathing of the suburbs means that often the other overriding representation, particularly intergenerationally, is the desire to escape. In *The Diary of a Nobody*, in a telling exchange, Pooter's son, Lupin, says to his father: 'I am not going to rot away my life in the suburbs' (Grossmith and Grossmith, 1919: 238), and so too is this reflected in many of the song lyrics from suburbia. As Huq (2013: 57) observes, 'the restlessness at the sterility of their surroundings was a key factor in the pop expressing suburban ennui'. The work of urban planner Nick Green (2005) and social historian Keith Gildart (2013) has thematically addressed how rock bands in the 1960s and 1970s captured this expression of discontentment, with lyrical themes reflecting wider sociopolitical narratives as well as detailing the minutiae of suburban life. This can be seen too in rock journalist Jon Savage's 1992 chronicle of punk, *England's Dreaming*, and the formative role played in the development of the genre by disgruntled youth escaping from the suburbs, and in what Simon Frith (1997) has called the existence of a 'suburban sensibility in British rock and pop'. Examples abound, many collected and explored by journalist John Harris who has also done much to document music from the suburbs: XTC from Swindon and their hatred of what they coined 'Respectable Street' (Virgin, 1981); The Jam from Woking in Surrey and their classic 'A Town Called Malice' (Polydor, 1982) where 'the ghost of a steam train' trundles by, 'bound for nowhere'; The Smiths from Salford outside Manchester who sang about how they felt their part of England 'dragged you down' in 'William It Was Really Nothing' (Rough Trade, 1984); The Pet Shop Boys from the Newcastle suburb of Brunton Park standing in 'suburban hell' ('Suburbia', Parlophone, 1986); 'The Bromley contingent' including Billy Idol and Siouxsie Sioux from the suburb of South London described by Simon Frith (1997: 271) as 'the most significant suburb in British pop history'; and, perhaps most famously of all, The Members from Camberley (also in Surrey) and their track 'The Sound of the Suburbs' (Virgin, 1979) depicting the young kids starting rock bands who 'just want to be free'. In many ways then, my own musical career spent writing music about my life in the suburbs was nothing new, and indeed I am one in a long line of musicians drawing inspiration from this particular England and wanting to tell stories of the suburban experience. What was different, at least in the context of the literature and music outlined here, was my medium: rap music.

Rap: Music of the City, in the Suburbs?
The suburbs are seen by many – particularly American scholars on the subject – as anathema to rap music. The former graffiti artist and political activist William Wimsatt even titled his 1994 study of hip-hop culture *Bomb the Suburbs*,[1] and Kembrew McLeod (1999: 145) notes that in hip-hop culture: 'To be inauthentic, or fake, means being soft, following mass trends by listening to commercial rap music, and identifying oneself with White, mainstream culture that is geographically located in the suburbs'. Certainly, arguments such as these speak to the specificities of rap (and broader hip-hop culture encompassing the 'elements' of – depending on the broadness of the definition – emceeing/rapping, DJ'ing, graffiti, and breakdancing) in the context of the United States. However, beyond the centrality of race (something I will come to momentarily), they highlight the core *geographic* component, for many, of rap music whereby it is typically thought of as representing a quintessentially urban experience. Indeed, for many years up until at least 2020, the genre was regularly subsumed within the broader genre category of what was called, at the time, 'urban music', or in America sometimes as 'urban contemporary' – umbrella terms which incorporated a range of genres including rap, R&B, soul and others. The term 'urban' in the UK was long contentious; musically, as far back as 2004 the MC Wiley, in his track 'Wot Do U Call It?' (XL, 2004), parodied the imprecision around the terms used to define the music he was making at a period now thought of as being the emergence of what came to be called grime. Eventually the term 'urban' fell out of popular use for a variety of reasons related to the unacceptable racial connotations of how the term was applied.[2] Nonetheless, the persistence of the

label – which had existed in various guises since it was coined by the US DJ Frankie Crocker in 1974 essentially for marketing purposes to make music made by Black artists more acceptable to White audiences – reinforced the notion that whilst rap might be consumed *from* the suburbs, it was not a product *of* the suburbs.

However, this conceptualisation is not universally the case. In France, for example, the suburbs and rap have been seen to go hand-in-hand. Here, rap music from the *banlieues* – particularly of Paris – has been chronicled by scholars such as André Prévos (1998, 2001), Alain-Philippe Durand (2002), and Karim Hammou (2016) who outline the emergence of this musical form among those who have come to be stigmatised as *jeune de banlieue*, translated by Hammou (2016: 72) as a 'young suburban non-White working-class male'. With reference to Paris, the doughnut shape of the city inverses the stereotypical 'suburban cliché' (Wunsch, 1995) of inner-city poverty and suburban wealth; the opposite is the case in Paris which arguably is an exemplary illustration of what Hedley Smyth (2003: 87) somewhat viscerally calls 'a compact city within a doughnut of decay'. This 'decay' – although not a term I would personally use – existing beyond the *Périphérique* ring road which encircles the city was seen to be reflected in French riots between 2005 and 2007 which were very much driven by suburban unrest from the *banlieues* of Paris, yes, but Lyon and Lille too (Haddad and Balz, 2006; Moran, 2011). Indeed, the aftermath of earlier suburban civil unrest was dramatised in the acclaimed 1995 film *La Haine* directed by Mathieu Kassovitz; a spellbinding black-and-white depiction of the lives of youths from immigrant families in the Paris suburb of Chanteloup-les-Vignes in the wake of rioting. Musically, Hisham Aidi (2004: 118) suggests: 'The culture of France's suburban ghettoes is heavily influenced by the trends of the American inner city', with hip-hop culture and rap music being a manifestation of this. Examples include rapper Kekra from Courbevoie (a Paris suburb), and rap group *Lunatic* – whom I loved listening to as a teenager despite not understanding any of the words – from the Parisian suburbs of Boulogne-Billancourt and Issy-les-Moulineaux. Indeed, *Lunatic* on their album *Mauvais Œil* (45 Scientific, 2001) had a track called 'Banlieue Ouest' – Western suburbs – containing lyrics which compared their experiences of suburban Paris to that of Sarajevo, alluding to the Bosnian War between 1992 and 1995.

Thus, what the case of rap in France highlights, among other things, is that rap is perhaps not *necessarily* intrinsically of the inner city per se, but of something else.

One notion is that this 'something else' is the shared experiences of marginalisation. This idea that rap is an important vehicle for giving a voice to the marginalised is emphasised in the context of the UK in recent work by music scholar Justin Williams (2020). However, it is important to confront the idea that, of course, marginalisation is often constituted by class and, crucially, race. That is, what the Paris suburbs and the New York inner city (for example) share is their racial diversity and non-Whiteness, facilitating the emergence of a cultural form of artistic expression understood to be specifically Black. Indeed, 'urban music' as a now-defunct genre category has instead come to be referred to today in 2024 as 'Black music'. Race – in particular, being Black – and its relationship to authenticity in hip hop has been extensively delineated in work by Anthony Kwame Harrison (2009: 84), who refers to 'the Great Race Debate' as the 'most monumental of all hip hop authenticity debates'. Certainly, the White consumption of Black cultural practices long pre-dates hip hop – articulated perhaps first in the famous 1957 essay 'The White Negro' (Mailer, 1957) and later detailed in, among others, Simon Jones's (1988) work *Black Culture, White Youth* – but Harrison notes that the mainstreaming of hip hop engendered what he describes as 'hip hop's expanding inclusivity' (Harrison, 2009: 100) where White rappers were increasingly able to gain prestige and acclaim in what is principally a Black cultural space via microsociological evaluations of rappers for their forms of subcultural capital (Thornton, 1995). Indeed, it is in this context that I grew up listening to rap music which was, without me being aware of it from the ethnic homogeneity of my suburban England, renegotiating and reconstructing understandings of race and rap. For example, Eminem was propelled to public attention with his first single 'My Name Is' (Aftermath/Interscope, 1999) when I was in my second year of secondary school (Year 8) in Surrey and his influence was profound not just for me but for hip hop, as a form of Black cultural and artistic practice, more broadly (Rodman, 2009). This profundity, I would suggest, was rooted in the fact that White rappers from earlier eras had often been figures of comedy – e.g. Vanilla Ice – with perhaps only really the Beastie Boys securing a perception of credibility (Stratton, 2008). However, Eminem was 'the first white solo artist to maintain long-term hip-hop success and cultural credibility' (Grealy, 2008: 851), and was, *crucially*, able to secure this credibility amongst 'both white and black audiences' (Verstegen, 2011: 872).

Harrison (2009), in his rich exploration, does not suggest that these processes of 'expanding inclusivity' mean that the wider debate around race and authenticity, nor over rap as a particular and special Black art form, have been settled, and indeed the negotiation of authenticity by White rappers continues to be a subject of scholarly attention (Harkness, 2011; Hess, 2005). However, it appeared to me at least, as a young kid listening to rap, perhaps from a place of cultural ignorance, that being White and rapping was not necessarily being foregrounded as entirely problematic per se in the post-Eminem era (see Cutler, 2003 for more on this theme in work which relates specifically to Eminem). That being said, even if ideas of rap, authenticity and identity had been framed by some as being more about *place* than race – notably, according to American historian Robin Kelley's (1996: 137) work on gangsta rap in post-industrial Los Angeles which advanced, as he described it, a 'ghettocentric' idea located in 'the 'hood' instead of simply related to skin colour – being White *and* suburban perhaps complicates this understanding vis-à-vis how marginalisation is defined, understood and experienced. When we think about rappers from the suburbs of Paris, for example, they are marginalised on various intersecting metrics – sociopolitically, economically i.e. in terms of class, geographically, and, of course, racially (Kaplan, 2015). There is overlap with understandings of life in the English suburbs here as a huge number of academic studies have demonstrated the increased racial diversity of contemporary suburban life (Phillips et al., 2007; Huq, 2008; Watson and Saha, 2013; Tyler, 2020). However, many of the suburbs in these studies skirt and encircle major cities including London. The suburbs of the England I know did not; they were not racially diverse when I lived there and still are not today. That is, my experience of suburbia is not one of racial diversity at all; I am not Black, nor did I grow up with any connection to Black people or Black culture (aside from the music I was listening to). As a child, I moved house seven times, attended five primary schools and two secondary schools across four English counties, and the number of Black students across all seven schools could likely be counted on the hands of two people. The statistics below were taken from the 2021 Census, and show, in the order I lived in them as a child, the Local Authority Districts in which I grew up: Tuxford in Nottinghamshire, Louth in Lincolnshire, Fetcham in Surrey, and the outskirts of Norwich. I am in my thirties today and I suspect that when I lived in each of these places in the late 1980s and 1990s, the numbers were even more stark:

Tuxford (Nottinghamshire) (Bassetlaw Local Authority): 96.5% White,[3] 0.6% Black[4]
Louth (Lincolnshire) (East Lindsey Local Authority): 97.7% White, 0.2% Black
Fetcham (Surrey) (Mole Valley Local Authority): 92.8% White, 0.8% Black
Norwich suburbs (South Norfolk Local Authority): 95.5% White, 0.8% Black[5]
(ONS, 2022)

My stereotypical delineations of the various different Englands which began this book are visions of England seen (in one sense at least) through my relatively narrow racial prism. In this sense, I was producing rap music that was not of the city, nor was I statistically speaking marginalised by class, although I problematise quantitative understandings of class in the next two chapters and examine Schmidt's (1998) notions of perceptual marginality rooted in the experience of peripherality later. Likewise, nor was I marginalised ethnically, nor did I geographically inhabit localities which afforded me any lived experience of ethnic marginalisation or Black culture. However, as I will explore in greater detail in chapters two and three, I did feel that the lives me and my friends lived in our suburban enclave of England were geographically marginalised and, critically, *culturally* marginalised and maligned (see Cullen and Pretes (2000) for more on the use of the term marginal). Our experiences were peripheral to national conversations and were *experienced* as peripheral. From my perspective, our lives, in the England which I felt no one cared about, were seen as trivial and unimportant, and indeed, as outlined above, often mocked, derided and scorned. We lived in an England outside of the tranquillity of English rurality, of great poets with National Trust housing and the protectionism of organisations like Rural England, and certainly outside the creative excitement of major cities where subcultures, fashions, accents and music 'came from'. I grew up listening to rap music from cities – from New York, Los Angeles and London – where rappers documented lives which were powerful and incredibly culturally meaningful.[6] I suppose an obvious question to ask is: why were they meaningful to me – in what ways did they speak to me and why did they captivate me? This is a question I want to return to and which I think I only truly was able to understand via the process of writing this book. For now, I can state that simply, like them, I wanted to document my life, and perhaps more broadly *our lives*, as I felt our lives were worthy of documentation, and that rap offered me a vehicle to explore that. I wanted to write songs about the things I saw every day, like the rappers I so admired, but about *our lives*: drinking in Wetherspoons, driving around in my Mum's hatchback, fights happening outside takeaways and in nightclubs, my job at an insurance company, friends experiencing hopelessness or joining the army and going off to fight in wars, and the dreams we shared growing up in the place we did.

One artistic figure is critical to mention here who perhaps, aside from Eminem, did more for young people from my background who loved rap music and wanted to rap than anyone else: Mike Skinner and his musical output as 'The Streets'. Here was someone who was White, suburban, and whilst it was hard to be precise about his class from listening to the lyrics alone, one did not get the sense of someone growing up in poverty necessarily. Skinner's debut album *Original Pirate Material* released by Locked On/679 Records in 2002 – when I was fifteen – was perhaps the first time I, or other people like me, heard someone rapping about the things we lived and experienced on a daily basis. It was a form of rap outside of the grime music from the housing estates of Bow in East London or hip hop from the housing projects of Queensbridge in New York or Compton in Los Angeles. His style was not even typical rapping; he spoke with an off-beat conversational informality in a Brummie accent on tracks like 'Has It Come To This?' about an England I knew – an England of boy racers, kebab shops, being afraid to walk through the underpass because of the scary blokes you might bump into, and smoking weed while playing Nintendo 64 with your mates; lyrics delivered by a man who openly and pointedly in the track said: 'think I'm ghetto? Stop dreaming'. The endeavour of Skinner was magnificently captured by scholar of music Caspar Melville (2004) as: 'a kind of ballad of no-place, anyplace, Nowheresville UK. Listening to Mike Skinner transports you to the almost deserted top deck of the replacement bus running between Manningtree and Harwich town...[His music is] distinctly sub-urban – the land of asbos,[7] twockers[8] and daytime drinkers [and he] is the hip hop balladeer of the suburbs'.

What Mike Skinner did was to take perhaps the central injunction which underlines hip-hop music, to 'keep it real' (Clay, 2003) – an injunction I will be examining in this book in more detail – and apply this to a version of England which this music had not engaged with before, and to tell stories of this England. As Angus Harrison (2017) wrote for music publication *The Fader*, Skinner's visions of England 'found immediate recognition in an audience who weren't being represented elsewhere'. Indeed, this was the case with me. His reimagining and reformulation of authenticity in rap was nothing less than revolutionary and inspirational, and offered the possibility that what mattered in rap was to tell stories which communicated feelings of broadly defined and broadly understood marginalisation (Osumare, 2001) – whether Black or White, from the city or suburb, and, perhaps, working-class or otherwise. This is what I wanted to do, and indeed throughout my career it was no surprise to hear my music being compared to that of Mike Skinner in publications like *NME* (Patterson, 2012) and *Wonderland* (Tsjeng, 2013).

Knowing by Doing

I first started writing rap lyrics in 2005, three years after hearing Mike Skinner for the first time. A few years earlier, the film *8 Mile* had been released; a semi-autobiographical portrayal of struggling Detroit-based rapper Jimmy 'B-Rabbit' Smith played by Eminem, featuring him finding his artistic voice through rap battles – essentially rhythmic competitions where two MCs hurl abuse at each other with varying levels of complexity and humour. I entered two or three local battles at a nightclub in Norwich which were well attended by – unusually for Norwich – an international and diverse crowd drawn largely from the military bases in the wider county, and from that point became engrossed in the idea of documenting my life and the lives of my peer group and all the apparent commonplace humdrum of our suburban lives. My initial tracks were what I now can see were fairly standard 'UK hip hop' derived from an era which feels long-forgotten now in which British rap sat firmly in the shadow of, and keen to imitate, its American older brother. These were instrumental beats drawn

Fig 1.1 Press photograph of Context (me) by Robin Mellor. Reprinted with permission.

from rappers in the United States with me rapping over the top with a focus on abstract metaphors and multi-syllable rhyme schemes, recorded whilst stood under a duvet with a second-hand USB microphone from Cash Converters in the box room of the run-down terraced house me, my girlfriend (now wife) and our mate Tom shared on the outskirts of Norwich.

After some initial EPs where I was trying to find my voice, with early tracks earning some support from BBC Radio 1 (notably one called 'The Harrier' and another called 'Frantic') I musically started to more fully articulate the stories of our lives in 2011 with the track entitled 'Off With Their Heads'. This song, and the video which featured Ed Sheeran led to a heightened interest in my sound, with media outlets like *NME*, *The Independent*, *HuffPost* and *MTV* increasingly supporting my releases. At this time, I was also regularly being invited to MC for drum and bass and dubstep stars when they would come to perform in Norwich, hosting for some of the biggest global names in these scenes like Andy C, Shy FX, Rusko, Benga, Plastician, Alix Perez and SpectraSoul. Later that year, my single 'Listening to Burial' was daytime playlisted on BBC Radio 1 – meaning it was played every day for a week across the range of daytime shows – following huge support from the BBC's regional and national 'Introducing' initiative which had launched a few years earlier in 2007 to support unsigned talent across the United Kingdom. I achieved this playlisting with no radio plugger or management. After moving to London later that year, I was announced as the winner of MTV's Brand New for 2012, the first unsigned act to earn a place on the annual list of artists MTV tipped for success in the future, appearing alongside musicians who – unlike me – would go on to be global stars like Lana Del Ray and Charli XCX. My next single, 'Drowning', featuring an elaborate underwater music video, was heavily supported on MTV, reaching number 14 in their rap chart, and the following year I signed a global publishing and songwriting deal with Sony Music Publishing. I went on to collaborate with perhaps my ultimate artistic inspiration, Mike Skinner of The Streets, on a track which, looking back, was the emblematic synthesis of what I had been trying to achieve in capturing prosaic ordinariness – 'Small Town Lad Sentiments' – and performed at festivals including Reading, Leeds, Wireless and BBC Radio 1's Big Weekend.

I released two more EPs entitled *Stealing My Older Brother's Tapes* – which was number 1 on DJ Semtex's Hip-Hop Mixtape Chart on BBC Radio 1Xtra – and *Hindsight is the Purest Form of Romance*, and my music was being shared on social media platforms by acts like Ellie Goulding and Plan B. In 2015 I signed a major recording deal and released the track 'In the Bag' which was daytime playlisted on BBC Radio 1Xtra. However, by this point I had begun to grow weary of a musical career and was simultaneously approaching the end of my academic studies too, having undertaken a BA, an MA and a PhD sequentially. This, alongside other forms of existential angst about the trajectory of my life, led me to slowly drift away from music as being my career focus, and increasingly academia came to provide me with the sense of purpose and indeed happiness which music-making often, upsettingly, failed to give me. In some ways I miss being a musician every day; in other ways, my life is happier without the pain and struggle. Perhaps I am just a better academic than I was a musician? Who knows? Nearly a decade on, I think I have come to learn that what I love is words, and if writing them on a page yields me contentment greater than, or at least comparable to, saying them in a microphone, then perhaps these two identities are more closely connected than perhaps first appears

Fig 1.2 Artwork from my EP *Hindsight is the Purest Form of Romance* showing me and my Grandad.

(see Back (2023) for more). Indeed, the scope of this book seeks to articulate the closeness of this connection in its most intimate and explicit way.

Music as the Medium, Music as the Method
This book is an introspective examination of my musical practice in the form of my rap lyrics written as a young man in my early to mid-twenties. However, it remains unclear, even to me, whether what I will attempt to achieve herein represents what has come to be called 'practice-based research' (Bulley and Sahin, 2021). That is, my practice – the lyrics, when they were written – was not undertaken with any clear research

question, within any kind of conceptual architecture, as an example of theory-informed praxis, nor are the artefacts (the songs and their lyrics) representative – at least to me – of what the world of higher education would articulate in REF-speak[9] as 'outputs'. They were songs written by a songwriter building a musical career. Yet, at the same time, given the position within which I find myself today as an academic, it occurred to me that these songs might represent subjects of critical and analytical research; as methodological artefacts of practice to be retrospectively and self-reflexively interrogated as sources of potential insight, befitting definitions (ambiguous as they are) of this kind of 'practice-based' approach to research (such as by Nelson, 2013: 6). My musical practice is the basis of enquiry and representative of what we might think of as the evidence base in this book. However, it was never intended to be so and indeed the form the analysis takes, which you now hold in your hands or read on your screen, is that of a more traditional academic monograph which has not gone on to iteratively inform future practice in that I, sadly, don't write songs anymore. Thus, conceptually, the picture is a messy one.

Perhaps the label ascribed to the endeavour is irrelevant. What matters more is that this work sits within a broad body of literature – within which I propose it should be understood – which analyses and centralises music (and rap specifically) from a particular perspective. There are two approaches which have informed my thinking here. First are traditional forms of scholarship on hip hop in England and the wider United Kingdom. Following early academic interest in the emergence of hip hop in the UK (Hesmondhalgh and Melville, 2001), we find today well-established academic analysis of rap music and the lives of rappers. A great deal of this focuses on London with examples from the genres of UK hip hop (Speers, 2017) or grime (White, 2017; de Lacey, 2023) – or indeed both (Bramwell, 2015) – with a smaller range of scholarly works looking at rap careers in other metropolitan areas such as Manchester (Paor-Evans, 2018; Reisner and Rymajdo, 2022) or Bristol (Bramwell and Butterworth, 2020). However, increasingly an interest is emerging in rap music across the UK (Williams, 2020; Ekpoudom, 2024). My own doctoral work was an exploration of my rap career in Norwich (albeit triangulated with two other case studies from the grime and UK hip-hop scenes in London) examining themes of emotional anguish, conditions of creativity and methods of self-promotion (Musgrave, 2014). More recent work is extending this interest in rap careers and musical identities in provincial, less cosmopolitan and even rural contexts. Notable here is the work of ethnomusicologist Adam Paor-Evans (2020a, 2020b) and his work located in the West Country which innovatively highlights how hip hop's linguistic and cultural conventions are being sociogeographically renegotiated within these new rap scenes. Paor-Evans (2020b: 423) suggests that a discussion of hip hop which 'reaches out from the cities to rurality...[is one] that hip-hop culture is desperate for', and indeed I wanted to write this book to form part of that discussion.

The second body of work this book sits within foregrounds the analysis of rap *lyrics*, as opposed to rap careers. This is part of a wider intellectual project which treats rap lyrical interpretation as a form of media analysis and hermeneutic enquiry. Historically, this tended to focus on the more controversial content of the genre (Krohn and Suazo, 1995), but today it encompasses broader analytical themes ranging from the politics of artists like Immortal Technique (Vito, 2015) to multilingualism amongst Nigerian rappers (Akande, 2013). Two books in this field warrant highlighting. The first is Adam Bradley's (2009) *Book of Rhymes: The Poetics of Hip Hop*. This offers an aesthetic – as opposed to anthropological or sociological – perspective on rap lyrics, informed by semiotic textual reading, taking seriously the task of delineating linguistic and stylistic features of the genre such as rhythm, wordplay and signifying. In championing the poetic nature of the genre the author highlights the capacity to treat the transcription and interpretation of lyrics as analogous to that of traditional written poetry, not unlike the approach I will adopt. This method can be seen to be exemplified in a non-rap context in the poetry collections of singer-songwriter Patti Smith, some of which are 'lyric books as poetry anthologies', e.g. *Patti Smith Complete* (1998), while others are books which began life as poems and later were recorded as songs, e.g. *The Coral Sea* (1996). Likewise, and perhaps even more closely related to my own endeavour, Paul Weller (2007) of suburban outfit The Jam published a collection of lyrics entitled *Suburban 100* recounting the ways in which his music captured a specific expression of life in the suburbs of Surrey. The other key contribution in this area is by novelist, music journalist and record label owner Will Ashon (2018) and his work *Chamber Music: About the Wu-Tang (in 36 Pieces)*. Taking as its central focus the classic LP *Enter the Wu-Tang (36 Chambers)* (Loud Records, 1993) by the Staten Island-based rap collective the Wu-Tang Clan, Ashon dissects the apparently bewildering and often oblique wordplay of tracks from the album, situating them within broader conceptual themes ranging from the ravages of crack cocaine, jazz saxophony, hip-hop history and martial arts, and contextualising them within African American oral and written traditions. Indeed, I recall in school being fascinated by the book *The Wu-Tang Manual* (2004) written by the group's founding member Rza which likewise evaluates the MCs' lyrics in rigorous annotated depth. This was similarly undertaken years later by rapper Jay-Z (2010) in his book *Decoded* where he explored his own lyrics. Whilst I am by no means suggesting my lyrics should be thought of as being on a par with these giants of the genre, the approach adopted heavily influenced what I will undertake in this book.

Context as George, George as Context

There are two further bodies of literature which I situate this book within. These are perhaps more tangential, and certainly less musically focused, but nonetheless represent what I consider to be a fascinating related field of enquiry which connect together the cultural and personal ambitions of this book. The first of these is autofiction: the apparently antithetical, even oxymoronic, bringing together of autobiography and fiction. Whilst the term has been hugely problematised by Armaud Schmitt (2010), the notion of forms of creative work derived from autobiographical experience has a long history. With reference to artistic lives, one might think of Henri Murger's 1851 work *Scènes de la vie de bohème* (published in English in 1883 as *The Bohemians of the Latin Quarter*) – which later went on to form the basis of Puccini's 1896 opera *La bohème* – based on his experiences of impoverished, Parisian garret-living amongst poets, or James Joyce's 1916 classic *A Portrait of the Artist as a Young Man*. It appears to me that this literary approach shares much in common with rap music, with its reliance on close observation, storytelling, and a focus on sharing intimate perspectives and experiences, thus raising fascinating questions around the nature of 'truth', and how one separates the *autobiographical* from the *fiction* – although certainly autobiographies are hard to empirically validate (Schmitt, 2017). Indeed, this debate by extension speaks to controversies within thinking about rap lyrics regarding the extent to which the lyrics that rappers write about their lives and their circumstances can reasonably be said to be 'true' (something I will address in detail in chapter three).

However, at this juncture, I highlight *autofiction* as a genre of literature with which this book at least forms a conversation insofar as these works are defined as having a *psychoanalytic* element (Gasparini, 2004); in other words, they are works concerned with 'conveying the intricacies of the self [via] a very specific form of autobiographical expression' (Schmitt, 2010: 126). That is to say, via highly personal and reflexive self-disclosure (which my lyrics always were to me), autofiction writers try to articulate, even reform and imagine, who they see and understand themselves to be. This is, at least partially, what I see the task of this book as: to take my lyrical forms of disclosure, and years later interrogate both them and my own life in order to reveal something of suburban England, but *also* to enrich how I perceive and articulate myself. Perhaps the most compelling recent example of this from within the genre of autofiction concerns Edouard Louis's 2014 work *En finir avec Eddy Bellegueule* (translated as *The End of Eddy*). It recounts the authors' experiences as a young gay man growing up in depressed Northern France, experiencing and witnessing violence, alcoholism, racism, threats and fear. Whilst presented as a novel, the book is – according to the author – based on real events. The psychoanalytic component to the text is that the author was born Eddy Bellegueule, but via the act of disclosure-laden writing and analysis-of-self via heavyweights of French thought, came to recast himself as a new man – Edouard Louis – which indeed is now his legal name; a metamorphosis from ostracised, parochial outsider to 'member of the French intellectual elite' (Adetunji, 2017). The relationship between the experience of provincialism, methodological innovativeness, and the centrality of self-analysis in Louis's work chimes closely with the endeavour in my own writing herein too.

The final approach which has informed this book is a methodological one. Autoethnography – the use of personal experiences (*auto*) to make sense of cultural practices (*ethno*) in an analytically systematic way (*graphy*) (Ellis et al., 2011) – centralises one's own autobiographical, intimate subjectivity to interrogate specific phenomena within scholastic frameworks. Here, rejecting assumptions or evaluative criteria relating to scientific 'objectivity' or neutrality (Bochner, 2002), authors embrace autobiographical tenets of storytelling and narrative to reveal something about wider cultural experiences. The work of Arthur Bochner and Carolyn Ellis (2016) has done much to personally inspire me in terms of how the method can afford us as researchers the opportunity to write analytically about our own lives to potentially produce what they describe as *Evocative Autoethnography*. In a specifically musical context, work by Brydie-Leigh Bartleet and Ellis (2009) delineates various kinds of *Music Autoethnographies*, both as listeners and as performers, with the ways in which musicians can use autoethnographic approaches to reflect on their own creative practice in 'culturally insightful ways' fleshed out further by Bartleet (2009: 713). In drawing on my life and upbringing, and connecting this to my artistic practice as a musician – telling George, in order to tell Context, to reveal something of suburban England – this book builds on my earlier published work on this subject which conceptualises products (and by-products) of artistic career building as ripe for reflexive self-analysis (Musgrave, 2017): analysis which, as per the psychoanalytic ambitions of autofiction, it is hoped, both provides an insightful way of understanding provincial England and also fulfils a personal desire to better understand myself (see Wright and Chung (2001) for an overview of the 'therapeutic' impact of writing). In this respect, I agree with communications scholar Arthur Bochner (2001: 138) when he says that the stories of our own lives inform and are reconstituted by the academic work we do and interests we have, and to this extent: 'the therapeutic and the scholarly are mutually implicated in our projects'.

Goals

England is a country I feel like I have seen various sides of and is the country I know best. That being said, I would never claim to know England as a whole well, nor is this book an attempt to understand or map England as per, for instance, the classic *English Journey* (Priestley, 1934). This book does not claim to, nor attempt to, grapple or negotiate with the big questions which circulate around England or Englishness, an endeavour perhaps most famously articulated by George Orwell in essays like *The Lion and the Unicorn* with all of his profoundly critical yet simultaneously optimistically patriotic ambivalence (Orwell et al., 1980). Likewise, whilst this book uses music and concepts of narrative to explore questions of class and identity, it can in no way claim to be the kind of tour de force of class in England represented by authors such as E.P. Thompson (1963) or, more recently, by the sociologist Daniel Smith (2023). Nor could I even claim to understand 'the English' – however such a heterogenous body might be defined – in all their complexities and oddities as many others have attempted – notably, again, Thompson (1965) or Jeremy Paxman (2007). Indeed, I remember waking up on the morning of the 24th June 2016 after the United Kingdom had voted to leave the European Union (although, the figures really demonstrated that it was England and Wales that voted to leave, not Northern Ireland or Scotland) and thinking that perhaps I did not really understand this country after all. Perhaps I don't. However, it is the place I know *best*, and for this reason this book is not called *The Britain No One Cares About*, or even *The United Kingdom No One Cares About*. Scotland, Wales and Northern Ireland have their own stories, histories, nuances, and identities best left to be told by authors from these places who can appropriately tell them. I can only speak about what I know, after all, and that is England; for better or for worse.

What is it I hope to achieve with this book? In the first instance, I wanted to bring together a number of disciplines which so fascinate me but which I had not yet been afforded the cognitive space to meaningfully engage with, and which the co-existence of my musical career and lived experiences provided the conditions for a relatively unique exploration of, namely: autoethnography, psychogeography, personality and narrative psychology, cultural perspectives on class, psychoanalysis, and cognitive perspectives on Bourdieusian theory, among others. In bringing these approaches together, I want to look again at my lyrics and ask what these subjective, complicated, biased, evocative, imperfect, descriptive stories of my life reveal about a part of England which has often been thought of as, at worst, a source of derision or embarrassment and, at best, something to be met with an uncomfortable, knowing smile with gritted teeth beneath. In this sense, the first ambition is to ask if we can use lyrics to understand geographies.

However, the book has another ambition which is a highly personal one. When envisioning this work, I felt that it did not fit neatly into any kind of predefined agenda, nor did it even necessarily explicitly chime with the main thrust of my wider work which focuses on mental health and wellbeing in the music industry (Gross and Musgrave, 2020; Musgrave, 2022, 2023a, 2023b; Musgrave et al., 2023). I only knew that, having left my musical career behind, I wanted to return to the pages of scribbled notes and lyrics written during a defining period in my life which had been documented in this specific manner, and look again at them to perhaps better understand myself as a person, where I have come from, and the understandings of the Englands I have lived in – some of which I have a very uneasy and fraught relationship with. In this sense, I wanted to ask whether conceptualising my lyrics as a source of data was methodologically reasonable and, if so, what analysing this data might reveal. I suppose, in essence, I wanted to explore whether I could take the nickname quoted at the beginning of this book and given to me by the DJ MistaJam – who, live on air on BBC Radio 1Xtra in 2013 referred to me as 'Middle England's Poet Laureate' – and produce my own, limited and modest, poetry anthology of rap lyrics. Therefore, this book is, unashamedly, what the American anthropologist Clifford Geertz (1988: 97) might have categorised as an 'author-saturated text' where 'the self the text creates and the self that creates the text are represented as being very near to identical'. This may appear immodest, even narcissistic, to some. However, modesty and rapping do not make for comfortable bedfellows. As such, I make no apology for it.

At its heart, however, this book is about the power of stories. It is about the power of music as a form of storytelling to tell the stories of places. It is about the power of the stories in lyrics as sources of data to tell us things which other kinds of data cannot. It is about the power of the stories we tell ourselves about England and about the kind of country we think we live in.[10] It is about the psychological power of the stories told to us by our families which shape the ways we see, perceive and understand the world around us. It is about the power of telling stories as a way of negotiating our understandings of who we are. It is about the power of listening to stories in order to problematise and get behind the over-confidence of terminological oversimplifications and statistical representations of places, of class, and of identity. It is an appeal to the power of the qualitative and the centrality of narrative. It is my attestation, simply, that stories matter.

Notes

1. Amusingly, Wimsatt revised his position sixteen years later with his book *Please Don't Bomb the Suburbs* (Wimsatt, 2010).
2. See Andrews (2018), Caramanica (2020), Saeed (2020) and Young (2020) for a detailed outline.
3. This figure has been derived by adding together all five definitions of White in the Census data: White: English, Welsh, Scottish, Northern Irish or British / White: Irish / White: Gypsy or Irish Traveller / White: Roma / White: Other White.
4. This figure has been derived by adding together all three definitions of Black in the census data: Black, Black British, Black Welsh, Caribbean or African: African / Black, Black British, Black Welsh, Caribbean or African: Caribbean / Black, Black British, Black Welsh, Caribbean or African: Other Black.
5. These illustrative figures do not include other ethnic measures in the Census data, e.g. 'Mixed or Multiple Ethnic Groups' subcategorised as including White and Asian, White and Black African, White and Black Caribbean, or Other Mixed or Multiple Ethnic Groups.
6. Inspired by the writer, author and broadcaster Sean Street (2014), and drawing on the poignant work of Jude Rogers (2022), I have made a series of playlists which can be heard whilst reading this book if of interest to readers. The first of these playlists 'Finding rap' is given at the end of this chapter. The tracks in this playlist represent the first rap songs I ever heard and the tracks which sparked my interest in the genre.
7. An acronym for Anti-Social Behaviour Orders, a controversial mechanism for preventing anti-social behaviour introduced under Tony Blair's New Labour government in 1998, and documented in the work of Donoghue (2010).
8. TWOC is an acronym for car theft – Taking Without Owners' Consent.
9. The Research Excellence Framework (REF) is a tool used to measure and rank the research 'outputs' (books, journal articles, etc.) of university departments for the purpose of distributing funding (see Sayer (2014) and Padro-Guerra (2022) for more).
10. Indeed, the editor of the New Statesman Jason Cowley highlights this in the title of his 2022 work *Who are we now? Stories of Modern England*.

Playlist 1: Finding Rap

2Pac – 'Bury Me a G'
2Pac – 'Pour Out a Little Liquor'
Wu-Tang Clan – 'Triumph'
N.W.A. – 'Alwayz Into Somethin''
Ice Cube – 'Ghetto Bird'
Eminem – 'If I Had'
Fugees – 'Nappy Heads'
Gang Starr – 'Above the Clouds'
Mack 10 and Tha Dogg Pound – 'Nothin' But the Cavi Hit'
Lone Catalysts – 'Due Process'
P Diddy – 'Victory'
Wu-Syndicate – 'Latunza Hit'
Ice Cube – 'It Was a Good Day'
Wu-Tang Clan – 'Severe Punishment'
Jay-Z – 'If I Should Die'

You can hear the playlist here: tiny.cc/md0cvz

2

Who Do We Think We Are? 'Context' in Context

My life has been defined by processes of self-articulation and relentlessly driven by narrative; by the stories of my family which have come to tell the story of who I am, who others think I am, and who I think I might be. They have defined how I see the world and how I live in the world, and ultimately would come to inform how these perceptions were reflected musically. We all tell stories about ourselves; about who we are – or who we think we are – where we are 'from' (geographically, historically, culturally), where we are going, and even where we belong – if such a thing doesn't sound too trite. But I suppose with two English teachers for parents, the stories I was told and encouraged to tell had a certain literary quality, often told as if imbued with a *telos* and loaded with expectation and belief. Central to these ideas has always been the interconnections between class and identity. Therefore, this chapter will address the following questions: who do I think I am, what stories have defined my life, and how have the places I consider myself to have 'come from' informed the ways I have both thought about, and then come to musically represent, these places? In essence, the lyrics I wrote in my twenties as Context were stories which reflected my subjective understandings of the places in which I grew up. Therefore, this chapter maps the central role of stories in my life, and what ultimately led me to use narrative storytelling in the form of lyrics to articulate the geographies of my upbringing.

To do this, I want to tell my story. I will sketch the history of my immediate family according to the narrative arc I have always been told; certainly unable to capture the fullness of the lives of those closest to me, but at least a close approximation of how their journeys, the places we have lived, and the music they loved, have influenced my thinking. In essence, I suppose the telling of this story is an attempt to put Context in context, by tracing back my experiences of the England no one cares about – in Yorkshire, in Nottinghamshire, in Lincolnshire, in Surrey and in Norfolk – and to sketch out in more precise sociological detail how the stories my family told me about who I was, where I was going, and who they thought we were, profoundly shaped both the person I became and the kind of music I would write.

George & Edith

In some respects, the lives of my paternal grandparents have acted as something akin to statistical indexing; the benchmark from which concepts of 'progress', however uncomfortably defined, would come to be measured in my family. They were born and grew up in South Yorkshire, in an area just outside Barnsley called Worsbrough. My Grandad – George Musgrave – was a coal miner. At the age of eleven he had passed what was then called the scholarship exam to attend the Barnsley and District Holgate Grammar School, but his parents could not afford the uniforms. So, instead, in 1936, when he was fourteen years old, he went down the pit, first at Barrow Colliery, and then later Rockingham and Grimethorpe. Barrow was somewhat infamous for an accident almost thirty years earlier when seven men had been thrown from the cage and fallen to their deaths in a shaft following what was described at an inquest as 'carelessness' by two cage operators (Elliott, 2017). George was the fifth generation of Barnsley coal miners; his Dad (Albert), Grandfather (Allen), Great Grandfather (George) and Great-Great Grandfather (Benjamin) had all spent their working lives in the mines, with most of them living on the same street in Barnsley – Cutty Lane – and getting married in the same church, St Mary's, about three quarters of a mile away. Researching my family history and reading their marriage certificates signed with wobbly crosses from not being able to write their own names or hold a pen, and reading about their lives as child hurriers down the mines, little boys in the dark, pulling corfs filled with coal, strapped to their waists or over their shoulders with leather belts, through tiny tunnels, is humbling and deeply upsetting (see White (1931: 40) or Garrisi (2017: 447–445) for more on 'hurrying' in Victorian England). Over 150 years of unimaginable, stoic toil and poverty which was plain to see; one of my Grandad's memories of his Dad were the blue lacerations all over his back from crawling underground and the

Fig 2.1 Me on Cutty Lane, Barnsley.

angry, black scars on his face from where deep cuts had been packed with coal dust. Indeed, this memory calls to mind Orwell's evocative depiction of miners' faces in *The Road to Wigan Pier* as having 'a blue stain like tattooing…veined like Roquefort cheeses' (Orwell, 2021: 24).

I remember, when I was perhaps twelve or thirteen, Grandad telling me about his first day down the pit: a little child walking down an enormous black tunnel holding the reins of a white pit pony. It was like being read a novel from an era which you thank God doesn't exist anymore. He told me and my younger brother that on that day the other miners left him down there in the pitch black at the end of the shift, perhaps as a first-day joke, perhaps because he was just another child down there in the dark, easily forgotten. He remembered having to lick his finger to find the direction of air and followed it until he found a tunnel to climb back up and then walk home, alone. He never really told us about the work he did, and when I got older and my Dad told me about it I understood why; you don't sleep soundly for some time once you hear that someone you love, when they were not much older than you, spent their days lying flat on their back, hundreds of metres deep underground, with claustrophobic black rock eighteen inches in front of their face held up by flimsy props of wood, chipping away tonnes of stone all day. Every day. He once said he had been so exhausted lying there, that when he imagined the seam collapsing and killing him, his thought was: 'sod it, let it happen'. In the life of relative privilege which I lived, this working life of 'hand filling' mining – as described by Schofield (2003) – was, mercifully, unimaginable. He only left the pit due to ill-health, with the dust, pollution and of course tobacco in his lungs eventually meaning he died in 2002, a few months before his eightieth birthday, which seemed a fairly spectacular age to reach.

He was a wonderful man. My lasting memory of him is his smell: old tobacco in a musty pipe, his wax jacket and flat cap with the aromas of cold and rain, the faint stench of his two West Highland White Terriers Thomas and Bosun, and the John Smiths bitter on his breath. For the majority of my life I barely remember speaking to him. He didn't speak much at all apart from stock catchphrases like 'aye, 'appen' (meaning maybe), or exchanging brevities with my Dad when they would go into the next room or down the pub. When he did say a few words my Nan would always scream at him to 'shut tha mouth, gob on legs'. I also remember how his face felt when I used to hug him: bristles like razors where the harshness of his skin was juxtaposed with the softness of his voice. It also always struck me that he seemed to be freakishly strong for a man so small. I can't remember how tall he was, but he once described holding steady at his 'fighting weight' (pronounced 'feeting wait') of ten and a half stone. He had once made dumbbells out of old pieces of metal which, as a child, I remember being completely in awe of as he curled them up and down, while me and my brother couldn't even pick them up together with all our force. My Dad still has them. I still struggle to pick them up. Then again, when my Grandad did pick-and-shovel mining his quota was two tonnes of coal an hour for eight hours; if you're not strong when you start work, you certainly are when you finish. He also had very diverse interests. He used to make magnificently detailed, elegant boats out of discarded scraps of wood which I was always amazed by. In typical fashion, he did not keep these, throwing them out 'for t'bin lorry' one day. He loved reading Dickens and had a full collection of his novels. He also loved music, particularly Artie Shaw and his Orchestra, as well as opera. Just before he died, my Dad recorded Puccini's *Tosca* for him to listen to in hospital. The last thing I remember him saying to me when I was sixteen was 'look after your Dad. He's getting old'.

My Nan – Edith Musgrave née Hallhouse – was unforgettable. A huge lady in every sense of the word, she thought of herself as something of a character. I remember her laughing with an infectious hoot. She would utter almost incomprehensible phrases in the thickest Yorkshire accent like 'tha talks like a tuppence ha'penny book' (meaning, you sound like you are telling a made-up story from a cheap book), or say wildly inappropriate things, like when she approached a bald woman in a discount shop and said 'don't be embarrassed tha's bald'. Once, some ramblers were walking past her house, so she ran to her upstairs bedroom window and threw sweets at them like confetti at a wedding procession. Me and my brother (generally) loved spending time with her; she made an enormous fuss of us and plied us with toffees wrapped in nondescript packaging of blue, green and purple paper which I have since never been able to find in any shops. I remember at their house in Worsbrough making the potion from Roald Dahl's *George's Marvellous Medicine* together and sleeping under an electric blanket in their spare room watching the lights from the passing traffic arch across the ceiling above. Her story is perhaps of less 'obvious' literary note than my Grandad's. My Dad told me how, as a child, she had walked into her living room to find her Mum dead in a chair from tuberculosis and had tried to wake her by offering her a small handful of sweets. She was seven years old. This, along with the fact that she used to have newspapers for tablecloths in her house as a child, is one of the only things I know about her life. She never spoke of it, and even my Dad knows little about it; I suppose much of it has been lost to time like so many working-class stories. I am conscious as I write this, moved to tears, that this may be the first and last time their lives have ever been

Fig 2.2 Me and my brother in Worsbrough, where our grandparents' ashes are scattered.

documented in any form aside from their birth, marriage, death, and perhaps my Grandad's army records from the War when, for the first time, he saw anywhere outside of Barnsley.

George & Victoria

My Dad – also called George Musgrave, but referred to by his middle name, Glynn – was born in 1946. He grew up on a street called Westfields in Worsbrough, in a British Iron and Steel Federation house; an unmistakeable post-war prefabricated style of house where the bottom half was made of bricks and the top half of steel. My Nan, like many miners' wives,[1] never wanted her son to go down the pit like many of his friends at primary school and like so many Musgrave men before him. Given this, he was brought up with an unease about his environment which would come to define his entire life. At the end of primary school he passed the 'eleven-plus' exam to attend the same grammar school as his Dad. Unlike his Dad, he went. His relationship with this moment always struck me as holding mixed and even contradictory emotions. On the one hand, local kids used to shout abuse at him on his way to school, he lamented how socially excluded he felt in that environment, and like all Northern, Labour-voting men of a certain age and background, continues to loathe the grammar school system and spits on the floor at the utterance of Margaret Thatcher's name. On the other hand, it is hard to believe that without attending grammar school his life would have taken the screeching divergence from his family's history, and the eventual emergence of a life of relative prosperity which would await him where mining was something for stories and memories. That being said, my Dad told me that the mines never leave you: he once described the lasting sensory memories of his childhood bedroom as being the smell from the slaughterhouse at the end of his garden, the sound of the siren from Barrow pit signalling an accident, and the sight of fire flicking and dancing across his ceiling from the flames bellowing high above the colliery across the valley.

Music was always a big part of my Dad's life. When he was ten his parents saved up and bought him an Eavestaff piano and music was often heard in the house. In an age of rationing and utilitarian furniture, it seems unsurprising that much of the music he grew up hearing came from the perceived glamour of the United States with sounds produced by Fender Stratocasters and Marshall amplifiers which were far away, in every sense, from the coalfields of South Yorkshire.[2] Most of the music he heard was either from my Nan singing songs like *You Are My Sunshine* or *Let's Twist Again* or from the radio; the BBC's *Family Favourites* shows on a Sunday afternoon, with songs by Jo Stafford like *You'll Never Know* or *You Belong to Me*, were particularly memorable. The Red Lion pub in Worsbrough had a jukebox and when the records were worn-out they would sell them cheaply, so my Grandad bought a radiogram and would pick up 45 rpm records by acts like The Platters, The Everly Brothers, and The Coasters. When my Dad was fifteen he started playing guitar in bands, performing instrumental versions of songs by The Shadows in working men's clubs and pubs. He continued to play in bands throughout my childhood, performing cover versions of tracks by acts like Dire Straits, Chris Rea, The Rolling Stones, and Fleetwood Mac, sharing the same bill with acts including The Drifters, The Walker Brothers, Brian Poole and the Tremeloes, and Simon Dupree and the Big Sound. He taught me to play the guitar when I was six or seven, and when my little brother got a drum kit one Christmas we would do 'shows' of rock band covers for our family.

After leaving school, my Dad worked in various jobs including a library and then Samuel Fox and Company steel works in Stocksbridge. He later trained to become an English teacher, gaining a CertEd and later a BA from the Open University. Here, he studied a course which he said would define much of how he thought about education throughout his life: E202 *Schooling and Society*. The course was, in fact, nationally embroiled in controversy following critical comments in the *Times Educational Supplement* over what the publication suggested was the 'propaganda' of the course's 'Marxist' readings and perspectives.[3] My Dad eventually became a head of department, working for twenty years at Valley Comprehensive School in Worksop – an ex-mining town in Nottinghamshire on the other side of Sheffield from Barnsley. The first six years of my life were spent about thirteen miles away from Worksop; a place where, in the early 2000s it was reported that in the wake of the destruction of the mining industry in the 1980s, one in three households had been impacted by heroin (BBC, 2002), news which was so shocking that it even reached the *Chicago Tribune* (Hundley, 2003). To this day, aside from a few notable exceptions of brilliant students, my Dad talks with a resigned dismissal of the years he spent in that school; that he began his career convinced he would make a difference, but that he doesn't believe he did. He once told an incoming newly qualified teacher: 'the day you walk through those gates and don't feel yourself change, is the day you need to leave'; a comment which speaks to his own powerful sense of the relationship between places and their disciplining forces which shape our behaviour and cognition. A running joke in our family was that he was given crystal whisky glasses upon retirement, and lamented: 'I gave that place twenty years and all I got were three chipped glasses'. He stopped working full-time when we were very young, returning for varying lengths of time to work at other schools part-time and later teaching inmates in prison.

After meeting my Mum (Victoria Musgrave née Hall), they had me, another George Musgrave, and not long after were married in a town called Retford in north Nottinghamshire. My brother William arrived two years later. In a very powerful way, my Mum is the bridge that connects and separates the lives of my grandparents and the life I currently live, which I continually remind myself when I walk around certain parts of London they could not begin to comprehend and doubtless would feel hugely uncomfortable in. The ambition, the drive, the push, the tenacity and the competitiveness which has so driven my life has entirely come from my Mum, who is, to me, nothing short of a superwoman. Born in 1953 in Manchester, the nuances of class were prominent in her upbringing. Her Dad (my 'Gramps', with whom I was not particularly close) – William Hall – had grown up in poverty, with both of his parents working in domestic service. However, unlike my Grandad, Gramps passed his scholarship exam and went to the school which would change his life: the Warwick School, an elite all-boys public school. Here, seeing other lads arrive in Bentleys and Rolls Royces while he was mocked for his accent and living in a rented house, he grew up to be thoroughly embarrassed of his roots, veiling them in secrecy, and was astutely aware of cultural dimensions of class, reflected in his love of opera as a mechanism of acceptance, for example. When my Mum was a young child, the family moved to a middle-class area of Manchester, Hale, facilitated by Gramps's relative wealth as a scrap metal dealer. However, my Mum recalls that she and her brother and sisters were told never to tell other people what he did for a living and instead describe him as a metallurgical scientist. Ensuring the family could meet the expectations of class respectability was key; my Mum was sent to elocution lessons to ensure she didn't develop a Northern accent and recalled noticing her Mum's speech change. Gramps even became a local Conservative councillor, and when he changed careers to work with second-hand furniture he insisted that he be called an antiques dealer.

By the age of fourteen my Mum was effectively a full-time carer for her Mum who had multiple sclerosis (which, again, had to be kept a secret). She died when my Mum was a teenager, and when Gramps got remarried my Mum went to a further education college to do an OND in Business Studies, Secretarial Skills and Languages to try and work in an airline to get away. She worked briefly at Manchester Airport but then moved to London, working in temp roles doing secretarial work. After marrying her husband (John), they moved to their first house, a bungalow near Orpington, where she had my older siblings Simon and Caroline. Here, she was a full-time Mum for many years doing odd-jobs here and there selling educational books or collecting information for the census. However, she had always wanted to be a teacher, and after moving to Retford (where she would meet my Dad and get remarried) she decided to go back to school. Her journey, from doing A levels at night-school with young children, going to Sheffield Hallam, to eventually becoming a headteacher and later what various education secretaries (namely David Blunkett in 1997 and Estelle Morris in 2002) came to call a 'super head', was always, in my mind, meteoric. Whilst she always rejected the 'super head' title and felt uncomfortable with it (Leggett, 2012), I feel it captured much of a term which years later I would come to associate very much with her: self-efficacy. This is defined by the psychologist Albert Bandura (1994: 71) as: 'people's beliefs about their capabilities to produce designated levels of performance that exercise influence over events that affect their lives'. In other words, self-efficacy reflects a subjective belief that you can achieve something, and this belief has been empirically seen to connect to goal-setting behaviour (Bandura, 1977, 1997). My Mum, when we were growing up as children, was always the emblem of modelling self-efficacy, and instilled this belief in me too, although surveying the literature it is hard to ascertain quite where this self-belief came from. In the end, much of my Mum's self-efficacy in fact became a source of the angst between her and my Dad. However, together, their relationship facilitated the emergence of the kind of narrative richness which would define my life: my Dad had the immediate proximity to *the* class struggle of the day (the miner's strike) from the heart of the Yorkshire coalfields, and my Mum was able to articulate the class-anxiety, the social striving, the ambitiousness and the utility of education which together their relationship represented.

George & Charlotte

Let me try and connect this story now with the themes I want to address in this book: the places we are from and how these places are represented and constructed. The complicated element here is that I am not really 'from' anywhere. My entire childhood, essentially, consisted of our family moving house every few years to follow my Mum up the career ladder. However, I can chart each of the places I have lived and how this patchwork of English market towns and suburbs ultimately came to act as the compositional backdrop to the music I would later write. Inspired by sociological 'live methods' (Back and Puwar, 2013) and what the *Sociological Review* (2019) has described as 'walking sociologically', as well as the psychogeography of authors like Iain Sinclair (2002) and Peter Ackroyd (see Tso (2020) for a wonderful collection on these authors and others) as well as colleagues such as Caroline Knowles (2022) and Keith Negus (Negus and Sledmere, 2022), I returned to each of these places when writing this book. I wanted to walk the routes I used to take to school, to return to the local parks, to sit at the bus stops, to stand outside the houses I once lived in, to see the hills I used to skateboard down, and also to just wander and breathe in each of these places. In seeing them with older – and perhaps wiser – eyes, I wanted to draw on traditions of ethnographic methods and thus kept diary notes, referred to by the sociologist Lisa Mckenzie (2017: 269) as 'ethnographic vignettes', which I would later return to and piece together. All of these places were perfectly nice. Some were beautiful, most were ordinary – the kind of England no one cares about – and, aside from one very notable exception, I was wonderfully happy in all of them.

Tuxford and Louth

The first place I ever lived was Tuxford, a small town in North Nottinghamshire not far from Retford where my parents got married. I lived here from the time I was born in 1986 until I was six. We temporarily moved from here to the adorable nearby village of East Drayton for a few years, but between February 1988 and October 1989 interest rates increased from 9% to 15%, meaning my parents had to sell the house and moved back to Tuxford, to the house (strangely) next-door to where we had moved from. You cannot help but experience Tuxford as somewhere that people are passing through. It's a small town carved in half by a particularly grim part of the A1 where ancient woodland lies clogged with an astonishing amount of litter and the fields are punctuated with the incongruous sites of sex shops and American diners. Every road in Tuxford seems to be a main road. Cars, haulage lorries, workmen's vans and sixteen-wheelers aching from the weight of vehicles stacked like Jenga blocks heading for either showrooms or scrapheaps hurtle past; it's there and then it's gone. As Lisa Mckenzie (2017: 269) writes of her experiences in similar towns and villages scattered throughout Nottinghamshire: 'The end of the village comes as quickly and unexpectedly as it started'. It is paradoxical to experience the speed of everyone moving past you in a geographical context typified by 'extremely low levels of mobility – whether moving in or out' (ibid.: 275). A handful of windswept bus stops act as what they describe as 'Your Rural Link to Town', running between Retford and Nottingham seven times a day, if they turn up. Beauticians and trinket shops, a working men's club and a food bank, faded Georgian splendour and council houses, the obligatory grand church and carpeted pub, and – bizarrely – a windmill, all sit nestled amongst the smell of chip shops and petrol, plonked in the middle of the Nottinghamshire countryside of enormous dormant chimney stacks and cack-splattered tractors. I remember it fondly as the only house I ever lived in where my whole family – me, my Mum, my Dad, all three of my brothers and my sister – all lived together, even if just temporarily. My older brother Simon went to Tuxford Comprehensive and some of his mates still live in Tuxford and Retford. I can picture myself as a kid watching my Mum on a little trampoline in our kitchen, jumping up and down on another diet to Bruce Hornsby tracks, and can remember lying in bed gazing at the twinkling Christmas lights that used to hang from the lamppost outside my bedroom window, listening to the sound of the traffic rush by.

    When I was six years old we moved first to a bungalow on the outskirts of a town called Louth in Lincolnshire for a few months, and then to a village a few miles away; a tiny strip of a few houses, a pub, a school and a post office surrounded by the undulating hills of the Wolds which I remember as a child looking magnificent in the county's serene desolation, covered in snow and glistening white in brief moments of December sunshine. Not long after moving here, my Mum had been sufficiently promoted to deputy headteacher that they were able to buy the cottage opposite our house for my grandparents to live in, meaning that my grandparents used to walk me and my brother to school and spent a lot of time with us. Although schooling was tricky here (I moved schools three times in one academic year for various reasons), it was a wonderful place to be a little boy and I remember it with only happiness: skateboarding in Cleethorpes and ordering copies of Thrasher skateboarding magazine to the village shop to feel connected to an America which still felt like a place to dream about; trips to Mablethorpe or walks in Hubbard's Hills and coming home to make Yorkshire puddings with my Nan; watching my sister (Caroline) dance around the kitchen to Whigfield's 'Saturday Night' (Extreme Records, 1992) and watching *The Clothes Show*, or listening to the tracks my brother (Simon) would play when he came to stay like the rapper Ice Cube's album *Lethal Injection* (Priority Records, 1993), or hardcore tapes like *Kaos Theory* (Telstar, 1992) containing the music he heard on his nights out at the Skegness Pleasuredome; playing Mortal Kombat, Super Street Fighter II, and Earthworm Jim with my younger brother (William) on the Sega Megadrive and watching *Live and Kicking, Finders Keepers* and *Art Attack* together, and cycling round the village on Simon's yellow and blue Falcon Pro Kappa BMX, which I thought was extremely cool.

Sociopolitically, Louth, and indeed the wider county of Lincolnshire, is a strange place in its apparent disconnectedness and insularity. Louth is part of East Lindsey, which voted 70.7% to leave the European Union in 2016 – the third highest Leave vote in the UK. In 2022, the British news and opinion website *UnHerd* published the results of a poll it had conducted alongside the polling-data platform Focaldata entitled 'UnHerd Britain 2023'. Encompassing 10,000 respondents, their research revealed nearly every single one of the 632 constituencies in Britain agreed (strongly or mildly) with the statement: 'Britain was wrong to leave the EU'. Only three constituencies disagreed, all in Lincolnshire: Boston and Skegness, South Holland and The Deepings, and, where I lived as a child, Louth and Horncastle. The work of historian James Broun (2020) on identity in South Lincolnshire in the late 1980s – not far from both Tuxford and Louth, from a similar period to when I lived there in the early 1990s – highlights beautifully how contemporary Euroscepticism is emblematic of much longer historical patterns of 'a traditional, paternalistic and rural shade of Toryism' (ibid.: 334) which typifies the political sensibilities of many in the area. The wider county of Lincolnshire has long rejected outsiders (whether English 'townies' in the 1980s, or EU migrants in the 2010s), rooted in what Broun describes as: 'an increasingly defensive and conservative set of ideas rooted in nostalgia, localism, lament for the loss of productive employment, inverse snobbery towards newly affluent service workers, anti-metropolitan and anti-elite sentiments, and feelings of powerlessness' (ibid.: 335). Some of these subjectivities are captured by Sally Brooks (2019) who writes of Lincolnshire's 'politics of the rural'. Indeed, the provincialism and peripherality which typifies this part of the world is reflected in cultural and artistic production which suffers from enormous challenges, particularly with reference to diversity on various metrics. This is delineated in work for Arts Council England, which includes many references to the challenges faced by areas including Louth such as: sparse transportation and connectivity, a population which is older and more ethnically homogenous than the national average, an absence of cultural diversity, a challenging absence of infrastructure and funding, and a lack of national representation (Madhavan and Nair, 2016).

The parts of Tuxford and Louth I lived in as a child are not 'suburbs' in the classic sense; they are market towns and villages. However, as Broun (2020: 349) highlights, the emergence of a new commuter class in new-build housing estates in areas like these meant that increasingly 'towns and villages became "suburban"' throughout the 1980s and into the 1990s. However, as per the aforementioned work of Stevie Smith (1972), Rupa Huq (2013: 6) and Gail Cunningham (2004: 424), suburbia is not simply geographic and both of these places are alike in their shared experience of remoteness. Certainly, the next two big house moves – to Surrey and then to Norwich – would be the moves that would come to define my songwriting and provide the range of experiences which textured my understanding of the kinds of England no one cares about, and the lives of those living there. In a sense, though, I see all of the places I lived as being connected, broken only when I moved to London as an adult and started my own family. However, what I remember most clearly from both Tuxford and Louth is the music my parents played. These songs are so powerful that when my parents eventually got divorced when me and my brother were teenagers, we refused to listen to them; if ever our Mum tried to play them, we would shout 'turn this DM [divorce music] off'.[4] I don't think I could listen to most of them until I was perhaps thirty, so intense was the loss they represented. In the same way that the work of Tim Baker (2022) uses literature to poignantly 'read back' his mother, I can likewise 'listen back' to my parents. It is as if these songs contain within them the stories of their love and its eventual passing, capturing the way relationships – with those we love (like 'Wonderful Tonight' by Eric Clapton or 'Baby Can I Hold You Tonight' by Tracy Chapman), those we used to love (like 'Do You Remember' by Phil Collins or 'Hello' by Lionel Richie), and places we live and dream of (like 'The River Runs Low' by Bruce Hornsby and The Range or 'Sailing to Philadelphia' by Mark Knopfler) – play out over the course of our lives. If I close my eyes and play certain songs, I can see them dancing together in our living room to Eric Clapton, or driving and holding hands with me and my brother sat in the backseat playing Tracy Chapman or Chris Rea; times which I know now were the all too fleeting moments before rancour and heartbreak took over: when they were happy, and in love, and we were a family.

Fetcham and the Outer-London Suburbs

When I was nine we moved again – our sixth house move and my fifth primary school – first to a small flat in Epsom for a few months and eventually settling in Fetcham, which sits within the Mole Valley in Surrey. It lies just outside the M25 and about twenty miles from Central London. In hindsight it is here, and more formatively later when we moved to Norwich, that the interpretations and representations of suburbia which would emerge in my lyrics began to ferment most clearly. Fetcham itself is a deeply uninspiring place, described not unfairly in my view by architectural critics Ian Nairn and Nikolaus Pevsner (2002: 244) in their work *The Buildings of England: Surrey* as the 'dispirited fag-end of Leatherhead, the start of the characterless chain of suburbanisation that follows road and railway all the way to Guildford'. It is hard for me to speak – to employ the terminology of Meyers and Marcus (1995: 2) – 'cleanly' and without bias about the relative merits or flaws of Fetcham as a place, largely because I had an appalling time at school throughout the time I lived there. Much of this stemmed from the fact that I was not great at making friends and didn't conform to the ideals of what the local boys thought was acceptable (namely playing football, which I never liked nor was I good at). Suburbia, at least in my experience, tends to punish non-conformity in all its guises. Therefore, I overwhelmingly remember it as a place of loneliness and sadness. This is not to say I was unhappy all the time – I have some great memories from there too – but I find it hard not to be angry and resentful.

If I could change one thing about my childhood, it would be that we ever moved there and I ever had to experience feeling the way I did at school there. Being punched or kneed in the face for trying to join in, or having paint thrown all over me, or having my bike taken off me and thrown in a river are just three examples of a series of experiences I frankly could have done without.

When driving back to Fetcham for this book from my North London home down through the mansion blocks of Maida Vale, the pink and purple and red stucco townhouses of Notting Hill, past the Green in Shepherd's Bush where groups of men sat playing dominos, around the mania of Hammersmith Broadway, over the Thames through Putney, and then past Roehampton heading towards Surrey, the changing architectural make-up made it clear that the Georgians or Victorians with their flair for ornate detailing, grand windows and decorative railings had not ventured this far, and I was now entering the post-Edwardian eras and all the horrific, post-war housing dreariness which followed, signalling one's arrival in suburbia. As I drove past New Malden towards Surbiton that morning, I was struck upon noticing that I was flanked on one side of the busy A3 by unkempt 1930s semis, with dilapidated windowsills and triple glazing to keep out the noise and pollution, sitting opposite a building site, surrounded by black hoarding emblazoned with large, bold, white lettering advertising new-build apartments as: 'Modern Suburban Living'. How bleak, I thought.

The composition of the 'village' of Fetcham (which I suspect is how it tries to describe itself with the same kind of fanciful agrestic vernacular employed by London 'villages' too) is overwhelmingly residential, typified by tired bungalows and plain semi-detached houses. There are various cul-de-sacs comprised of an odd mix of overgrown grass outside mundane-at-best or dishevelled-at-worst low-rise, mid-century housing, interspersed with occasional grand homes which doubtless *Location, Location, Location* on Channel 4 would describe as characteristic of 'leafy Surrey'. The relative blandness of the housing is encapsulated in a local planning document which states, matter-of-factly: 'Designs are typical of suburban housing in this part of South East England with little local distinctiveness' (Mole Valley, 2010: 14). There is a small and unexciting high street, with a large abandoned petrol station on the corner which sits boarded up with its windows smashed and its lettering faded. There was little sign of life on the day I visited; it seemed ironic to me that a place with so few pedestrians could feel so incredibly pedestrian. However, most apparent was the proliferation of flags; Union Jacks and St George's Crosses seemed to be everywhere, leaving me wondering what the choice of flags said about the persons choosing to fly them. Indeed, Susanne Reichl (2004) in her semiotic analysis of these two emblems of Britishness and Englishness as methods of polysemic meaning-making, explores the tensions around how these symbols are read and by whom, and the centrality of context in decoding flags as signifiers. How did I read them on the day I visited this place I used to live? As per journalist Poppy Noor's (2018) desire to 'reclaim' the St George's Cross from its connotations with the far right, I find it personally a real shame that the flying of flags in England has come (entirely understandably) to be so negatively understood as symbolising 'not welcome' by many; as a symbol of violence and of hatred. Indeed, when designing the cover for this book, I was all too cognisant – indeed wary – of how the colours, chosen to evoke the national symbol of England for a book about one person's perception of one side of England, were themselves highly loaded. I suppose, as work by political scientist Lenka Dražanová (2014) on national identity so powerfully shows, pride and exclusion are often two sides of the same coin. That being said, in Fetcham, I saw them flying proudly outside tatty pet shops or the local off-licence adjacent to a large banner reading 'The Sunday Telegraph' and 'Sky News' in a homage to Rupert Murdoch, leading me to wonder precisely what they were so proud of, as surely it couldn't be this place. Even the street names seemed to belie the lack of imagination, with the high street simply called 'The Street'.

Walking around on that sunny afternoon I found myself continually asking: why on Earth did my parents ever move us here? To this bland and sterile place. As suggested, I doubtless lack objectivity about this particular suburb – although much like Hegelund (2005) I prefer to think of objectivity more as a scale than a dichotomy – and whilst I would loathe living in a place like this now, I am sure many of Fetcham's residents love it. Indeed, I note some have passionately defended the area against its description as the 'fag-end of Leatherhead' praising its community spirit and the beauty of the surrounding countryside (van Klaveren, 2016). Revisiting, I am

Fig 2.3 Off-licence in Fetcham.

unconvinced. Indeed my view of the residents, so tarnished by my own time there, has encountered little to enamour me since; in 2007 I recall reading that some locals had abused and humiliated army veterans using the local swimming pool for rehabilitation sessions on the grounds that their loss of limbs was scaring people and that they had not paid the full entrance fee (Crane, 2007; Harding et al., 2007).

I suspect my younger brother remembers this place differently to me, having made friends and generally 'fitted in' better somehow. Most of my good memories from here are with him and two other boys (Liam and Thomas), skateboarding or cycling around the local area or playing GoldenEye on the Nintendo 64. Looking back, as children, I don't think my brother would have been as lonely without me as I would have been without him. Perhaps he will tell me differently if he reads this. Perhaps not. I ended my afternoon by walking to my old youth club which I found abandoned; long grass and scattered litter outside a rusty and decaying basketball court with kids' names scrawled on the walls as markers of presence and perhaps expressions of a desire to be remembered. Looking around at the tawdriness and the mundanity, wondering what the young people writing their names on these walls felt when they scribbled away just as I had, I kept thinking: why did I ever care about this place? Why didn't I just tell all those lads I wanted so much to like me, but didn't, to just fuck off? I suppose when you're eleven or twelve, you do care. One of the joys of getting older is not caring.

On my drive home back into London I stopped at a pub – The Elgin – not far from me and my wife's first flat on Ladbroke Grove and sat outside to have a beer and experience the life I was now so thankful to live: the packed hissing buses, the old drunk blokes smashed outside the Kensington Park Hotel (KPH) pub, the tourists wheeling suitcases out of their Airbnbs, doubtless off to find 'that' blue door (Schoonhoven, 2006), the families leaving the North Kensington Library with kids holding armfuls of books, the nannies and assorted W11 pram-mafia outside Notting Hill Prep School, the screams from the flower vendor, the chat in different languages from the tables outside Fez Mangal, the thunder of the Hammersmith and City line trains over the bridge, the school kids with boxes from Chicken Cottage blaring music out of their phones, the young couples staring in horror at the prices of flats in the window of Winkworth, the band lugging their guitars and amplifiers into Sarm music studios, the glamorous group of women in magnificent West African dresses crossing the road, the hipsters in ridiculous woolly hats in the blazing sun, the beautiful Victorian houses painted in various shades of green, blue, and white. This was not pedestrian. This was alive.

Norwich and the Suburbs

If Fetcham was the suburb I despised, Norwich and the surrounding areas represented a new chapter in my relationship with suburbia; one infinitely more Janus-faced, rooted in a mixture of adoration and exasperation. We moved to Norfolk when I was thirteen and lived in a rural village outside Norwich. However, much of my time was spent in the nearby suburb of Hethersett because my friends lived there and it was good for skateboarding. I remember this time with great fondness: filming 'Sponsor Me' skateboard videos in the playgrounds of the local schools; drinking cider and pretending to like it on playing fields on cold November nights; nicking copies of Max Power from the corner shop and imagining the cars we would soup-up with body kits and neon lights and drive around once we passed our driving tests and weren't dependent either on the tedious unreliability of semi-rural buses or on parental taxis; and smoking squidgy hash and having a whitey in a supermarket car park and trying not to be sick in the back of my mate's Dad's car when he came to pick us up. These are the suburban good times.

I love Norwich even if only for the fact that it was the place where I met my wife, Charlotte. We met at school when we were fourteen sitting next to each other in Spanish and Business Studies and have been together since we were sixteen years old. We moved in together while still at school when she moved into my Mum's house, stayed together when we were apart at university, travelling back and forth to see each other every weekend, got married on our fifteen-year anniversary, and now have two beautiful children. Much of me finding myself as an adult, outside of but still internalising the story of my family, begins when I met her.

When we finished school at eighteen, we moved into a shared house with Charlotte's childhood friend Tom. We lived, as doubtless many young people when living independently for the first time do, in a tired terraced house just outside the city centre with plaster peeling off the walls hidden by rap posters, dangerous gaps in decrepit floorboards, and a near-daily hunt for weed which seemed to preoccupy our entire peer group. During this time we both worked for the insurer Norwich Union, now called Aviva; an employer which, it seemed, everyone we met had worked for in Norwich at some point. Whilst I had always held jobs while I was at school (washing dishes in a Moroccan restaurant and working in a local pub) this was my first experience of the daily rhythm of a kind of office life which is so typical for millions of workers. Each day I would walk into the city, over the bridge across the ring road, in my ill-fitting Next suit, mid-2000s chunky, shiny tie, Pod school shoes, lanyard, and an iPod loaded with rap albums, and experience the dullness of handling customer service queries about car insurance. On the one hand, this all felt somewhat empowering; being paid a proper monthly salary and having conversations with people which, for the first time since I had moved to Norwich, did not revolve around school with people who knew my Mum as their headteacher. On the other hand, there was something deeply dispiriting about it. I remember that on the outside of the office building there was imposing, stencilled graffiti which you could not help but see and reflect on each time you saw

Fig 2.4 Graffiti outside the Norwich Union (now Aviva) building in Norwich.
Source: Michael Dales https://mynameismwd.org/. Reprinted with permission.

it which read: 'Why do you do this every single day?' In the end, I loved Norwich until I didn't, and I will let the lyrics and their analysis which will follow later unpack more of that relationship.

What is so interesting about many places in England is how their appearances can often mask what lies beneath. In much the same way that the despicable content and actions of so many politicians are concealed as respectable by virtue of their public school accents even as they punish the most disadvantaged in society, so too can cobbled streets, quaint second-hand bookshops and pretty Edwardian bandstands obscure the experiences of many who live there. Norwich is a fantastic example of this. On the one hand, it is a beautiful little city; indeed, as it calls itself, 'A Fine City'. It was England's first UNESCO City of Literature, with quirky shops and charmingly wonky ancient medieval buildings on pretty lanes; a city of majestic cathedrals with cloisters and manicured gardens; of delightful looking pubs on high streets with independent retailers run by friendly old hippies selling incense and bongs and grinders and radical political pamphlets; where Grade II listing seems commonplace, an open air market sells food and trinkets at prices which are reassuringly inexpensive, and friendliness is seemingly pervasive and infectious. At the same time, Norwich is a city greeted with either a knowing chuckle or outright derision by many, informed by its association with comedic figures like Alan Partridge, or celebrity TV chef Delia Smith and her now infamous 'let's be 'avin you' half-time speech at Carrow Road football stadium (Galea-Pace, 2022a).

At the same time, Norwich is surrounded by a kind of quiet, unnewsworthy poverty; the kind unlikely to earn the attention of major government funding initiatives or to take on mainstream cultural significance as sites of either artistic production or political resistance – like, for instance, Newham and Tower Hamlets in East London (White, 2021), Toxteth in Liverpool (Frost and Phillips, 2011), or St Pauls in Bristol (Hyder, 2014). The city is encircled by housing estates such as North Earlham, Larkman, Marlpit (together, NELM), Lakenham and Mile Cross, the majority of which were built in the 1920s as part of the post-First World War 'Homes Fit for Heroes' building boom. Indeed, outside of London boroughs, metropolitan districts and unitary authorities, Norwich City Council is the biggest local authority landlord of housing in

England (Norwich City Council, 2022). Ethnographic work by Ben Rogaly and Becky Taylor centred on the NELM estates has done much to enrich our understanding of the lives of residents, their complex negotiations of belonging and class, and their forms of situational identity work performed within what Sibley (1995) refers to as *Geographies of Exclusion*. This work is particularly insightful given its emphasis on how sociopolitical marginalisation intersects with *geographical* marginalisation too (Taylor and Rogaly, 2007; Rogaly and Taylor, 2009a, 2009b). In other words, not only are political, social, and markers of identity (race, gender, class, sexuality, etc.), mechanisms of inclusion of exclusion but, simply, where people are born and live are too.

We can see the inequality of the city reflected quantitatively. Data taken from the UK Government's *English Indices of Deprivation* 2019 (UK GOV, 2019) show that many of these areas, identified spatially as LSOAs (Lower Layer Super Output Areas, which highlight clusters of streets), contained within electoral wards such as Mancroft, Catton Grove, Mile Cross, Nelson, Town Close, and Crome, are among the 10% of most deprived LSOAs in England. Two images of an interactive map taken from the Department for Communities and Local Government (DCLG) showing Norwich are included here. The map on the left shows inner Norwich, while the map on the right highlights Norwich within the broader county of Norfolk. The darker the shading the more deprived the LSOA – as seen in the housing estates surrounding the city – and the lighter the shading the less deprived the LSOA – as seen both in the wider rural countryside and in the wealthier 'Golden Triangle' area in the south west of the city. In this context, deprivation is calculated using various facets including: income, employment, education skills and training, health and disability, crime, barriers to housing and services, and the 'living environment' (all data-points of which are downloadable from the UK Government website).

What this data reveals – and of course this is true of almost anywhere in the world – is that you could ask two groups of people how they see and experience a place, and you are likely to get two wildly different answers. This leads me to ask a broad conceptual and methodological question which has concerned many, from demographers and statisticians to anthropologists and sociologists: in the face of such inequality and

Fig 2.5 DCLG Map of 'Indices of Deprivation 2019' showing inner Norwich (left) and Norwich in the wider context of the county of Norfolk (right).
Source: http://dclgapps.communities.gov.uk/imd/iod_index.html.

indeed diversity of experience, how can we come to understand a place? In other words, what mechanisms can effectively tell the story of a place when the numbers on a screen say such different things about people's relational and affective geographic experiences? What I want to explore in subsequent chapters is the extent to which music-making as a form of storytelling can act as one part of the methodological picture to enrich our understandings of people's experiences. Before that, however, I want to conclude with the final part of my story.

My Story: Class and Identity

Connecting each of the places I grew up in (Tuxford, Louth, Fetcham and Norwich) and my experiences of them, are the fraught and uneasy connections between the lives of my grandparents and parents, and the life I was living, or perhaps more accurately, the life my parents wanted to live and aspired for me to live. At the heart of this is the blurred, messy notion of that longstanding English obsession, class, in particular: how class is experienced, reproduced and understood over extended generational temporalities; the subtle and even unconscious acquisition, exercising, and communication of privileged forms of knowledge and value; and the subjective ways we define ourselves and craft conceptualisations of identity based on notions of perceived 'fit'.

When I was five years old and living in Tuxford, my parents took me to see the University of Cambridge on a day out and my Mum told me it was where I would go when I grew up. I do not know why she believed this or how she knew this. She had no real basis for thinking it other than the fact that she thought I was clever (or what she used to jokingly describe as 'a cognitive child'). We had no connection to an elite university like this; my Mum had gone to Sheffield Hallam as a mature student after night-school, and my Dad the Open University. I can intensely remember walking through King's College Chapel, standing next to my Mum, with no idea of what the place meant or what it would come to mean in my life, staring up at the vast ceiling which I would continue to look up at for years to come. Despite my reluctance to even apply there when I was in school (some of which, it turned out, was well-founded and some of which was not), going there was one my greatest achievements and it simply would not have happened without my Mum who, in hindsight, had a vision rooted in her own astonishing self-efficacy and made it happen, as she always did. This is not to say that my Dad was not central to this process; in terms of cultivating my interests in social and political issues even as a child, growing up in a house where I could speak to a man of immense knowledge every day, and encouraging a practice of critical reading, he was key and intellectually inspiring – but my Mum was highly focused on the utility of skills like these in a goal-setting sense. As is the case for thousands of other young people every year, gaining admission to Cambridge meant more to my family than simply winning a place at university; I will never forget the way my Dad hugged me and cried when I handed him my letter offering me a place. The photograph shown here, on the left, was taken by my Dad on the day we visited when I was five. It shows me, my Mum and my brother walking down Senate House Passage. The image on the right is the three of us almost twenty years later, on the day I graduated. This is one of the most precious images and memories of my life. However, this picture contains more than just three members of a family; it holds within it the story which so *defined* my family and defined my life. It is an emblem of my familial narrative.

Fig 2.6 Left: my brother (3), my Mum, me (5) – Right: my Mum, me (22), my brother (20) at my graduation.

In my final year at university, my Dad wrote me a letter, as he often had done throughout my time there, usually containing his typical mixture of newspaper clippings alongside scribbled lamentations, but this one containing part way through the phrase 'From Grimethorpe to Cambridge in two generations'. These seven words seemed to capture an enormous amount. I often felt that my path to Cambridge was part of a journey that my family was on which, in basic terms, started with my grandparents and in a way was being realised with me; as if my attending this university was emblematic of an exercise in social climbing, recognition and meaning which transcended my own personal autobiography. After all, depending on how one cuts the cake, my journey to Cambridge can be read two ways. On the one hand, it is fairly mundane – a White, male, middle-class kid from a high-achieving state boarding school with statistically reasonably high household income, with parents from professional occupations. On the other hand, this journey can be situated within the more powerful intergenerational narrative which always assumed a degree of literary prominence in our familial oral history which captures with more nuanced sociological insight what concepts like privilege or fit or ease really look *and feel like* as psychological experiences. In other words, to refer back to the phraseology of Bourdieu, the *cognition* of sociology.

I want to unravel this claim in a bit more detail. On the one hand, we might think of these constant glances to the coal fields of my family's past as being simply a kind of 'family folklore' (Loveday, 2014). On the other hand, as a teenager at school I never thought Cambridge was for people 'like me'; it seemed a distant institution for those with more refined accents from more refined places, with more refined tastes and comfy in more refined spaces. As I said as a teenager: it was for 'posh knobs'. I think now, that if even I – with all of the aforementioned apparently identifiable markers of privilege – could think that, how must so many others feel, and how can we explain the transmission of a mechanism of perceived exclusion, and social and cultural unease, in a meaningful way which is so masked by oversimplifications of class? And yet I did feel it. Intensely. Excluded with the door apparently wide open, albeit – honestly – whilst possessing the requisite reserves of cultural capital to effectively manage it. That being said, this unease did often transcend perception alone. Two funny stories highlight this. I recall in my first year walking into the bar at Clare College and a group of lads in magnificently condescending Received Pronunciation saying 'Oh wow, look, a chav' and laughing before I threw beer on them and threatened them. Another example was at a house party in my second year, where a wealthy, internationally schooled German student said to me, 'I read about you before I came to this country. You are what they call a "typical English lout"'. At the same time, this story of long-term class movement, and its example as a case study of the shifting composition of social relations in modern England, contains within it fissures and scars which inform how the identities of, in particular, me and my Dad played out, and which were playing out across my Mum's entire life informed by the class-shame of her upbringing, and which reflect in some ways the lack of subtlety in blunt conceptualisations of class which cannot, I would suggest, be understood solely by the job one does or the money one earns, and requires a cultural understanding.

When I was fourteen years old and living in Norwich, my parents bought a house that they could, one day, retire to. It was back in

Lincolnshire and I suspect was supposed to represent not only a returning to a place where we had all been happy once, but also a culmination of everything they had worked to achieve; a signalling of an arrival at a place which perhaps only exists in our own minds – of respectability, of achievement, and of purpose. The first time my family saw it we were blown away by the fact that it had an outdoor swimming pool. It seemed unimaginably lavish. It was situated in a picturesque village not far from where we had all once lived together – me, my brother, my sister, my Mum and Dad on one side of the road, and our grandparents in a cottage on the other side. A sweeping curved road led you down to a tranquil village pond with weeping willow trees cascading over the water, and the house itself was perched atop a small hill with a gated entrance. It was, we thought, magnificent. My parents never got to retire there; less than two years after buying it, when I was fifteen, they were divorced, the house was sold, and my Dad was living in a one-bedroom house on a 1990s estate in a Norwich suburb. This rather unceremonious and heart-breaking end to their story often struck me as having something of the myth of Sisyphus about it: the social ambition of pushing an enormous boulder up a hill only for it to roll back down again so close to the imagined summit.

Immediately after my parents bought this 'dream house', my grandparents came over to see it and were visibly uncomfortable. I recall looking through the kitchen window, on a blazingly hot afternoon, watching my Dad and Grandad sit on the front patio, admiring this scene of pastoral repose, drinking beer in silence. For what seemed like forever, they said nothing to each other. What could they say? It was like Wittgenstein's lion had learned to speak, but whatever they said could not be understood by anyone who heard it. To me, that moment of not knowing what to say or how to say it and the palpable sense of unease, seemed emblematic of a class chasm that had ruptured between them, and which had been splintering and cracking from the second my Dad had put his pencil down on his desk at the end of his eleven-plus examination. The only thing to do was just to keep drinking. And say nowt.

This awkwardness at the life our family had arrived at, and the place me and my brother were so often reminded that we 'came from' (although of course we never lived and experienced it), permeated much of our lives like an embodied transgenerational phantom. The year before this incident of 'silence on the patio', we had moved from suburban Surrey to Norfolk. I will never forget how, on the first day of school, as we left the door in our uniforms, my Dad knelt down and said to me and my brother, 'remember, these people are not like us'. I didn't really know what he meant at the time, but I think I do now: that the kinds of people he imagined lived in a place like this, and he imagined went to a school like this which he had caricatured as posh, knew nothing of the life he and my Mum had worked so hard to make sure that we did not need to live. Of course, this says so much more about how he saw (and continues to see) the world – the class confrontation, the antagonism, the exclusion, the resentment, the injustices (both perceived and real) – but the comment was profoundly telling. It speaks to my Dad's uneasy sense of who he was – and is – in certain social settings. When writing this book I asked him, today, out of curiosity, what class he thinks he is. He could not answer. Perhaps he thought the question did not matter? Perhaps at his age he feels ambivalent about his own class identity (the work of sociologist of class Mike Savage (2001) on class ambivalence is fascinating on this subject)? Instead, he made reference to a formative film he had seen as a nine- or ten-year-old, *Young at Heart*, where Frank Sinatra plays a songwriter – Alex Burke – whom my Dad had seen as an outsider, which he, even as a child, had so identified with. After he told me this I researched the film, and read a fascinating character study by media scholar Karen McNally (2007: 132) on Sinatra's portrayal and representation in this film as being that of a 'resentful non-conformist', marked by a 'consistent sense of class alienation' (ibid.: 117) that 'defines his existence' (ibid.: 132). The parallels with my Dad are striking, as is the fact that this kind of distant Hollywood media could speak so directly to the experiences of his life, not unlike the rap music which I would find such affinity with in my own life. The capacity of forms of media to speak to our lived experience, even when thousands of miles away and an apparent lifetime apart, I find hugely powerful.

Similar things to this comment on my first day at a new school happened throughout my life; representative of the class-ridden chips on our shoulders that my family carried about. For instance, on the day before my Cambridge entrance interview, much to my Mum's dismay and horror, I shaved my hair as short as I could make it and put lines in my eyebrows and speed stripes in the side of my head. I also wore tracksuit bottoms and trainers to my interview, petulantly insisting that the invitation had told me to wear a suit, and that this had the word 'suit' in it. I remember waiting to go in for the first part of my interview – a discussion about an extract of Thomas Hobbes's 1651 classic political text *Leviathan* which we had been given ten minutes earlier to read – surrounded by what looked like unfathomably polished sixth formers in suits proper, thinking 'these people are not like me'. Today, I know how stupid I was; many of them were, in lots of ways, precisely like me, but this highlights how powerful the stories in my family had become. Another example of this is that when I graduated from Cambridge, I will never forget all the other parents arriving in their finery and hats as if attired for royalty – including my Mum – and my Dad rocking up in a T shirt and jeans. Even at the apparent culmination of the journey we had been on, in his words 'from Grimethorpe to Cambridge', he could not resist a final, and perhaps unconscious, 'fuck you' to everyone else there: people who were, I suspect, in his mind, not like us.

Notes

1 See Carol Giesen's (2021) work on the families of coal miners in West Virginia for a beautiful account.
2 When writing this book, I asked my Dad to make a playlist of songs he remembered hearing growing up in the 1940s and '50s. The tracks he chose are given in Playlist 2: 'Daydreaming in Worsbrough' at the end of this chapter.
3 Reflections on this course, its units, and the broader theme of sociology of education in the 1970s have been fascinatingly detailed by one of the course tutors at the time, Martyn Hammersley (2016).
4 Alongside my younger brother, we have collected these songs in Playlist 3: 'When they were happy' at the end of this chapter.

Playlist 2: Daydreaming in Worsbrough

Artie Shaw – 'Stardust'
Artie Shaw – 'Begin the Beguine'
The Mills Brothers – 'You Always Hurt the One You Love'
Jo Stafford – 'You Belong to Me'
The Jimmy Dorsey Orchestra – 'Amapola'
Connie Francis – 'I'll Get By (as Long as I Have You)'
Nat King Cole – 'Don't Get Around Much Anymore'
Perry Como – 'Some Enchanted Evening'
Nina Simone – 'My Baby Just Cares for Me'
Fats Domino – 'Blueberry Hill'
The Platters – 'The Great Pretender'
The Everly Brothers – 'Bye Bye Love'
Eddie Cochran – 'Summertime Blues'
The Coasters – 'Yakety Yak'
Ritchie Valens – 'La Bamba'
The Shirelles – 'Will You Still Love Me Tomorrow?'
Martha Reeves and The Vandellas – 'Dancing in the Street'
Wilson Pickett – 'In the Midnight Hour'
The Spencer Davis Group – 'Gimme Some Lovin''
Sam and Dave – 'Soul Man'
Carl Mann – 'Pretend'

You can hear the playlist here: tiny.cc/960cvz

Playlist 3: When They Were Happy

Bruce Hornsby and The Range – 'The Way It Is'
Bruce Hornsby and The Range – 'The River Runs Low'
Jon Secada – 'Just Another Day'
Eurythmics – 'Who's That Girl?'
Chris Rea – 'Candles'
Mark Knopfler – 'Sailing to Philadelphia'
TOTO – 'Rosanna'
Players – 'How Long (Has This Been Going On)?'
Eric Clapton – 'Wonderful Tonight'
Lionel Richie – 'Hello'
Tina Turner – 'On Silent Wings'
Tracy Chapman – 'Baby Can I Hold You Tonight?'
Mike and The Mechanics – 'Beggar On a Beach of Gold'
Cyndi Lauper – 'Time After Time'
Eurythmics – 'Miracle of Love'
Eurythmics – 'I Saved the World Today'
Eric Clapton – 'Layla'
Alison Moyet – 'Invisible'
Bruce Hornsby and The Range – 'Mandolin Rain'
Phil Collins – 'Do You Remember'
Phil Collins – 'Against All Odds (Take a Look at Me Now)'
Dire Straits – 'Sultans of Swing'
Bruce Hornsby and The Range – 'Every Little Kiss'
Chris Rea – 'Josephine'

You can hear the playlist here: tiny.cc/i60cvz

3

What Stories Do, Why Stories Matter

Thus far I have sought to tell what I have characterised as 'my story'; the narrative arc that has broadly defined my life driven by, among other things: childhood labelling (me being thought of as 'the clever one'); class alienation, positional jockeying and consciously perceived unease; my family's exploration of the relationship between geography and psychology reflected in our multiple house and school moves and the impact (both positive and negative) this had on me; and, crucially, intergenerational social mobility and (semi)suburban aspiration. This is not a story which I have moulded from memory to suit the argumentation of this book: this is an active, orally transmitted, teleological, shared family story – an explanatory mechanism of meaning-making which has been read like pages from fiction since I was a child by parents who, as English teachers, were themselves profoundly invested in the act of storytelling. A nice example of this commitment to and investment in narrative is that when my Dad first introduced my Mum to my Grandad in the Strafford Arms pub not far from Worsbrough, her first thoughts were of the poems and novels of D.H. Lawrence, particularly his 1913 work *Sons and Lovers* and the short story *Odour of Chrysanthemums* (1914). Indeed, Lawrence was from Eastwood, a mining community not far from where we first lived in Nottinghamshire, and my Mum asked my Grandad about life as a miner based on her reading of these stories; the camaraderie and community of men living and working together. His reply: 'don't be bloody daft lass'. Stories, to my Mum and my Dad (if not my grandparents), mattered.

In this chapter I want to bring together a triadic conceptual framework which connects the thematic enquiry of storytelling and its impact, to try and make sense of how this recital of familial narration ultimately connects to the lyrics which this book seeks to better understand: lyrics which are, themselves, stories. In other words, having told my story, I want to now explain, in a broader conceptual sense, beyond the individual examples and instances of focused apertures and vignettes above, what stories *do* to us, why stories *matter*, and why rap music and songwriting came to act – at least for a time in my life – as my principle form of storytelling. In order to do this, I want to build a three-stage argument. Firstly, I suggest that narratives can be profoundly connected to our understanding of what psychologists refer to as 'the self', and that these vehicles of identity construction can exist intergenerationally too. In other words, who we see ourselves as and understand ourselves as (or at least who we think we might be) can be driven by stories which extend further than our own autobiographies. Secondly, building on this, I want to propose that these narrative-based identities of extended temporalities come to shape the ways we see and understand the world, our place within it, and our relationship to others. This concept is not without detractors, and I engage with those who might disagree, but I suggest that stories can come to be relationally connected to the subjective experience of class – or what sociologist Diane Reay (2005) calls 'the psychic economy of social class' – and that this was certainly the case in my life. Finally, connecting both of these arguments together, I propose that, for me, music-making as an act of storytelling came to be the primary method by which I was able to try and articulate the stories of my life and in doing so try and make sense of who I was and the world of those around me. Thus, I conclude by drawing on Foucault's concept of 'technologies of the self' and its application in the work of sociologist of music Tia DeNora, to suggest that music was one of these 'technologies' for me, and that this was therefore why I felt it was so important to use rap music to tell *my* story.

Stories and Identity

Stories matter. In a range of settings, on a range of topics, and in a range of disciplines, narrative storytelling has been shown to be powerful and impactful. Literature highlights how stories can be used to improve 'narrative leadership' within companies (Fleming, 2001; Sintonen and Auvinen, 2009; Wines and Hamilton, 2009), as vehicles to improve how we learn mathematics (Borasi et al., 1990) or law (DeVito, 2013), and as sources of motivation in times of warfare (Johnson et al., 2017). Stories have been seen to engender demonstrable improvements in various contexts, from communication in children with limited language (Brinton and Fujiki, 2017), advertising (Lien and Chen, 2013), and even medical practices (Newman, 2003; Watson, 2008). Stories have been highlighted as forces for strengthening neighbourhood relations (Slingerland et al., 2021), devices for improving methods of working in the construction industry (Leung and Fong, 2011), guides for practice in paediatric medicine (Optiz et al., 2016), and tools for advancing social justice (Charmaz, 2016). Evolutionary biologist Stephen Gould famously suggested that human beings should be defined as 'the primates who tell stories', a quote drawn on by psychologist of human judgement Robyn Dawes in his 1999 paper which suggested that human brains more effectively process stories (instead of statistics) to inform decision-making, referring to humans as 'primates whose cognitive capacity shuts down in the absence of a story'. The work of Jonathan Gottschall (2012) fascinatingly weaves together findings from neuroscience, psychology and beyond to highlight the centrality of narrative in the survival of the human species, and a beautifully crafted paper by American novelist Scott Sanders (1997) argues more compellingly than I why and how stories are so central to our lives – to entertain, to empathise, to teach, and to learn. Stories are key to how children develop, learn and understand (Tatar, 2009), and, more broadly, stories from the *Epic of Gilgamesh* and the Bible to *The Tale of Genji* and *Don Quixote* have been influential in shaping human history and even entire civilisations (Puchner, 2018). This centrality of storytelling has been captured most elegantly, in my opinion, by the poet Muriel Rukeyser (2006) who writes, in 'The Speed of Darkness': 'the universe is made up of stories, not of atoms'.

There is perhaps one academic discipline where storytelling has been (and continues to be) foregrounded as core to the practice of articulating who a person is and the development of forms of self-knowledge: psychoanalysis. As argued by professor of psychiatry Nancy Kulish (2022: 835) 'stories are central to the entire psychoanalytic process', and this can be seen in foundational texts such as Sigmund Freud and Joseph Breuer's *Studies in Hysteria* (1895 / 2004) where patients such as 'Anna O' were described as having daydreams in a 'private theatre'. Via this dramaturgical language and the central positioning of the importance of narrative revealed in the short stories of his patients, Goldsmith (2006: 84) suggests that Freud was 'negotiat[ing] a space between literature and science from which psychoanalysis could speak'. Indeed, as explored in the introductory chapter, many of the texts of autofiction which have so inspired my own thinking, such as *The End of Eddy* (Louis, 2014), have a psychoanalytic component insofar as they seek to use narrative to better understand (and even change) one's self. In sociology too, the role of narratives as methods of self-understanding, informed at least in part by psychoanalysis, has been conceptualised as 'the narrative turn' in social sciences. Arthur Bochner in his paper 'Narrative's virtues' classifies this concept beautifully as a turn:

away from facts and toward meanings; away from master narratives and toward local stories; away from idolizing categorical thought and abstracted theory and toward embracing the values of irony, emotionality, and activism; away from assuming the stance of the disinterested spectator and toward assuming the posture of a feeling, embodied, and vulnerable observer; away from writing essays and toward telling stories.

(Bochner, 2001: 134–135)

This position is not without detractors, and indeed the conclusion of this chapter will afford engagement with many insightful and fair oppositions. However, as suggested earlier, one of the central ambitions of this book is to explore the connections between my (life) story, the stories told in my music, and what those stories reveal not only about a side of England but also about who I am as a person. In order to examine this, I will begin this chapter by looking more closely at the relationship between stories and selves, and more specifically its application in my own life where longer ancestral stories came to be so formative, via literature from narrative psychology on the intergenerational self. After unpacking in more precise detail what we mean by the term 'the self', I will look at how longer-term understandings and articulations of identity rooted in storytelling come to manifest and engender meaning.

The Intergenerational Self

Much psychological literature on identity formation positions narrative storytelling as crucial in the development of 'the self'. The concept of the self is a rather sprawling, perhaps even nebulous, concept in psychology but one which is synthesised nicely by social psychologist Roy Baumeister (2010: 139) as encompassing a reflexive consciousness whereby you can 'be aware of yourself and know things about yourself'. With reference to self-knowing, then, narratives are understood by many to be key in this process. Dan McAdams (2001: 100) in his life story model, for example, suggests that narratives can provide 'unity and purpose [to our lives] by constructing internalized and evolving narratives of the self'. This takes place by stories facilitating three processes: the reconceptualising of our personal histories, a better understanding of our present, and the mapping and anticipating of our futures. Thus, via the use of psychosocial narrative constructions with thematic and *causal* coherence, we use stories – particularly in emerging and early adulthood – to provide meaning to our lives; e.g. this event or experience happened to me, which has consequently made me the person I am today. In this sense, this body of work by McAdams (1985, 1993, 1996) provides a theoretical architecture for Jerome Bruner's (1990) constructivist contention that narratives are *Acts of Meaning* – mechanisms which facilitate an interpretation of the self and the expression of those meanings in our practices from a psychological position which is distinctly *cultural* (as opposed to, say, solely biological or neurological).

Work by Kate McLean and colleagues (2007) brings together Dan McAdams's (1993) concept of our selective autobiographical 'life story', Jerome Bruner's (1990) cultural psychology, and the idea of 'self-concept' i.e. evaluative or descriptive beliefs about ourselves and who we see ourselves as being (Kernis and Goldman, 2003). In doing so, they propose *a reciprocal relationship between stories and selves*. In other words, the authors suggest that we use stories about our lives to develop and maintain understandings of the self; that is, our self-concept vis-à-vis who we understand ourselves to be and who we see ourselves as. Narratives are therefore, in the lives of many people, methods which allow us to construct and make sense of the world around us (Bruner, 1991). Thus, we use stories via the emergence of autobiographical memory which 'connects us to our selves, our families, our communities, and our cultures' (Fivush et al., 2011: 321).

Enveloped as we are in contemporary society in forms of digital media, we are by extension surrounded by stories; from films in the cinema and songs on the radio to Instagram 'Stories' on social media feeds. Indeed, these forms of technologically driven, narrative-rich media have been suggested to be important particularly in adolescents' development of self (McLean and Breen, 2014). However, another fundamental site of narrative storytelling – as my own life highlights – is the family. Whether in day-to-day dinnertime conversations (Bohanek et al., 2009), as vehicles for imparting lessons (Ryan et al., 2004), or in constructing family mythologies as emblems of personal or familial values (Stone, 2004), families, as personality psychologist Avril Thorne (2000: 45) so succinctly concludes, 'collude in self making'. It is in this context of 'collusion' that more recent psychological literature has begun to unpack the concept of the intergenerational self: identity formation as a form of psychosocial development constructed and mediated over extended temporalities within families and across generations, providing positive outcomes both for tellers (in the form of generativity/wellbeing), and receivers (in the form of identity/meaning). The idea is fleshed out in a rich conceptual paper by psychologists Natalie Merrill and Robyn Fivush (2016) entitled 'Intergenerational narratives and identity across development'. This work brings together Erikson's (1963, 1968) theory of psychosocial development, Bronfenbrenner's (1979) ecological systems approach, and Nelson and Fivush's (2004) sociocultural model of autobiographical memory to propose that:

> intergenerational narratives are simultaneously personal stories for the tellers and received stories for the listeners in ways that help define identity as an individual within a family and within a culture.... [S]torytelling [is] a culturally mediated linguistic form for weaving together the past, present and future in ways that create a meaningful identity [and] intergenerational narratives play a critical role in the psycho-social development of individuals in ways that vary across the life span.
> (Merrill and Fivush, 2016: 74)

The life story I sketched out in the previous chapter represents the intergenerational narrative of my family; told by my parents, received by me and my younger brother as children, weaving together connections and differences between the socially and culturally splintering but emotionally connected roots of my immediate ancestry. Reflecting on this today, I can see how these stories were mechanisms of value transmission for both the tellers (my parents) and receivers (me and my younger brother) as per the literature in this area: the focus my Mum placed on hard work, striving, and competitiveness to move 'upwards' in some sense and how telling this story helped her make sense of her (and our) trajectory; the way in which education was the route to achievement for both my parents in breaking away from their histories to forge new futures for themselves and their children; and the anchoring of us as children as being 'from' somewhere as a conceptual place in the absence of any kind of geographical anchoring as we hopped all over the country moving house and school. Indeed, with reference to this final point, in 2011 I wrote a song called 'Off With Their Heads' which contained the lyric 'my background is a mining town, so you will never see me give up or start lying down'. Of course, I am not actually *from* a mining town in the sense that most people would understand the use of the term being 'from' somewhere. I never lived in Worsbrough, nor experienced poverty, and in lots of ways when I travel back there today it feels peculiar and almost foreign despite spending a great deal of time there as a young child. But in the contextually specific environs of my family I felt that I was, in a longer sense, a product of Worsbrough and that this *mattered* in my life, and was a great source of pride. It meant something to me and shaped how I saw and see the world. I was from there in the sense that my family were from there and we were all on a journey which could be traced back there: that is my background, and this place is part of my intergenerational identity which is poignant, special and a source of meaning which came to matter in large part *because* of the way it was canonised in an oral literary form from my earliest memory.

A final factor to consider vis-à-vis the transmission of this intergenerational self is the role that naming plays. Here I refer to the fact that me, my Dad and my Grandad all share the same name – George Musgrave – and the impact sharing that name has had. This name has given me immense pride and made the journey my family has been on all the more visceral and immediate. As Sofia Kotilainen (2012: 17) notes in a study of Finnish ancestral naming and its role in identity formation: 'In all ages an inherited family name has played an important part in the shaping of a person's identity', and I feel it has for me too. Likewise, the sense of history a name embodies can be a source of strength. An example I love of this comes from UK MC Skepta in his track 'Bullet from a Gun' (*Ignorance Is Bliss* – Boy

Better Know, 2019). In it, he raps about how understanding his name – Joseph Adenuga – in a broader historical context strengthened his feeling of purpose: 'Mum told me what my name really means and the power just kicked in. I found my way home then I saw my Grandad's name on a gravestone. The same as mine, already dead. Nothing to fear I've been here from time'. Evidence suggests that the impact of this process of homonymous 'namesaking' – 'one of the most enduring of human traditions' (McAndrew, 2022: 220) – is not entirely clear, evidenced in ambiguous findings on the role of shared names on parental attachment styles (Bird and McAndrew, 2019). However, all I can say for certain is that in my own life this feature of my family only served to strengthen and reinforce the power of the narrative of my family story. This literature therefore helps us understand why stories matter vis-à-vis identity and meaning. However, what is the *impact* – in a more practical and applied sense – of this construction of an intergenerational narrative? That is, what do these kinds of stories do to us beyond reflexive forms of meaning-making or feelings of pride both for tellers and receivers, and how do they come to shape not only the ways we interpret the world but also how we relate to others, i.e. how we live within the world relationally?

Life Stories as Relational Stories

For some authors, the impact of intergenerational stories is mixed. For instance, Merrill and Fivush (2016) cite work on the intergenerational experiences of highly traumatic events such the Holocaust (Wiseman et al., 2006) or Stalin's purges (Baker and Gippenreiter, 1998) and how the sharing of these stories within families and across generations demonstrates more contradictory and subtle outcomes for tellers in terms of generativity and wellbeing. Likewise, a body of research into intergenerational trauma and its transmission among groups including combat veterans (Dekel and Goldblatt, 2008) and refugee families (Sangalang and Vang, 2017) points to the power of the phenomenon notably in terms of *negative* outcomes with reference to health and wellbeing among descendants. However, the concept of the intergenerational self is critiqued somewhat differently in recent work by sociologist Sam Friedman and colleagues as being employed, perhaps even weaponised, to 'deflect privilege' (Friedman et al., 2021). Their work suggests that narratives across generations allow articulations of long-range social mobility – such as in my life – to be used by certain individuals to misidentify one's social class and in doing so fail to acknowledge someone's own structural privilege. Here, they cite data showing that 24% of people who come from what they describe as middle-class, 'professional and managerial backgrounds' identify as working class (ibid.: 716). For Friedman, the argument developed is that this represents a 'misidentification' of one's objective class position, and that narratives are the justificatory mechanisms which facilitate the denial of forms of structural *privilege*. For these authors, the argument seems to be that stories, for some, obfuscate and can come to act as a Gaussian blur of denial.

Whilst I find Friedman's broader analysis of class insightful and sophisticated (Friedman and Laurison, 2020), I found this work and indeed the media coverage that followed both fascinating and somewhat frustrating. On the one hand, I do not in any way claim to be or feel working class and never have, and in this sense do not fall into the demographic the paper seeks to understand. On the other hand, I find the argumentation problematic. For instance, is being defined as 'privileged' – where the term is used as a kind of catch-all descriptor instead of intersectionally – a reasonable categorisation based solely on the job a parent does, for example? This is the approach seen in Carey et al. (2020) in their work on job participation in the UK creative industries, for example, where being privileged (as they use the term) is understood as one parent working in higher or lower managerial, administrative or professional roles. This is not to suggest that having professional parents does not confer privileges; far from it, it confers many. But the picture is more complicated, and more interesting questions relate to *in what ways* privileges are conferred *or not*. Perhaps more importantly, how helpful and revealing is the term as a descriptor? In the field of work and enquiry I know best – music and cultural work – I would contend that being born and raised in London is a form of privilege – a geographic privilege – given the cultural and social opportunities not present in places like Norwich or Tuxford or Retford or Louth or Worsbrough; a privilege not captured by simple categories of employment. Indeed, empirical work on creative employment acknowledges this too, given the emergence of a 'London effect' (Oakley et al., 2017) where, drawing on data from the Office for National Statistics Longitudinal Study

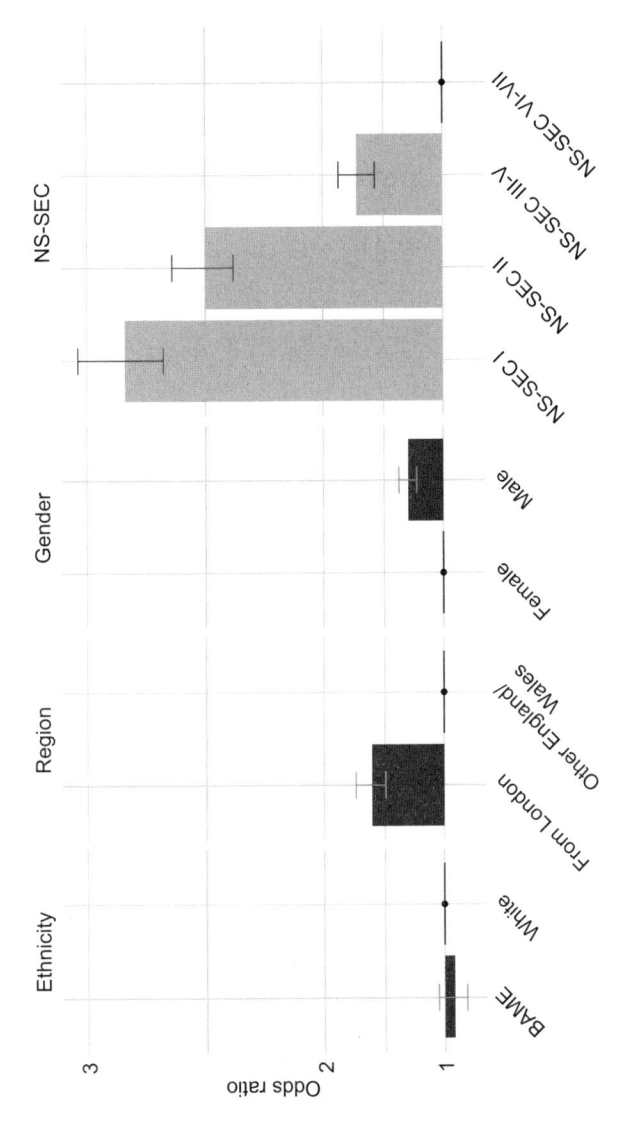

Fig 3.1 Figure from Brook et al. (2022: 11) showing what they describe as 'Odds ratios for covariates on probability of ever having core creative jobs,' based on data from the Office for National Statistics Longitudinal Study, authors' analysis.

dataset, Orian Brook and colleagues (2022) emphatically state that, statistically: 'being from London is positively and significantly associated with core creative work.'[1] Their data shows geography to be more important than gender, for example, in securing 'core creative work', and I have included a key graphic from this research here in which the impact of being 'From London' is clear. Of course, privilege is not evenly distributed among everyone growing up in London and, as the graphic shows, having parents in professional occupations was demonstrated in this research to be by far the most impactful variable. Likewise, the term is often employed in more subtle and intersectional ways which can account for this (Kliman, 2010). However, I would suggest it is an oversimplification to describe someone as privileged or not based on such narrow identifiers.

More substantively, I find the notion of professional or managerial work necessarily being *objectively* indicative of being middle class, or indeed as representing middle-class privilege, to be somewhat reductive. Indeed, the methodological variety of attempts to measure class speak, perhaps, to an unease about our collective ability to objectively measure and define someone's class position (see Savage et al., 2013) and the shortcomings of what journalist Polly Toynbee (2023) has referred to as 'the crude weighing scales of sociologists'. Perhaps my experiences are unusual, I do not know, but my wife, for example, is resoundingly middle class; arguably, depending on how one understands this most complex of terms, somewhat upper-middle class based on cultural markers of taste which I attest – drawing on Cook (2000) and Bourdieu (1979) – powerfully matter. However, her enormously cultured Mum was unemployed for almost all of her life, working occasionally as a bus driver and part-time chef in a local pub in Norfolk, and her Dad was an electrician. By this metric she would misidentify as being middle class when she was 'objectively' working class. However, this would be absurd given the transmission of class signifiers via her grandparents, one of whom on her Mum's side was a wealthy general practitioner and another of whom, on her Dad's side, recalled, as a young child, having a governess and told me when I was applying to Cambridge: 'All the men in our family attended Trinity'. However, even this too is insufficient and fails to capture the very real challenges (alongside the benefits) faced in her life connected to her upbringing. Much like in my own life, both mine and my wife's longer family histories define us and inform our cultural experiences of class, at least in some sense, and only understanding our narratives would reveal this. I suspect that while examples like ours are not generalisable, neither are they unique. In other words, mine and my wife's (and perhaps others' too) cultural and affective experiences of class – and the subtle, almost imperceptible delineations between working/lower-middle/middle/upper-middle class[2,3] which as Bourdieu (1987: 13) himself noted were not clear-cut and were more akin to 'a flame whose edges are in constant movement, oscillating around a line or surface', driven by aesthetic choices, attitudes, tastes, accents, opportunities, etc. – cannot be simply identified by the job a parent does at a particular age (as is seen in the Labour Force Survey (Social Mobility Commission, 2022) for example). Instead, these affective experiences of class are the products of forces beyond this which shape both how one sees the world and how one lives in it; forces which can linger for generations. Indeed, multigenerational data from families in Denmark by Rasmus Klokker and Mads Jæger (2022) showing high transmission of cultural capital from grandparents to grandchildren lends some empirical weight to this too.

Given this, I can appreciate that narratives might not be deflections nor 'misidentifications', but that their use instead attests to the *power* of stories in shaping the ways in which we psychosocially and culturally perceive and understand the world and ourselves; in other words, that life stories are relational stories with relational forces. By extension, this speaks to me, to sociologists Roberto Franozi (1998), Beverley Skeggs (2000), Lisa Mckenzie (2012, 2013, 2017), Joy White (2020) and others, as well as to a much longer historical traditional in anthropological ethnographic texts (Cornwell, 1984), of the need to both tell and *understand* people's stories. As sociologist and leading proponent of narrative analysis Catherine Kohler Riessman (1993: 4) suggests: 'precisely because they are essential meaning-making structures, narratives must be preserved, not fractured, by investigators, who must respect respondents' ways of constructing meaning and analyse how it is accomplished'. Literature on the intergenerational self and separately on intergenerational trauma might feature differences in outcomes, but many agree that the stories do *matter* to people – it is the *ways* in which they matter and the impacts on practices and relationships which are debated.

Ontological Complicity

In the context of stories and class, the impact of narratives has been captured beautifully by sociologist Diane Reay (2005) as a phenomenon she refers to as 'the psychic economy of social class', or 'the psychic landscape of social class'. She suggests that sociology has – aside from notable exceptions (Walkerdine, 1984; Skeggs, 2004) – too often ignored the affective, psychosocial dimensions and dynamics of class. Here, she makes reference to stories being the 'discourses that [we] draw on' with an 'easily discernible plot' (Reay, 2005: 922) to help us navigate the tensions of class identity, which in the context of educational achievement (Reay's area of research specialism) can mean feelings of self-realisation for middle-class university attendees (which to an extent chimes with my own experiences), and guilt or shame for working-class attendees.

Reay's argument, for me, calls to mind Pierre Bourdieu's (1981: 306) concept of 'ontological complicity', and by extension the work of Georg Theiner and Nikolaus Fogle (2018) on embodied, extended and distributed cognition which has done much to enrich my own understanding of this element of Bourdieu's body of work. Here, Bourdieu uses the analogy of fish, and explains ontological complicity as being the ease with which some feel and experience their social worlds. He suggests: '[the fish] does not feel the weight of the water, and it takes the world about itself for granted' (Bourdieu and Wacquant, 1992: 127). This wonderful analogy then, which we might reinterpret as being that 'one can learn to swim, but a fish swims without even knowing it is swimming', tells us something crucial about stories. It highlights that the subjective experience of Bourdieusian ontological complicity is insufficiently captured by quantitative accounts of class, or indeed of privilege. A more refined reading of the role that narratives play in the emergence of how we perceive the world is needed to better understand these phenomena as cognitive, affective and relational experiences.

Here, another of Bourdieu's concepts proves insightful: *habitus*. Habitus, for Bourdieu, represents a conceptual attempt to grapple with the sociological tension between the determinism of structuralism and its potential disavowal of agency (such as the kind of passivity Bourdieu rejected in Althusser's Marxism for example), and ideas of free will and choice (and to an extent the concept of self-efficacy too) which can disavow structural realities. Thus, the suggestion is that we all embody a set of dispositions captured terminologically as a *habitus*, simply defined by scholars of arts education Dawn Bennett and Pamela Burnard (2016: 135) as 'what people think, do and prefer'. These dispositions are cultivated via practices of socialisation, and thus whilst conceptualised as a strategic orientation they simultaneously exist on a semi-conscious – and therefore semi-unconscious – plane. As Bourdieu (1977: 72) in characteristically elegant fashion suggests, the habitus represents: 'systems of durable, transposable dispositions...collectively orchestrated without being the product of the orchestrating action of a conductor'. Habitus, then, as an embodied history structures how we perceive and understand the world; Bourdieu calls the habitus: 'structured structures predisposed to function as structuring structures' (ibid.) – the implication being that not only does our socialisation provide a structure with which we see the world, which is itself structured (a 'structured structure'), but also it structures (in an ongoing, forward-facing sense) how we go on to see and interpret the world in both thought and practice (a 'structuring structure'). In this respect, the habitus is defined beautifully by Bourdieu as 'the internalization of externality and the externalization of internality' (ibid.). As outlined by work into the psychology of narrative and the intergenerational self, stories are crucial in our construction of self and therefore, by extension, the habitus possesses an inherited endurability *rooted in narrative*.

Thus, consideration of the role that inherited stories play and their relationship to the social spaces one finds oneself within *beyond* mechanistic categorisations is needed. To connect this back to Bourdieu's analogy of fish and swimming, privilege (for example) as a descriptor of two people simply tells us that, in a context where swimming matters, both parties are statistically speaking likely to know *how* to swim and are likely to have certain advantages (or privileges) at an aggregate or population level over other swimmers, and of course over those who do not know how to swim; it says nothing of their potentially divergent experiences of being in the water as individuals. In other words, the perceptual ease or fit one feels with one's social world and one's relationship to that environment is complexly constituted and driven by factors beyond boxes which can be easily ticked on a form or labels ascribed as identifying characteristics which have, I would attest, become what Foucault (1966) might call the *episteme* of contemporary society.[4] In other words, labels often *hide* narratives, and identifiers can hide identities, and narratives did (at least in my life) really impact how I saw and experienced the world, my place within it, and my relational, subjective experience of class and identity. The transmission and production of an intergenerational self is founded on stories which are not trivial nor solely mechanisms of deflection, but entirely consequential vis-à-vis notions of ontological complicity and habitus: they shape and mould how we interpret and perceive (or not) the 'weight of the water' around us, and these narratives have extended temporalities which ripple and resonate relationally within our social worlds and across our lives and histories.

As a young person was I (or indeed, am I) 'privileged'? Of course. I possess identifying characteristics which confer privileges such as White, male, middle-class, cisgendered, heterosexual, professional parents, etc., and indeed part of that privilege is often not noticing the ways in which these characteristics confer certain privileges. My point is not whether these privileges exist (clearly they do), but to problematise the utility of the term as a descriptor in the way it is so often employed. That is, does understanding who I am in this narrow way capture the ways in which I came to intergenerationally understand, experience and live in the world around me in pockets of suburban England where the negotiations of class were playing out in real time as the dreams my parents had for me were forced to confront the challenges of our family's past and how we experienced being in these spaces? In other words, to offer a specific example, does it offer a way of understanding how someone like me with such apparent privilege on paper could feel such unease at the thought of attending somewhere like the University of Cambridge which I did not perceive as being 'for me', and where others who 'tick the same boxes as me' might not share this unease? No. Only by understanding my story can the nature of my ontological non-complicity (for lack of a better term) be understood. As Anoop Nayak (2006: 828) notes in his work on displaced masculinities: 'previous inscriptions of past cultures continue to be etched into the present'. Stories, then, are not *just* stories; they are formative. We know this from a variety of fields, for instance from data on how family narratives around personality types in children can come to be constitutive and identity forming (Bossard and Boll, 1955; Davies, 2014).

It is perhaps for all of these reasons that the stories of people's lives have always so fascinated me; why I have always been personally drawn to social disciplinary perspectives which have sought to understand the textured reality of people's everyday lives as opposed to the objective certainties of 'hard sciences', conceptual abstractions of mathematics, or what I so often see as the insufficiently subtle forms of quantitative social categorisation. My sense of self is inextricably entangled with my story and I am fascinated by the stories we tell, how we tell them, and the stories others tell; not least because, I propose, we are defined by stories – well, I am anyway. This is perhaps why I wanted to tell some of *my stories*, and, for me, rap music offered me a vehicle to *tell* those stories which so endure and shape us. Sociologists of narrative rightly acknowledge that a conceptual exploration of stories presents a methodological challenge vis-à-vis analysing them as forms of data. In my life, music became this method. To this extent, there is a third and final concept I want to use to connect the intergenerational self and ontological complicity, and this concerns how we understand and articulate ourselves and our stories – the 'constructing' or 'styling' of identity (Foucault, 1997) – through what Foucault (1988) calls 'technologies of the self', which I want to argue was captured, for me, in music-making.

Rap and Storytelling: Technologies of the Self

In a seminar given at the University of Vermont in 1982, Michel Foucault began to flesh out a new intellectual project exploring questions relating to the constitution of the self. In it, he mapped methods of self-understanding in society, from Christian spiritual takes on self-disclosure rooted in obedience and contemplation back to ancient Greek methods of understanding, cultivating, and articulating the self. He refers to these methods as 'technologies of the self': intellectual and behavioural practices which 'permit individuals to effect by their own means or with the help of others a certain number of operations on their own bodies and souls, thoughts, conduct, and way of being, so as to transform themselves in order to attain a certain state of happiness, purity, wisdom, perfection, or immortality' (Foucault, 1988: 18). Foucault thus highlights the connections between: (a) the things we think, feel and do; (b) the transformative impacts of these practices;

(c) their ramifications vis-à-vis consciousness, meaning and selfhood; and (d) the cultural contexts in which these things take place. These technologies manifest in a variety of different forms, many of which have great parallels with the role and function of music in my own life. For instance, Foucault outlines how the Stoic conceptualisation of the Socratic principle of 'taking care of oneself' centred the role of meditative reflection of conscience. Particularly interesting here is the importance of writing in the culture of taking care of oneself as an introspective act. Giving examples from Socrates to the fifth-century AD *Confessions* of Saint Augustine, Foucault notes:

A relation developed between writing and vigilance. Attention was paid to nuances of life, mood, and reading, and the experience of oneself was intensified and widened by virtue of this act of writing.... Taking care of oneself became linked to a constant writing activity. The self is something to write about, a theme or object (subject) of writing activity [e.g.] taking notes on oneself to be reread, writing treatises and letters to friends to help them, and keeping notebooks.

(Foucault, 1988: 27–28)

Here then, the link between this kind of constant diary keeping and self-examination of thoughts and feelings as a technology of the self for better understanding and articulating who we understand ourselves to be chimes closely with my own use of music, i.e. using music as a way to articulate myself and the tensions I wanted to negotiate in my life. Indeed, music is understood to be particularly powerful in this way, with work by sociologist of music Tia DeNora positing music as 'a resource for the identification work of "knowing how one feels" – a building material of "subjectivity"' (DeNora, 1999: 41). She empirically explores via interviews how individuals *use* music through their listening habits to both better understand, and then subsequently meet, their needs (to feel, to remember, to forget, to relax, to focus). Thus, she suggests that 'the sense of "self" is locatable in music' (ibid.: 49), and that 'music provides a material rendering of self-identity: a material in and with which to identify identity' (ibid.: 51). In other words, the ways in which we listen to music facilitate a richness of both self-understanding and self-articulation.

I would suggest that this is even more applicable if we consider musical *production* as opposed to solely consumption – which is the focus of DeNora's paper – i.e. thinking of music as storytelling (Abebe, 2021), and the function of this storytelling for the teller as a form of identity work. DeNora highlights the fact that much of identity work is concerned with, drawing a phrase from Erving Goffman (1956), a 'presentation of self to other(s)...: [a] "projection" of biography' (DeNora, 1999: 45). This 'projection' is particularly acute when looked at in the context of music-making and songwriting. For example, empirical ethnographic work on music-making by inmates in a Norwegian prison by Kjetil Hjørnevik et al. (2022) highlights this wonderfully. Drawing on work which explores music in therapeutic settings (Ansdell, 2005) or as a vehicle for social justice (Foster, 2015), the authors locate the emergence of a musical 'life story' (Bonde et al., 2013) as representing a form of biographical storytelling which affords insights into 'people's lives, histories and aspirations' (Hjørnevik et al., 2022: 4). These musical stories, they suggest, afford practitioners the opportunity to forge a sense of identity with narrative coherence and meaning, and in doing so to also articulate something of the institution within which this meaning-making takes place, engendering a 'co-construction of life narratives' (ibid.: 16). As novelist and critic John Berger (1984: 72) noted: 'Events are always to hand. But the coherence of these events...is an imaginative construction'. Music, in this instance, is part of this mechanism of construction.

This body of work on music and identity-making speaks to my own experiences. In my early adulthood, rap music was the vehicle through which I was able to tell the stories of my life and the lives of those around me, informed, as it was, by precise microsociological detailing of my immediate world. I would do this continually: on the bus, when people told me stories, on nights out, in the pub, at work. For almost a decade between 2007 and 2016 I recorded my thoughts and feelings on an almost daily basis largely in the 'Notes' section of an iPhone, and in this sense my engagement with technology and music-making produced an environment within which music as a technology of the self came to define my life and how I understood who I was – or, at least, who thought I was or, perhaps, how I wanted others to think of me. Indeed, Foucault cites a letter written by Marcus Aurelius to Fronto in AD 144–145 as being emblematic of a kind of self-reflection rooted in writing, featuring a 'meticulous concern with the details of daily life [which] are important because they are you – what you thought, what you felt' (Foucault, 1988: 28–29). To an extent, I shared this 'meticulous concern'.

I can, therefore, connect the three threads of the argument in this chapter together: in the context of my life, the development of my intergenerational self engendered a desire to negotiate questions of place, identity, class, meaning, and belonging – reflected in my own subjective experience of ontological complicity – which music as a technology of the self allowed me to participate in. This is why I loved, and continue to love, music as a form of storytelling. I wanted to find a way to tell the stories of my suburban background and the lives me and my friends were living. This was not a salacious or even particularly exciting story, but knowing how much stories mattered to me I felt compelled, even obliged, to tell it. This is what I wanted my music to be: a story of our lives. If I am being true to myself, did I do this in the way I wanted to and hoped? No. I never made a seminal album – I never even made the album I always hoped I would. Nor did I make a seminal track. But I did speak honestly, and through this honesty I did help to better understand the person I was, am, and who I wanted to be, even if sonically and musically my career perhaps did not go as far as I once dreamed it might. The lyrics I wrote about my life represent precious fragments of identity work undertaken in my mid-twenties wherein I was constructing not only myself, but also my peer group and the place(s) in which I lived as affective, sensory, vivid experiences rooted in mundanity, anxiety and hope.

Conclusion: The Flames on the Ceiling

In the previous chapter, I made reference to a conversation I had with my Dad in which he suggested that, for him, despite breaking away from a life in the pit like those before him, the mines never left him: they were an enduring sensory experience. He identified these precisely as memories from his childhood bedroom: the sound of the siren from the pit signalling an accident and the shadows of the flames on his ceiling booming from the colliery. What I have tried to articulate here is that the stories we tell and hear *are the flames on the ceiling*. In my life, these flames flickered and shone, smouldered and smoked, in the form of the stories my family told and how they shaped who I understood myself to be; the intergenerational narrative which so moulded my experience of ontological complicity, and which later found voice in the form of rap music as a technology of the self. This speaks to what we might think of as the endurability of the habitus, whereby class, as Diane Reay (2005: 924) beautifully attests, 'troubles the soul and preys on the psyche'. Friedman (2016: 145) illuminates wonderfully the emotional and 'psychological imprint of social mobility' among those who are mobile within a generation; I would suggest that this 'imprint' carries even further. In other words, class, particularly in its constitution and foundation in the family: 'is something beneath your clothes, under your skin, in your reflexes, in your psyche, at the very core of your being' (Kuhn, 1995: 98). The stories of meaning we tell and hear are part of that 'core'. Thus, narrative, to me, matters and always has and lingers as the flames on the ceiling. My music told my story (or at least part of it), and this is where that story comes from.

It is important to conclude here by considering the perspectives of those who have problematised the role of storytelling in our lives. Philosopher Galen Strawson (2004, 2018: 45), for example, suggests that the injunction to articulate one's life via narrative *and* the normative notion that this is a good or moral thing – phenomena he labels the *psychological* and the *ethical Narrativity theses* – are together what he describes as 'a fallacy of our age'. He rejects both premises on the grounds that many do *not* see their lives in terms of stories, and that in fact not doing so is superior given that one becomes, as fellow philosopher Graeme Nicholson (2009: 106) proposes, 'less weighed down by a portentous presentation of one's ego'. However, many *do* agree with the importance of the interrelationship between stories and selves and yet still problematise the cultural place of narrative within contemporary society. Interestingly, a recent intervention has come from a literary theorist – Peter Brooks – who, himself, back in 1984 had articulated the key role stories play in our lives in his book *Reading for the Plot*. Almost forty years on, he has come to revise his position to suggest that we have been, as his latest book is entitled, *Seduced by Story* (Brooks, 2022). In it, he argues that we have, in contemporary society, become subject to a 'hyperinflation of story' (ibid.: 10) whereby our 'mindless valorization of storytelling' (ibid.: 9) means we are insufficiently critical of the stories we hear all around us. He does not suggest that stories are themselves dangerous – indeed, he proposes that close and critical reading of novels, for instance, offers us the chance to empathise and reach new understandings on various perspectives – but that stories have been culturally elevated and privileged to the degree that they are no longer treated with proper scrutiny nor scepticism. Likewise, while Jonathan Gottschall suggested in 2012 that stories were essential to human survival, almost ten years later in 2021, his re-evaluation – *The Story Paradox* – suggests that our desire for, and acceptance of, stories is increasingly leading many to fall victim to, for example, conspiracy theories.

A particularly interesting methodological debate vis-à-vis the place of stories in social science exists in the realm of illness narratives in health research. This longstanding debate between sociologists of different methodological persuasions has been ongoing since the late 1990s and concerns the extent to which the use of narratives meets the threshold of acceptability for what some define as meaningful, critical sociological enquiry. The various facets of this extended, fraught and contentious debate have been helpfully delineated in a paper by health sociologist Carol Thomas (2010: 655). Her paper contrasts the more orthodox, 'traditional sociological ethnography' of thinkers such as Paul Atkinson (1997) and Atkinson's collaborative work with David Silverman (1997) in which they excoriate the emergence of what they coin 'the interview society' with its pseudo-therapeutic ambitions and the 'blind alley' represented by the narrative turn, against the 'poststructuralist inspired methodological loosening-up' (Thomas, 2010: 655) of advocates of the narrative turn such as Arthur Bochner (2001), Arthur Frank (2000, 2002), and Elliot Mishler (2005). A range of critiques are advanced by, in particular, Paul Atkinson regarding what he sees as the moralising and sentimentality of narrative approaches which lack methodological robustness and which privilege narratives in various ways over other forms of data. In opposition, Arthur Bochner and others have rejected the narrow way in which the discipline of sociology is conceptualised by Atkinson, preferring instead to embrace epistemological diversity in the field, and thus highlighting the ethics of a form of qualitative research which both is reflective and acknowledges the ways in which narrative representations are meaningful for the storytellers.

One of the central critiques advanced by Atkinson (1997, 1999, 2005) in his work on the 'proper' place of narrative in health research – and which connects clearly to Brook's (2022) reservations about the truthfulness of stories – is the idea of authenticity, which acts in these evaluations as a proxy for truth. In other words, the ways in which exponents of the narrative turn come to *privilege* storytelling as offering unique or special, and by extension more authentic and even truthful, insights, is for Atkinson (and more recently Brooks) a misnomer. He argues that stories are, like all forms of knowledge produced by actors, subjective social constructions, and therefore should not be understood as indicative or reflective of 'hyperauthenticity' (1997: 341). For Bochner and others, this is rather beside the point. They see stories as representing *a* truth and not *the* truth per se, and are of the view that the self-understandings sought by storytellers and their truths should be embraced as methodologically distinct practices within social research. Whichever side of the debate one lands on (and personally I find much to align with in Thomas's (2010) position that we should treat stories seriously as per Bochner, but apply scepticism and methodological precision as per Atkinson), this particular argument presents fascinating questions vis-à-vis truth. How true are the stories I was told growing up, how true are my understandings of who I am in the world, and therefore – crucially for the purposes of this book – how 'honest' and true, in fact, are the stories I came to tell in the rap music I wrote? How can we disentangle the layers of subjectivity within all of these overlapping and mutually constitutive narrative forms? If I am to use the stories I wrote in my music as forms of data to be analysed (informed by the positions of *both* Bochner and Atkinson), how reasonable is this? I suggested earlier that I felt my music was honest, but how accurate is this claim? Unpacking the extent to which we might think of lyrics, and in particular rap lyrics, as truthful, is thus the task of the next chapter before examining the lyrics themselves.

Notes

1 'Core creative work' is defined in their research drawing on Hesmondhalgh (2013), Throsby (2008) and Pratt (1997) as 'a principal set of cultural occupations, which includes artists, musicians and actors, and those working in publishing, media, libraries, museums and galleries' (Brook et al., 2022).
2 This calls to mind George Orwell's claim in *The Road to Wigan Pier* that he belonged to the 'lower-upper-middle-class'.
3 Whilst others have sought to offer new definitions of class – e.g. 'emergent service workers' and 'precariat' (Savage et al., 2013) – these are not, I would suggest, regularly used by most of the British public.
4 The works of theorists Satya Mohanty (1993, 2018) and Kenan Malik (2023) are insightful on this subject.

4

Lyrics, Truth, and Ethnography

The focus of this books is the role that lyrics as stories can play in our collective acts of construction and representation. However, before looking at my own lyrics and examining what the stories they tell might (or might not) tell us in the next chapter, it is important to take a bit of time to ask challenging questions around the applicability of lyrics as a data source, as I propose to do herein. What is the function of song lyrics, and, if we understand them as forms of narrative storytelling as was suggested in the previous chapter, how should we treat these stories with reference to the critiques of Brooks (2022) and Atkinson (1997) around concepts such as truth, reality or authenticity? In other words: what do, or can, lyrics *do*? In the first instance, as sociomusicologist Simon Frith (1989: 80) noted over thirty years ago, it is important to delineate between what are described as 'folk' forms of music which might reasonably be said – by proponents of theories of folk realness at least (see Palmer, 1975) – to be 'the authentic expression of popular experiences and need', against genres such as pop which have a more mass-market orientation and which may be written by professional songwriters with distinct aims and ambitions. With reference to the former, genres referred to by Frith include country, soul and rock, with blues being highlighted in the work of Michael Haralambos (1974: 117) as being a genre which 'concentrates almost entirely on experience.... [T]his is the way it is, and this is how I am suffering'. Frith (1989: 85) problematises this oversimplification, however, suggesting instead that the function of lyrics must be understood as being about more than content alone, and that genres such as blues are 'not simply documentary'. Instead, lyrics are, for Frith, not just about what is said but *how* it is said, and how the syntax, cadence, prosody and delivery of words convey emotions and meanings which can be interpreted by listeners in a complex interrelationship between fantasy and reality, fiction and truth, idealisation and accuracy.

That being said, an interesting place to begin is a consideration of what lyrics might *tell us* about the lyricist, and to use this to then ask to what extent and in what circumstances we might think of lyrics and the stories they tell as being true or truthful. Nick Cave in a recent article with British newspaper *The Guardian* suggested that: 'Songs have the capacity to be revealing, acutely so.... They are little dangerous bombs of truth' (O'Hagan, 2022). But what kinds of truth? Frith's article raises interesting questions around how folk genres, often emanating from socially marginalised groups, might be understood as 'authentically' or 'accurately' communicating the experiences of those telling their stories through music. This is a topic which can be seen receiving a great deal of scrutiny today in the context of rap lyrics, particularly in their use in criminal proceedings, a phenomenon referred to by Erik Nielson and Andrea Dennis (2019) as *Rap on Trial*. Thus, the first part of this chapter will look at the extent to which it is reasonable to think of the stories contained in rap lyrics as truthful and to interpret them literally. I will suggest that the ambiguity within the genre perhaps makes truth an insufficient prism for evaluation. Instead, part two will turn to a broader examination of what forms of experiences and hidden *subjectivities* lyrics might qualitatively reveal, and in this sense examine their applicability as a data source from a variety of perspectives, including in public health and music therapy among victims of trauma as an expressive medium. Part three will try and bring the first two discursive sections together, and suggest that scholarship which highlights the ethnographic potential of rap music offers an insightful perspective to better understand what the specific stories contained in the lyrics of this family of genres (encompassing rap, grime, drill and others) *can* tell us, particularly about geographical spaces and artists' experiences of them.

The Truth, the Whole Truth, and Nothing but the Truth?

In a range of court cases from around the world – from Young Thug in Atlanta (United States), to drill group 1011 in London (United Kingdom), and Ammo (real name Lamar Skeet) in Toronto (Canada) – defendant-composed rap lyrics have, over the previous thirty years, been increasingly cited as evidence in criminal proceedings, and in several instances been crucial in securing convictions for prosecutors. Their evidential utility has been encouraged by bodies including the United States Department for Justice (Lyddane, 2006), and their permissibility and judicial rationale predicated on a number of theories of relevance, outlined in great detail (and synthesised here) by legal scholar Andrea Dennis (2007: 8–12). Firstly, rap lyrics are often legally admitted on the grounds that they are a confession or inculpatory statement; in other words, if a rapper is being accused of dealing drugs, and has written rap lyrics about dealing drugs, the latter is viewed as a confession of the former. Dennis (2007: 8) notes that despite lyrics technically qualifying as hearsay, they are exempt from hearsay rules and generally deemed admissible and relevant as substantive evidence given their being framed as an admission of guilt. Secondly, rap lyrics can be considered relevant as indicative of intent or motive; in other words, if a rapper is being accused of a specific murder, and has written lyrics depicting murder more generally, this demonstrates intent to murder, or that the murder they are being accused of is more probable. The third rationale is that lyrics can act as 'character evidence', indicative of a defendant's knowledge of the crimes they are being accused of; the example cited by Dennis (2007: 11) is that of a rapper charged with drug distribution who had authored lyrics which included drug dealing terminology. In the United Kingdom, this kind of character evidence is captured under the Criminal Justice Act 2003 as evidence of, or a disposition towards, misconduct. This is, for example, similar to the rationale used in the criminal case against Oscar Wilde in 1895 for homosexuality where his creative work – in this case, his novel *The Nature of Dorian Gray* – was used to question his 'moral character' given the use of homosexual themes in the book (Frankel, 2012: 16). Finally, whilst rap lyrics permitted as evidence in court have, on occasion, been deemed to be prejudicial, they are often not deemed to be *unfairly* prejudicial,[1] and thus lyrics are often admitted with various provisos stated to juries.

Central to the admission of rap lyrics as evidence is the tendency of courts to interpret the lyrics literally as statements of fact and that they are autobiographical in nature. As Dennis (2007: 15) notes: 'courts are likening rap music lyricists to journalists, autobiographers, or diary-keepers'. This is suggested to be particularly the case with rap music – in particular a sub-derivation defined as 'gangsta rap' (which is somewhat broadly and often mistakenly applied) and its perceived link with genuine gang members with its injunction to 'keep it real' (a phenomenon specific to rap music related to a form of culturally codified authenticity which I will delineate and problematise in greater detail later). In other words, the authenticity or accuracy of statements by rappers is understood by many to be core to the identity of the musicians in a way that is not the case with, say, operatic tenors when singing about violence or murder.

Much of this is hugely problematic, and the literal interpretation of rap lyrics and their use as evidence in criminal proceedings has been critiqued from various perspectives. Musicologically, Nicholas Stoia and colleagues (2018: 355) note the existence of various stylistic and genre-specific tropes and stock lyric formulas within rap music – such as bragging, hypermasculinity, or being combative and/or competitive – which 'makes their interpretation as autobiographical particularly dubious'. Likewise, courts and juries often fail to appreciate the artistic elements in rap music, e.g. use of metaphors or other literary devices, seeing it purely as descriptive. In this sense, audiences lack the relevant understandings to appreciate rap music as artistry and instead see it, in the words of Jay-Z (2010: 56), as just the authors, simply, 'reading out of their diaries'. Thirdly, rap lyrics are often insufficiently contextualised in legislative contexts, for instance acknowledging that a wider climate of commercialisation of rap music engenders pressures on up-and-coming musicians to conform to ideals within the genre – of toughness or strength, for instance – which may be written for commercial appeal or driven by a desire to entertain, as opposed to being rooted in accuracy. Fourthly, there are questions raised around inequality, where more famous rappers might be more likely to be interpreted as acting as a 'character' – such as in the case of rapper Beanie Sigel (Caruso, 2006) – than younger, aspiring rappers, who also lack financial resources to aid in their defence. Finally, and most crucially, salient questions around race and racism are crucial to reflect upon in the relative singling-out of *rap* lyrics in particular, meaning criminal proceedings are typically focused against young Black men. Indeed, racism connects many of these critiques above. Whilst lyrics from other musical forms have been used in court (such as 'white power' music in a case of racially motivated aggravated assault[2]), there can be little doubt that rap lyrics are grossly over-represented in court cases as permissible evidence. According to criminologist Lambros Fatsis (2019), alongside many of the other scholars cited thus far in this chapter, much of the inability of courtrooms and juries to disentangle the literal from the metaphorical, and the biographical from the artistic, stems from the fact that (often) White prosecutors and jurors do not understand this form of Black cultural expression and indeed can only view it through this narrow prism. More than this though, it strikes me that the stories in rap lyrics are often themselves racially weaponised in order to *tell a story* about young Black men as violent, dangerous, criminals which has racialised narrative coherence, i.e. that chimes with racist preconceptions.[3] For all of these reasons, Charis Kubrin and Erik Nielson (2014: 204) suggest that courts must: 'be careful not to assume that the lyrics are autobiographical'.

Whilst all of these arguments are entirely reasonable and fair, it is important to consider another side of the equation. I would propose that we *cannot* say that every lyric written in rap songs is a fiction being performed by a character or an actor, just as we cannot say that every rap lyric can be read literally in accordance with standard principles of conversation. In other words, we cannot establish a simplistic dichotomy that rap lyrics are either 'acting' on the one hand or being 'truthful' on the other. Indeed, 'lyrics from rappers range from truthful accounts to exaggerated fantasies' (Keyes, 2002: 4), and in this sense the disentangling of the accuracy or truthfulness of rap lyrics is, in fact, more nuanced and complicated given that the contents contain what Jonathan Ilan (2020: 995), in his work on the criminalisation of UK drill, calls a 'fact-fiction hybridity'. Some lyrics in drill, to take a UK example of a subgenre of rap, *are* in fact autobiographical: sometimes where we hear a drill artist say they are dealing drugs, or running a wider 'county lines' operation, they have been convicted of these crimes, assuming one has faith in the conviction (Kirk, 2019; BBC, 2022; The Law Pages, 2022). Or, sometimes when we hear a drill rapper rap about having a gun, they have been arrested for possession of a firearm (Zayed, 2023). Likewise, sometimes when a drill rapper paints a picture of a life of violence where they refer to a threat of being killed, this is also tragically true (Cobain, 2018). This has been seen to be the case in grime too; when Crazy Titch (real name Carl Dobson) rapped about shooting guns in tracks such as the N.A.S.T.Y Crew song 'Cock Back' and others, the extent to which one can argue that he might be entirely playing a character is problematised given that in 2006 he was sentenced to thirty years in prison for shooting dead a music producer (Muir, 2006), although it is important to note that Dobson has insisted he is innocent and at the time of writing a petition calling for a retrial is available. Indeed, these cases push back against the claim of Stoia et al. (2018: 357) who suggest 'ultimately, though, rappers are actors'. In the case of these young men, it appears that they were not, and the range of UK drill artists (some of whom are also alleged gang members) in prison as of 2023 further problematises this claim (DrillaSE, 2023). These cases, and many others, challenge notions that rap lyrics should be rejected as fiction on the grounds that their 'primary purpose is to entertain' (Kubrin and Nielson, 2014: 197); after all, real-life can be entertainment too, such as the way that political events are often presented as unfolding akin to 'drama' (MacKuen, 1983). Much of rap *is* true.

However, much of it is not. Some rap lyrics – even within the same song or bars, sitting adjacent to or within statements of fact – *are* fiction; fictions rooted in the construction of a persona likely to be perceived as credible and authentic by fans and others, drawing on wider genre-specific lyrical tropes, exaggerating and boasting about elements of their own life, and pulling together and embellishing stories from their wider friendship group and/or community, reconceptualised and repurposed in the first person in an act of creative and artistic expression. Separating fact from fiction is enormously complex and requires a level of cultural sophistication which often the public, legal authorities or juries may lack (see Ilan, 2012). Indeed, as per Kubrin and Nielson (2014: 197), rappers have a 'complex and creative manipulation of identity, both on and off the stage'. Thus, on the one hand, the notion that rap lyrics act as evidential material to be read entirely literally in all circumstances is of course absurd, *and yet at the same time* it is hard to make the case that rap lyrics are entirely performative whilst simultaneously praising their representation of lived experience and astute social commentary. We cannot say the bits we like are true, but the bits we don't are not. In this sense, perhaps 'accuracy' or 'truth' are the wrong prisms through which to evaluate what the thoughts, dreams, statements and stories contained in rap lyrics are (or are not), or do (or do not do), and instead we might ask instead what we might reasonably understand them to *reveal*.

The (Lyric) Book of Revelations

Whilst we can question the truthfulness of lyrics, it undoubtedly remains the case that lyrics do tell us things. For example, outside of hip hop they have been analysed in order to reveal wider structural features of the music industry, such as creative innovation and diversity based on lyrical themes and its inverse relationship to concentrations of power by record companies (Peterson and Berger, 1975). They can reflect wider societal norms, or even (controversially) shape them (Davis, 1985). They might tell us about, or perhaps inform, broader cultural attitudes to sexuality and romantic love (Dukes et al., 2003; Madanikia and Bartholemew, 2014), attitudes towards illegal drugs (Markert, 2007), or conceptualisations of gender (Shin, 2016). Work by Lin Qiu and colleagues (2021) suggests lyrics can reflect socioeconomic conditions, in research which showed a relationship between levels of unemployment and lyrical themes of anger. Lyrics can share new forms of language and slang (Coleman, 2014: 68), reveal the rich influences of immigration (Azzi, 1996: 443–447), tell us about the mood of society – be it optimistic or anxious (Pettijohn and Sacco, 2009) – and even reveal how societies emotionally respond to shocks such as COVID-19 (Putter et al., 2021). We might not be able to say that lyrics are always true, but they can reveal *truths*.

Can we make a similar case beyond these macro-conceptions of the revelatory capacity of lyrics and look instead more microsociologically to ask what they can tell us about the human being writing them? The work of singer-songwriter and public health scientist Tasha Golden is of particular interest here, articulating an epistemological and methodological position which espouses the benefits of unconventional knowledge-creation in the field of public health, focusing her work on victims of trauma. Golden, drawing on the work of scholars such as Allana Beavis and colleagues (2015) and justice-orientated qualitative researcher Kakali Bhattacharya (2009) among many others who have sought to decolonise qualitative research methodologies, posits that conventional methods of data collection – such as interviews or surveys, for example – have often failed to capture differences in how people communicate experiences, understandings, and meaning in their lives, particularly within specific populations who might be harder to reach (such as victims of trauma) (Golden and Wendel, 2020: 5). In simple terms, if researchers want to hear diverse experiences from diverse voices, they need to reimagine diverse ways of listening to them. An example of this is the methodology known as Photovoice where, simply put, participants take photographs and then collaboratively discuss and interpret the images to reflect on salient themes in their lives, which Professor of Social Work Kimberley Bender and colleagues (2017: 383) note has been seen to facilitate the sharing of 'experiences which would otherwise be difficult to express and process'. This notion too is captured by sociologist Lois Presser and criminologist Sveinung Sandberg (2015: 296) in their work which explores the use of creative outlets to understand stories of crime and recidivism, suggesting that arts methodologies can capture and reflect: '[the] stories people fear telling or for which they lack a vocabulary'. In essence, if we want to hear people's stories, we need to let them tell us, and the arts – data suggests – offers them a way of doing this.

Golden (2020: 966-967) advances the concept of the arts as valuable sources of *data* given the capacity of forms of creative expression to provide insights into the lives and experiences of those who create them. Indeed, her own work with incarcerated teenage women demonstrates the revelatory capacity of expressive prose, suggesting that: 'program participants share very different information through their poetry and stories than they share in surveys or screenings.... Providing trauma-informed, arts-based modes of communication, and valuing the results as *data*, has been critical to the development of accurate, first-hand, actionable knowledge' (ibid.: 961). Even more explicitly, Jill Sonke and colleagues (2019: 11) in a white paper produced for the University of Florida Center for Arts in Medicine suggest: 'As expressions of individual, community, and socio-cultural experience, arts and culture represent fundamental practices of knowledge-generation, experience, and connection; they therefore have merit as data'. This work therefore advances the notion that forms of creative storytelling (such as musical lyrics) tell us things about the person(s) producing them, and indeed can often reveal more than conventional approaches to knowledge-creation.

With more specific reference to lyrics as a source of data which can reveal insights about their writers, scholarship in the field of music therapy research offers further weight to these claims where lyric writing has been seen to reveal subjectivities and knowledges among a range of populations, notably those with particular vulnerabilities or pathologies. The work of music therapists Clare O'Callaghan and Denise Grocke (2009) brings together a body of research evidence in this field to highlight the ability of research adopting phenomenological methodologies to reveal songwriters' subjective, affective experiences. As they note: 'songwriting is a vehicle through which people with vulnerabilities can express what theorists regard as important.... Music therapists are urged to analyse their clients' song lyrics, to extend understanding of clients' lived experiences [and] what clients regard as important in their lives' (ibid.: 327). For example, work by another music therapist, Katrina McFerran and colleagues (2006), among female adolescents with anorexia nervosa found songwriting to be a mechanism to provide novel insights into how their condition was being experienced by promoting engagement with key themes around identity formation. Similarly, songwriting among participants with mental illness has been seen to reveal the challenges of living with a lifelong condition and sources of enjoyment, such as working in teams (O'Callaghan and Grocke, 2009). Indeed, I recall for a previous research project (Gross and Musgrave, 2020), interviewing a rock musician from Newcastle who employed fascinating phraseology when he suggested that he was: 'not a particularly articulate person, but in songs I get more precise and more complex arguments across'. Other contexts where lyric writing has yielded new insights include among bereaved adolescents (Dalton and Krout, 2006), and among asylum seekers and refugees (Harrison et al., 2019) – a study which is of particular interest to me given the ways in which songwriting was seen to reveal new insights about specific geographical places of meaning and importance in the lives of lyric writers.

Both of these fields of enquiry above (public health and music therapy) demonstrate the powerful capacity of lyrics to act as data sources and as mechanisms for revealing composers' subjectivities. However, how can we connect these insights to rap music specifically? That is, what can *rap* music reveal to us if we are to proceed from the notion advanced above that we are not using literal truth as the mechanism of interpretive analysis? In this first instance, an illuminating body of work advancing what has come to be termed 'hip hop therapy' (Tyson, 2002, 2003; Elligan, 2004; Tillie Allen, 2005; Levy, 2012) has highlighted the utility of the genre as a way of facilitating rapport and communication with at-risk young adults, such as in social work, to reflect authors' perspectives on issues such as racial identity, self-efficacy and female empowerment (Kobin and Tyson, 2006). This has been reflected too in the emergence of organisations such as Key Changes (n.d.), a North-London-based charity which works in partnership with NHS mental health services and health and social care agencies to offer music-focused therapeutic interventions (of which many focus on rap music) with individuals suffering from depression, anxiety, PTSD, schizophrenia and other conditions. Another example is Hip Hop Psyche which advocates for the use of hip hop in music therapy environments (Sule and Inkster, 2014, 2015).

However, what about the revelatory capacity of rap *outside* of these specific contexts which often adopt specific forms of guided songwriting, which focus on specific populations – notably those experiencing trauma of various kinds – and where the songwriting has a specific aim and purpose? We might answer this in two ways. Firstly, rappers, as per many musicians, often *are* victims of some kind of trauma and indeed it is those traumatic experiences which can draw them to music-making as a method of artistic expression (Swart, 2013). Work by Charis Kubrin (2006) highlights how this often can be particularly true of rappers, who are predominantly young Black men articulating themes emanating from the challenging inner-city social contexts in which they reside, reflected (in Kubrin's analysis) in lyrical themes of nihilism. Indeed, this has been the case ever since the emergence of rap as a genre, and arguably one of the earliest and finest rap records to achieve this so poignantly was 'The Message' by Grandmaster Flash and the Furious Five (Sugar Hill Records, 1982) with its depiction of poverty and decay in the New York City of the late 1970s and early 1980s.

Connected to this, I would suggest, one of the principal strengths of what rap lyrics can reveal is their subjective portrayal of the authors' lived experiences. In the words of Jay-Z (2010: 243): 'rhymes can make sense of the world in a way that regular speech can't'. This has been core to the analysis of rap music, from classics of the genre such as the aforementioned 'The Message', heralded for its 'candid depiction of inner-city life but also its ability to capture the physical and emotional suffering wrought by American inequality' (Kubrin and Nielson, 2014: 189), to grass-roots rap music in London and Bristol in the UK where the genre was seen to allow 'ordinary young people [to] construct translocal subjectivities through the production and use of rap lyrics' (Bramwell and Butterworth, 2019: 2513). That is, whilst the idea of literal truths can be problematised, many attest that rap does communicate the authors' truths, particularly spatially. Indeed, variations and subgenres of rap music have often been explicitly linked to the places which have produced them; their sonic soundscapes blended and woven with their immediate locales. While hip hop itself emanated from New York City (more specifically the Bronx, and even more specifically 1520 Sedgwick Avenue in the Bronx), specific derivations are similarly geographically constituted: gangsta rap came from South Central Los Angeles (Viator, 2020), drill from the South Side of Chicago (Evans and Baym, 2022), grime from East London – generally thought of as Bow (E3) more specifically – (Brar, 2021), trip hop (or 'Bristol sound') from Bristol (Wragg, 2016), crunk from Atlanta (Grem, 2006), and Miami bass from 'Liberty City, Goulds and Overtown' in Miami (Unterberger, 1999: 145). What this suggests, then, is that rap music is spatially constituted, a theme perhaps most robustly explored in the work of Murray Forman (2002) looking at US rap's relationship to spatial zones within cities and the capacity of rappers to map 'the cultural byways that delineate their localities' and where 'space is a dominant concern' (ibid.: 3). Thus, rap is deeply connected to articulations and understandings of *place*, and stories told about these places and the authors' experiences of them. By extension, rap might have the capacity to act as sources of data *about* these places.

Rap as Ethnography?

The argument thus far has proceeded as follows: (a) whilst we cannot read rap lyrics literally, there is often much truth within them which can reveal subjectivities for analysts to examine; (b) lyrics can, in certain circumstances, reasonably be said to act as sources of data; and (c) one element of rap music's status as a form of data lies in its depiction of place. Bringing many of these concepts together are two key papers which I want to look at in more detail. The first is by cultural scholar Lee Barron (2013) focused on grime music entitled 'The sound of street corner society' – a play on the title of the ethnographic classic *Street Corner Society* by Foot Whyte (1943) – and the second by sociologist David Beer (2014) viewing the lyrics of Jay-Z as a form of 'insider's ethnography'. Both have been influential in my own thinking about the capacity of rap lyrics to reveal geographic insights.

Barron's paper proposes that grime – which is, in essence, a British subgenre of rap music – can be read as a dataset given the ways in which the genre is itself distinctly ethnographic. Grime is understood to have emerged from the Bow area of London, with seminal contributions to the genre by artists like Wiley, Kano, Dizzee Rascal, Trim, Roll Deep, Ruff Squad and many others evoking the struggles and experiences of, predominantly, Black youngsters living in London's most deprived easterly boroughs (Hancox, 2018). Barron (2013: 536) describes the genre's vivid descriptions of everyday lived experience and the insider's emic depictions of the social conditions of inner-city life, rooted in close participant observation, which so typify grime as 'the sound of the ethnographic imagination'. Here, he draws inspiration from Paul Willis (2000: ix) who, in his innovative work which so creatively interprets the potential of qualitative methodologies, asks: 'what happens if we understand the raw materials of everyday lived cultures as if they were living art forms?'. As per work by Martin Stokes (1997) on the ethnographic nature of music in Turkey, Barron (2013) suggests that this is precisely how hip hop and grime music should be understood, i.e. that there is a proximity between grime and ethnography and that grime as a genre has the capacity to act as an ethnographic artefact. He notes: 'It is difficult to cite another contemporary mode of music which authentically achieves such a consistent geographically and socially distinctive focus on localised urban experiences' (ibid.: 543). Thus, whilst there are sociologies and ethnographies of rap and rappers (Bramwell, 2015; Speers, 2017; White, 2017; Paor-Evans, 2020a) the argument here is that rap *itself* is ethnographic.

In suggesting that 'the basis of hip-hop and grime music within lived urban environments does suggest an ethnographic air' (Barron, 2013: 543.), Barron's view is informed by various disciplinary perspectives. Perhaps most explicit is the concept of 'indigenous media' seen, for example, in the work of anthropologist Faye Ginsburg (1991: 104). This introduces the term 'ethnographic media' to refer to films produced by native North Americans, Indians of the Amazon Basin and Aboriginal Australians whereby their artistic output is understood to 'communicate something about that social or collective identity we call "culture," in order to mediate (one hopes) across gaps of space, time, knowledge, and prejudice'. The implication is that grime acts as a form of this. Barron cites the work of Hammersley and Atkinson (1997: 157) who note 'the social worlds studied by ethnographers have often been devoid of written documents other than those produced by the fieldworkers themselves' to suggest, much like Ginsburg, that this is *precisely* what grime represents – i.e. 'culture articulated from the level of the individual upward' (Barron, 2013: 539) and 'the articulation of culturally specific and particular urban ways of life' (ibid.: 542). Whilst anthropologists such as Debra Spitulnik (1993: 305) have pushed back against this concept of anthropological media on the basis that, potentially, *all media* can be ethnographic, and indeed critic and art historian Hal Foster (1995: 302) wholly rejected the emergence of what he described as the 'new quasi-anthropological paradigm' in art, Barron instead makes a very specific case that grime music is *particularly* ethnographic.

A similar argument to that of Barron is advanced by David Beer, who mounts a case perhaps even more explicitly aligned to the aims and ambitions of this particular book. Using as a case study the Jay-Z book *Decoded*, which as referenced in the opening chapter served in part as inspiration for my own endeavour, Beer (2014: 677) argues that forms of hip hop can represent a form of poetic urbanism rooted in close participation which can provide 'detailed accounts of place and region [and] provides us with an imaginative insider's ethnographic account of these often lost or hard to see urban lifeworlds'. Much like Barron, the centrality of participant observation is key to this assertion, noting how Jay-Z (2010: 203) himself acknowledges rap music to be typified by 'close observation'. Beer's insightful account is conceptually informed by sociologists who have captured microsociological detail with particular care and attention, notably Howard Becker who has suggested that forms of popular media including fiction, film and photography have acted as key sources of academic inspiration. Beer extends this to popular music and hip hop specifically given its ethnographic potential, crafted by 'insiders', i.e. from within the cultural world under enquiry. This kind of insider sociology or anthropology has a long tradition: e.g. Ralph Turner's (1947) work on naval officers based on his experiences in World War II, Donald Roy's (1959) work on factory workers struggling for autonomy based on his employment experiences, Fred Davis (1959) on taxi drivers (see Anderson (2006: 376) for a summary), as well as Guthrie Ramsey (2003) on 'Race Music', which centres largely around his evocative, and often poignant, reminiscence of growing up in Chicago, both listening to and playing jazz music.

Defining Ethnography

It is worth here zooming out to ask what ethnography is, how it has been defined and understood, and whether there are forms of methodological benchmarking against which we might more formally evaluate the suggestion of Barron and Beer. In other words, if we are to proceed from the suggestion at the end of the previous chapter that stories do have value but should be treated with methodological precision, can we be more precise about what ethnography is in order to apply these parameters to rap lyrics as stories? One can attempt this both conceptually and methodologically. Conceptually then, and being both necessarily brief and deferring to the expertise of the scholars cited herein for further reading, ethnography is a clustering together of methodological approaches and theoretical perspectives which seeks 'the understanding and representation of experience [and] presenting and explaining the culture in which this experience is located' (O'Reilly, 2012: 3). Whilst hugely varied with various subdisciplines (all with varying levels of scholarly robustness and epistemological presuppositions) the ambition of the discipline has remained the exposition of the research participant's 'relation to life, his vision of his world' (Malinowski, 1922: 25). Methodologically, this has been achieved by absorption within the culture under enquiry, be it cultures far away or closer to home. In the words of the classic foundational text of anthropology on the Trobriand Islands by Bronislaw Malinowski (1922: 7): 'Proper conditions for ethnographic work…can really only be achieved by camping right in their villages', and thereupon applying the ethnographic methodological staples of participant observation and field notes, interviews, and secondary textual analysis of artefacts undertaken within a theoretical schematic (such as functionalism, structural-functionalism, cultural materialism, diffusionism, interactionism, etc.) to guide and inform data collection and analysis. The approach has been used in a variety of cultural contexts to explore a range of cultural phenomena, with some of my personal favourites which I was introduced to as an undergraduate – and which I still find myself returning to in my teaching today – including a study of the politics of gender via dancing practices during Greek occasions of celebration by Jane Cowan (1990), and the classic text by Marcel Mauss on gift-giving (Mauss, 1954).

This is a sketched overview, but the question of what ethnography is and how it might be defined has been tackled systematically by sociologist Martyn Hammersley (2018) and offers a more robust interpretive framework to facilitate the analysis of rap music being attempted herein. He suggests the seven defining characteristics of ethnography as it:

1. being a relatively long-term (however defined) data collection process,
2. taking place in naturally occurring settings,
3. relying on participant observation, or personal engagement more generally,
4. employing a range of types of data,
5. being aimed at documenting what actually goes on, and
6. emphasising the significance of the meanings people give to objects, including themselves, in the course of their activities, in other words culture, and thus
7. being holistic in focus (ibid.: 4).

There are two key features it is worth drawing attention to here. The first is Hammersley's point regarding the centrality of participant observation, which is, he suggests '*the* core of ethnography' (ibid.: 8). This kind of close and precise observation is perhaps most elegantly captured in the symbolic interactionalism of Erving Goffman (1956) and might be undertaken from various perspectives. As outlined by Raymond Gold (1958), this can range from a complete outsider looking-in at one extreme – as so typified early ethnographic work from the first part of the twentieth century with its focus on non-Western cultures – to a complete 'insider' viewing what takes place around them – as so typified sociological enquiry from the Chicago school of sociology through to the emergence of what has been called 'anthropology at home' (Madden, 1999). The point is that, alongside other forms of methodological triangulation as suggested above, the heart of ethnography is, for many, observing.

The second feature of note is Hammersley's point vis-à-vis 'documenting what actually goes on'. It is worth stating here that I will, for the purposes of time, clarity and focus, avoid any ontological or epistemological interpretivist debate concerning the nature of truth in observable social behaviours. Indeed, I will return to this in the concluding chapter when I re-evaluate questions of 'realness' and 'keeping it real' in rap music and its relationship to truth. To return, the question posited then is: *what should ethnographers observe* in order to document what is going on? For sociologist Paul Atkinson (2015: 95), the distinctiveness of the kind of traditional ethnography he advances lies in a focus on what he refers to as 'the sensory and material means of mundane reality' (see also Psathas, 1980). This focus on quotidian experiences which has so defined the anthropological approach in essence from Malinowski onwards, and which has been comprehensively and beautifully analytically mapped in the work of Michael Sheringham (2006), and the capacity of these observations to reveal broader structural characteristics of society, means that ethnographers should seek to document and understand (and also, generally, explain) 'everyday performances [which] are quintessentially complex' (Atkinson, 2015: 86). Furthermore, the claim is often that these mundanities, studied by researchers in a small number of 'cases' or contexts, have the capacity to be revelatory.

To what extent can we map these ethnographic attributes onto forms of rap music to evaluate the claims of Barron and Beer? The key features for Barron (2013: 532) which make the songs of grime musicians ethnographic are: the ability of the music to provide listeners with 'insights into meanings of human existence from the standpoint of insiders, to uncover "the world of everyday life" (Jorgensen, 1989: 14-15), and the music's focus on 'participant observation in the most immediate, lived sense'. This focus on participant observation is also central in Beer's argument that the lyrics of Jay-Z offer ethnographic insight. In the first instance, I do not think we can say that rap lyrics in general strictly fulfil the essential criteria of ethnography outlined by Hammersley (2018), and indeed even their reconceptualisation as a more specific kind of 'urban ethnography' (Duneier et al., 2014) would also not stand up. Indeed, sociologist Loïc Wacquant (2002) has mounted a vociferous evisceration of key contributions to this subdiscipline on the grounds of methodological, conceptual and theoretical woolliness and frequent moralising. On the other hand, given the centrality of observation amongst certain rappers in specific areas of rap, and as suggested by Dan Hancox in his focused work on grime MC Dizzee Rascal, 'grime lyrics describe with molecular detail the dirt of the MCs' vividly quotidian lives' (Hancox, 2013: 175), I think it is reasonable to say that *some kinds of rap*, and *some kinds of rappers*, do produce forms of rap music which whilst not ethnographies, are *ethnographic* – a distinction which is elaborated in the work of Frank Lutz (1981).

There is then, here, what appears to be a degree of tension between the rejection of rap lyrics as autobiographical – seen in texts which refute their literal reading and subsequent racialised weaponisation in judicial contexts (Kubrin and Neilson, 2014; Stoia et al., 2018) – and the suggestion that the ways in which some of these lyrics portray their locality constitutes a form of ethnographic text to be read as a source of data (Barron, 2013; Beer, 2014). However, with the requisite understanding of the conventions and diversity of the genre and an appreciation for the pressures, constraints, styles and ambitions of the artists being evaluated, I think it is reasonable that both can, at once, be accurate readings of rap, broadly because one cannot homogenise 'rap' or 'rappers' as sharing these kinds of characteristics. In addition, of course, whilst making the claim that certain kinds of rap can be thought of as ethnographic, this is not to say that this is *only* what they are i.e. they often produce *more* than astute social commentary and given the nature of the medium often go further, for instance producing 'scenes', genres, movements, etc. With this is mind, it makes sense at this juncture to bring this conceptual discussion back 'down to Earth' and explore some examples of rap which, to me, represent the best of the ethnographic potential of rap – both from the UK and the US – to demonstrate the anthropological capacity of the genre.

Mobb Deep, Dizzee Rascal and The Streets

I have often enjoyed reading the series *33 1/3* from Bloomsbury Publishing which takes as its focus of analysis one album in its entirety, particularly the publication on NaS's seminal album *Illmatic* (Gasteier, 2009). However, if I were ever to participate in this series of books, I would choose an album by another resident of the same Queensbridge housing project – Mobb Deep, and their album *The Infamous*. This is perhaps my favourite album of all time. I can remember the first time I heard it; after my parents got divorced my Dad ended up living on a quintessential suburban, 1990s, new-build cul-de-sac and me and my brother would go and stay with him every other weekend. I recall that I listened to this album one night when I couldn't sleep, in the dark, wearing headphones, and it was an experience akin to going to the cinema.

The album depicts the experiences of rappers Prodigy and Havoc from the Queensbridge Houses in Queens, New York, the largest public housing project in North America. The image they paint of the streets off 40th and 41st Avenue is grim and nightmarish. The eerie, stripped-back production of drum loops, haunting piano samples and minor-key synths offers an almost spooky canvas onto which lyrics are painted which tell stories of nihilism, violence and the perennial threat of violence; of a suffocating, claustrophobic sense of being trapped, experiencing paranoia and fear; of urine-soaked stairways, drug use and drug dealing, shootings, hanging out on park benches drinking, and robbing people for no reason other than them being strangers. In essence, of course, this depiction of Queensbridge is a 'spatial imagining' much like the imaginings of England which began this book, and this takes place in the context of rappers needing to 'represent' local geographies which will be unpacked in more detail later (Forman, 2000). Beyond questions of accuracy, however, it is undeniable that like a director of a film, you feel the stifling pressure of the world they articulate in all its richness. Queensbridge was artistically represented in this album as a place of unimaginable bleakness described in precise detail: the street corners, the basketball courts, the park benches, the corner bodegas, the tower blocks, the street lights, the smoke. The way in which this world was described was unlike anything I had heard before and chimed with much of the anthropological literature I was reading which evoked similar spatial descriptions (albeit often of very different places around the world).

Interestingly, the Queensbridge housing projects sit on the banks of the Hudson River, with the skyline of Manhattan visible from some of the buildings. In the Netflix series *The Ozarks*, one of the leading characters Ruth Langmore (played by Julie Garner) is playing an album by another Queensbridge resident, NaS, in her headphones when she bumps into a rapper called Killer Mike in a diner. Reflecting on life in Queensbridge, Mike notes, making an inference from the work of Lauren Berlant (2011) on the concept of 'cruel optimism', that there is a component of psychogeography to music from this locale, which was in touching distance of unimaginable wealth, and yet was still in fact experienced as peripheral by those who live there, saying: 'I've always thought it was so hopeful and so fucking cruel at the same time'. These same sentiments have been expressed by the grime journalist Hattie Collins in her depiction of the area of East London where grime originated from too: an enclave of poverty sitting in the shadow of Canary Wharf (Collins, 2005). It is from here that the second example of ethnographic rap I want to highlight originates – Dizzee Rascal's 2003 album *Boy in Da Corner*. This again features lyrics which powerfully articulate his life in East London as a young man and the suffocating preoccupations of his life and upbringing. Indeed, this album is mentioned in the work of Barron (2013: 536) too, who foregrounds the ethnographic insight of the album, noting: 'This was an urban space characterised by deprivation and street violence, as the lyrics for the track "Brand New Day" illustrate with rhymes that stress teenage violence between rival estates and gun crime. Later in the song, the social horizons and life chances of living in such an area are further emphasised with a potent tinge of social hopelessness'. Part of what this album does is highlight rap's ability to articulate places with varying specificities; that is, if Mobb Deep were concerned with just a few streets and street corners, Dizzee Rascal slightly broadened this out to be an area of East London, while my third favourite example of ethnographic rap – by Mike Skinner – was not specifically of a place per se, but an abstract notion of suburban England. The album *Original Pirate Material*, which I began this book examining via the work of Caspar Melville (2004), represents perhaps the closest version of rap ethnography which connects to my life and lived experience, and which was a huge source of inspiration growing up.

There are many other examples I could have referred to here. Each of these three albums shares, to an extent, a feature in that their treatment of the everyday is often more realist (even bleak) than, say, the work of UK hip-hop MCs such as Ty or Roots Manuva when he raps about sitting here 'contented with this cheese on toast' in the track 'Witness (1 Hope)' (Big Dada/Ninja Tune, 2001). Indeed, Roots Manuva's debut album *Brand New Second Hand* (Big Dada, 1999) was important in my teenage years;

I remember going on a skateboarding holiday to Barcelona with my Dad and brother and endlessly playing the track 'Inna'. I loved its witty tale of Roots being in a bar with trendy people all around him, feeling out of place having 'only got five quid to spend' and 'cotching at the bar side, taking in the view. Press luck, trying to scrounge me a next pint of brew' before having a toke of hash, taking off his shirt, and the bouncers throwing him 'flat 'pon the floor'. More recently, acts such as Goldie Lookin Chain, Korrupt FM from the acclaimed BBC series *People Just Do Nothing*, and even – to an extent – Bad Boy Chiller Crew, all embody a satirising of more comedic forms of mundanity, and represent another dimension to the great variety within the rap genre even when viewing it through the relatively narrow prism of the ethnographic 'everyday' as undertaken here. Likewise, there are other global examples of rap documenting everyday life which those with closer linguistic and cultural understanding have done much to draw out. I am thinking here of rappers like MWR from Palestine (Bourgeois, 2019), La Etnia from Bogota in Colombia (Tickner, 2008) – and indeed countless other examples from across Latin America (see Castillo-Garsow and Nichols (2016) for a breathtaking overview) – Reggie Osei, O'Kenneth and others from Ghana advancing their own take on drill called Asakaa (Okirike, 2021), Thato Saul from South Africa, and the aforementioned Lunatic from France with their stories of life in the *banlieues* of Paris (Downing, 2020). I have chosen my three examples because they were salient, formative and important in my life and spoke to me, but one of the beautiful things about rap is the way this is taking place throughout the world and in a variety of ways.

I do not for one minute think that my work stands up to the ethnographic calibre of the great musical projects I have referred to here. Far from it; my own musical career was far more modest, typified by a level of success upon which I can look back proudly, with great fondness and with my head held high, but which – if I am honest – did not reach the kind of heights I had at one point in my life hoped it would. To be brutal and frank, of course I dreamed of bigger stages, bigger audiences and a greater level of success, which is of course defined subjectively and ambiguously by musicians (Hughes et al., 2013; Smith, 2014; Gross and Musgrave, 2020). Sonically and lyrically too, I do not think I stood up to these albums in terms of delivery, lyricism, skill or other measurable variables which might suggest lyrical quality. That being said: do I feel that I had something relevant to say that I felt was not being said elsewhere in the way I wanted to say it? Yes. Do I feel that I said the things I wanted to say in the ways I wanted to say them? To an extent. Do I feel that the lyrics I wrote during this period of my life contain within them some fragments of ethnographic insight to reveal something about a suburban way of life in England at the time they were written and thus warrant close reading and examination to elicit thematic areas of enquiry? I think so. It is on this basis that the next chapter will dive into my lyrics from this period of my life.

Notes

1 Defined by Dennis (2007: 12) as: 'the extent to which the point to be proved is disputed; adequacy of proof of the prior misconduct; probative force of the evidence; proponent's need for the evidence; availability of less prejudicial proof; inflammatory or prejudicial effect; similarity to the charged crime; effectiveness of limiting instructions; and the extent to which prior acts evidence prolongs proceedings'.
2 Chaddock vs State.
3 Former US Attorney Jason Shapiro's (2014) *Lawyers, Liars, and the Art of Storytelling: Using Stories to Advocate, Influence and Persuade* (itself drawn upon in the aforementioned critique of narrative by Peter Brooks) is insightful here on this phenomenon more broadly.

5

Small Town Lad Sentiments

Following the arguments developed previously regarding the capacity to derive specific insights from lyrics, I will now present a collection of songs which I wrote between approximately 2010 and 2014. I have chosen to include here the lyrics which relate specifically to the themes of this book – as opposed to the songs I wrote about, say, falling in love – and as such many of the tracks share overlapping ideas and concepts. Some of these were songs which I ultimately released, some were recorded but were not ready to share, some had interesting couplets pulled and recorded in other tracks, and many were just ideas which never found life beyond my iPhone 'Notes'. All of them draw on my experiences from living in Norwich and being brought up in Tuxford, Louth and Fetcham. Some of the tracks were written whilst I still lived in Norwich but the majority were articulated after I had moved to London, where Norwich and the surrounding area became a memory, the distance giving me a new perspective. This speaks to something intriguing about these lyrics, in that they broadly evoke a memory of a place and a life which, even as I wrote them, slipped further through my fingers. That is, as I left Norwich to finish my education in London, signed a songwriting deal with Sony Music Publishing and moved into being a full-time academic, so the world of parochial angst, frustration, fear, anxiety, drinking and fighting, all reflected in these lyrics, became increasingly distant; like writing about a ghost. To an extent I wonder if this is an existential problem of this form of ethnographic rap, rooted as it is in a place, a perspective, and a time of life which is fleeting; that almost with each letter written down, that life drifts increasingly towards being historical as opposed to present. In a sense, from the moment I closed the door on the last house I lived in in Norwich, and drove a hired van packed with boxes down the M11 to start a new life, so the place which provided me with my artistic inspiration faded in the rear-view mirror down the motorway and further from my reality. This calls to mind comments by the singer and songwriter of the suburban band XTC, Andy Partridge, who once said that he never left Swindon – 'a soft, gloopy, apathetic place…Averageville' – and that by staying 'it's given me something to kick against. It's the anvil you get to harden stuff up on' (Harris, 2010). Perhaps I lost my anvil. But, in hindsight, it was the right thing to do.

Small Town Lad Sentiments

Welcome to the breadline,
Where we're counting ten pence pieces, letters are sent with red lines.
Do they know the headlines?
Wonga loans[1] maxed out past the deadline,
And I say that I'll change on Monday: day-dreaming past my bedtime.
It's all too quick to hold true,
You go from getting stoned in your old room,
To freezing your nuts off out in the dole queue.
I'm scared that I'll waste away and I'll stay until my brain degrades,
And I'll be that old pisshead saying: 'I could have made it mate',
You know what these are?
Small town lad sentiments spoken until my Benson[2] ends.

End your week in the shops
Getting off your trolley, two bottles of Glen's voddy[3] until fears are lost,
And on Monday try and hide it from your boss
At your desk job, trapped with no power.
I used to try and make the days go faster with fag breaks for half an hour.
We grew up being told that actions speak louder than words,
But you need cash to act and I'm skint; fractions speak louder than verbs.
Recently I've had a vicious inkling that my ship is sinking
In a place where typing out a CV is wishful thinking.
You know what these are?
Small town lad sentiments spoken until my Benson ends.

When being bored as fuck grates you, call your mates, go blaze two.[4]
Play tunes of US rap and grime that you love but can't relate to.
We're feeling depressed,
Because we got told 'stay in school, that's your secret to success',
But fill a CV out, put it on their desk, are they fuck impressed.
Why do you think we give up and act crazily slack?
We're strewn from the beaten track and sign up for tours of duty in Iraq.
So, you know what these are?
Small town lad sentiments spoken until my Benson ends,
Told so that you go see sense again, you know what these are.

20Something

I'm in the same spot,
And my pocket's got all the same rocks that I got in the same squat,
The same scotch bottle, in the same shop.
Will I ever move?
Well, I know it would be clever to.
But just put on your school shoes,[5] go out and get leathered in a Wetherspoons.
With a pay packet this weak for the week I know mate it's peak,
Should I get wrecked up for the night, or keep it and eat for a week?
And you need to keep en garde, what's occurring is deep,
My mate sold his stuff to buy crack to smoke on his own while you sleep.
We're 20something...

Are we worthless mugs fussed about buying new shirts and drugs?
Smug. Strip clubs and jugs.
Buy you a tequila, swap for a tug.
It's that vanity song that asks where my sanity's gone,
And I'm pissed that the only cheque/check I seem to get is a reality one.
I feel useless and shit, it's as ruthless as this,
I'm a 20something in a caff with my fry-up mopping up my bean juice with my chips.
Now, I've got pages filled, we just try to pay the bills,
Pubs, girls, raves and pills, jaded thrills.
We're 20something...

I see some lads my age earning double what they pay me,
But the only double I get is the one that ends with JD [Jack Daniels].
I'm all alone at night thinking it's changed from playing Goldeneye,[6]
Now all we do is go phone a guy to get stuff to take through our nose or eye,[7]
Then I recall it for your Bose[8] with mics.
We're outspoken louts, spout gas from my lungs,
And when I'm gurning is the only time I bite my tongue.
I'm out lairy and lager fuelled, use strings until the strings on your heart are pulled,
These are tales of lads who fear ending up unremarkable.
We're 20something.

This Is Us

This is us, is it it for us?
Wonder are we under-attainers?
We're the kids dreaming in school uniforms and trainers.
Thinking that we'll be huge and that's why our nothingness pains us.
We were just watching [MTV] Cribs[9] all day at home and so, mate, can you blame us?
I'm thinking that living in a small town like this we'll just grow to be strangers.
Light pipes for your pipe dream of growing up to be famous.
Go and rob the off-licence just to get your name in the papers.
JD [Jack Daniels] shared amongst mates sitting on the pavement.

This place really takes the piss, caged in a desk job and you're making it.
Why do you think that my mates get shit faced and smack you in the face for the sake of it?
The suburbs dream of violence,
to be disturbing this silence...
Why do you think I'm in Budgens, grabbing Glens and put a few quid in,
Taking the coke lid off and tip it in then swigging, while my mate beside me is billing?[10]
There's no mystery why we get in the type of state that we get,
I maybe on some level do it to forget
That I'm in my mid-twenties and no-one's heard of me yet.
Out blind drunk, lost at night, bosh a line, got blood on my Lacoste tonight.
We can't think outside the box, we live there: ostracised.

Trying to be a top pick in the media mate
but honestly, I'm feeling afraid that at this rate,
I'll leave a non-existent Wikipedia page.
I've got that small town cabin fever madness,
Trapped in a maddening pattern of average.
But sobriety bores us, so pour us something enormous,
wonder what more is there for us? Middle England Pyramid stage[11] performance?
Dream on.
Soak the rag; lighter fluid poured on an old sock, inhale some drags,
Lynx cans in a plastic bag,
England wants words from this lad.
I'm a White Lightning[12] kid, Nikes and spliffs,
you know what I'm writing is tales of lads who spend their nights fighting pissed,
A 'Dispatches'[13] you might have missed...

Long Way from Nowhere

You work in a bar, I'm working in a call centre,[14] babe can you taste the resentment?
I'm living, and how else are we meant to?
That's why we're out getting higher than our rents are.
Log on, until pence are paid input the data hit enter.
Are we gambling our lives away?
That seems apt in a town with more bookies than job centres.
Sometimes I start to think how easily we could run.
We live a long way from nowhere, pack it up and we'd be done,
And leave this town where our lives revolve around minus funds.
But we'll say the same until next Saturday, up until we see the sun.

A parochial plot is written, I know just what is missing.
Rural, White Hart boozer, lock-in living,
In our twenties not got a pot to piss-in.
Smudged stamps on my hand, smudged make-up on your face:
We're each other's, displaced.
Red nail varnish, red lipstick, red wine glass, daydreaming in space.
We've past that Year 6 disco slow dance,
To a fifty pound a week romance.
We can leave together, I've got no plans.
Is that childish talk from a grown man?
I just wanted to give you more so that we could breathe more easily.
Are we leaving here, or are you leaving me?
Is optimism naivety?

Are we stuck where the kids have gone loony, smashing meow meow[15] for hours?
Don't be like my mate get nicked, strip searched, cold shower,
then belling me up he's so dour.
We know the feeling of what being parred is like,
Waiting for our lives to start like Jarndyce.[16]
Ambition's an affliction and losing's not a class feeling,
Seeing smudged fingerprints underneath a glass ceiling.
I tell tales of the sinners
In £100 jeans by D&G[17] but can't pay for their dinners.
I can't watch, get locked, trapped by your watch,
In a 9-to-5 trap play or get your pay docked.
To evade those in displayed socks[18] burn the hot rocks,
Locked in the stock room of Argos until your heart stops.

1.4 at 12

What do we know about 'Aston Martin Music'?[19]
This is 'For your Ford Fiesta when the city's darkened music'.
For driving while your mate is spangled in the back and off it,
To my knowledge packing two Os[20] in his pockets,
If we're pulled, toss it.
Drive by Mr. Pizza, see some loony with a bleeding face,
A paramedic's screaming please she needs some space.
Come and see a city transfixed on debt,
And see the reason that Smirnoff spells 'poisoned' in predictive text.[21]
That's what we're going to do,
In a 1.4 at 12am, the city we're running through.

You know that if you want to come and see how we're living, just come and ask me
- *We're in the Festa[22] mate*
If you want to come and see how we're living, see it from the backseat
- *Pass the lighter b'or[23]*

See the lads I know the type, side parting and their spliff's enormous,
That claim they're artists, put a 'piss' before it.
That's what they really are; a mastered art.
Seeing flowers by the roadside with candles lit, that's proper dark.
I know how things are and how they also aren't,
Free for those that can afford it, pricey for those that can't.[24]
So drive past abandoned shops and boarded up Little Chefs
With twenty-decks,[25] and joke how the chefs you know are cooking ket.[26]

See a bloke in the street twat his bird – have a word,
Bouncers bowled over and his face just landed on the kerb.
Pissed girls are standing with their blokes crying their eyes out,
In drunken rows that end in them saying that they want time out.
I'm stopping at a red light,
This Max Power nutter pulls alongside, the engine revs, he bezzes by.
But what do we know about 'Maybach Music'?
This is 'Lads in Ford Fiestas where's the K[27] at Music'.

I Can't Kickflip[28] Anymore

I can't kickflip anymore, I just realised it the other day,
It felt like a poignant metaphor of something special that's slipped away.
Nowadays we fall asleep on the sofa, and wake up on the same sofa.
That's indicative that our childhood is over.
How can it be that we just throw away our salary
Getting out of our minds to try and retain our sanity?
Now I'm gradually making everyone that I know mad at me,
As I backtrack tragically trapped in apathy atrophy.
I'm in the Festa smoking the green, MJ 'Smooth Criminal' lean.[29]
We live rural, Pot Noodles and bugle,[30]
Wrecked up on ket, up City, as usual.
Run slowly horses of the night,[31]
We're fucked off because our life's not working out in the type of way that we thought it might.
When did we go from having all of our questions answered,
to having all of our answers questioned?

I can't kickflip anymore, I just realised it the other day,
It felt like a poignant metaphor of something special that's slipped away.
Nowadays shop keepers just know what I'm on though,
White faced, king skins, Tangfastic Haribo.
I'm trying to be an average lad,
dreaming I can turn my stanzas into grands.
Instead we dick about, just hammering grams with our mates,
Why not at the level our salaries stand?
Where I come from there's one major employer,
Failure's our social paranoia.
I've got blind vision I can't brush off à la Goya.[32]
Sat here reflecting on the sights that we see,
I just came from a funeral saying 'rest in peace',
while the bloke's son laid a wreath handcuffed to police out on day release.
At the wake bring a bottle in your coat, to buy a coke
and top it up without leaving at closing time broke,
Then you'll only have to buy one round with your rolled-up note.

I can't kickflip anymore, I just realised it the other day,
It felt like a poignant metaphor of something special that's slipped away.
Nowadays, it's lairy season,
spending your evenings tweaking out and peaking.

Getting doner meat, drown it in garlic sauce, then throw in his face for no reason.
Will I be happy with BMW on my car keys?
Peaked too soon? No it can't be,
Sniffing coke you're panicking when you skip a heartbeat,
Burn the candle from both ends and get wax on Primark jeans.
I can't let go,
Dressed in all black, chain smoking, tristesse, Juliette Greco.[33]
I'm a man seeing a boy trapped in a mirror, a confessional sinner.
How do you define being a winner in a land of 'one man' dinners,
Playing 'social interaction for beginners'?

Stretch

    I need an alchemy that morphs my notes to rubber bands to stretch them out.
    I need to change the change I'm stressed without,
    And make my pounds stretch like my patience is,
    Everyone's doing lines off a mirror but never facing it.
    Ten quid to fund my dinners for a week, I'm chip shop chique,
    Wearing three figures on my feet.[34]
    My mate said it'll all change one day but I'm wondering when.
    Just say you're cool – pretend.
    I'm asking my mate 'have you got a tenner to lend'?
    I know I'm taking the piss but not got a penny to spend.
    Just got a Mayfair and a Glens, I'm a million miles from Mayfair and a Benz,
    Rudeboys staring; be wary of them.
    We're skint mate, let's get lairy again.
    I've only got one slice of bread left, only got one mile left in my tank,
    Only got one bar left on my phone, only got one pound left in the bank.

    I'm sick of the taste of own brand,
    Sick of the taste of value ready meals at home and,
    I'm sick of getting cut off my phone plan,
    Looking at people getting money thinking 'get with the program'.
    Sick of the waste of grown man,
    Sick of waking up thinking 'that night was sick', but feeling sick when I look at my balance paying the loans back.
    And now my mate's signing on saying 'I'm more than a box to tick,
    I'm not a prick,
    Fuck this, I'll take their cash and get off my tits'.
    It's a toxic mix;
    Lost kids in a mosh pit, crushed rocks sniffed to escape feeling boxed in.
    I've only got one slice of bread left, only got one mile left in my tank,
    Only got one bar left on my phone, only got one pound left in the bank.

Afghan Letters

Yes mate, you asked me to write you,
Not done it before but thought I'd try to.
I've put in pictures of us out on the piss and the new Fabric mix, it's sick.
I saw your girl out the other night, some pissed up twat was trying to try it on,
Five lads rocked up and I doubt he was going to get wrong.
We'll keep an eye on her while you're gone.
I saw a picture of the scan,
What a trip seeing his little hand.
But mate, this city never changes,
Same clubs, same drinks, same bed filled with different strangers.
And legit, when the news comes on I always think 'this is it'
'Another soldier killed in Helmand by an IED', I shit myself a little bit.

You told me can you write to me whenever you can,
Because where you all are
seems so far,
So I'm writing letters to Afghan,
Just like I said I would.
You said 'Mate I know, soon I will be coming home, but I need this'
So when I can,
I'll be writing letters to Afghan, like I said I would.

Yes mate, safe for your letter,
I know it's a bit weird for lads to write but it makes me feel better.
I know now why they call it Helmand,
Because it is: it's hell man.
How have I gone from going out shopping with my dole,
To being out in the desert getting shot at on patrol?
Mate I played your tracks to the lads in the squadron,
And they were like: 'Your mate's a problem!'[35]
But it's such a stress to see a man get killed and breathe his final breath,
I had to put one lad on a stretcher with his legs blown off, what could I
    say to him when he said he wished that he had been laid to rest?
But that's life I guess,
Can't let it turn you sour, just pray that you don't get shelled in the early
    hours.
Five weeks of this tour left and I'll be back in May,
Happy days,
Get home and smashed for days.

You told me can you write to me whenever you can,
Because where you all are
seems so far,
So I'm writing letters to Afghan,
Just like I said I would.
You said 'Mate I know, soon I will be coming home, but I need this'
So when I can,
I'll be writing letters to Afghan, like I said I would.

On the night he came back we went out on the piss and heard a firework crack,
And I could see the terror in his eyes as he snapped.
I could tell that single sound immediately took him back
To the place where the mortar bombs were falling by his head
And his mate was screaming, losing both his legs.
Best believe neither of us said a thing, it just went unsaid,
We went and got smashed out of our heads
But we both knew.
That's a paradox, one minute he's in the desert hammer cocked
As another man is shot,
Then we forget by buying grams and shots like we jacked Camelot,[36]
How could I handle not speaking on it?
I guess it's easier to stand and watch.

Choose Lager

Choose life, choose stress.
Choose white? Choose debt.
Choose strife, choose ket,
Choose looking at twenty years in regret.
Choose Primark, choose Glens.
Choose Rizla, choose Benz.
Choose waiting, choose friends,
Choose filtering through a digital lens.
Choose gear, choose gurning.
Choose Uni, choose learning.
Choose Job Centres, choose earning.
Choose Afghan: choose returning.
Choose Rightmove, choose begs.
Choose Red Bull, choose dregs,
Choose being awake when the only things open are hospitals and legs.
Choose filters, choose raves.
Choose Fosters, chews face.
Choose England, choose rain,
Choose quarter life crisis, choose pain.
Choose shouting, choose lager.
Choose hashtags, choose harder.
Choose lager, choose lager,
Choose H&M, we can't buy Prada...

Choose life, choose art.
Choose tax, choose charts.
Choose Wetherspoons, choose bars,
Choose birds in white tops wearing black bras.
Choose fighting, choose beats.
Choose concrete, choose streets.
Choose stop and search but then having gear and so legging it from police.
Choose cunts, choose frapes.
Choose legends, choose mates.
Choose Greggs, choose japes.
Choose labels, choose fakes.
Choose Mayfair, choose drags.
Choose Withnail, choose tabs.
Choose Fabric, choose lads,
Choose dealers who tick you twenty bags.
Choose Festas, choose Jäeger.

Choose indie, choose major.
Choose excess, choose danger,
Choose wanking over Page 3 in the paper.
Choose Poundland, choose cars.
Choose comedowns, choose pars.
Choose ra's. Choose looking back and thinking 'yeah, I had it large'.

Being 21 Goes

Still say 'When I grow up I want to be...'
Is that an adult in front of me?
Tell me 'grow up', fuck that, pass me my bumps and keys.
I've got fears of coming third like flunked degrees.
I love this city, it's my home but I mean
I've been out shitfaced in the same bars every week since I turned 18.
Piss my nights away,
Wish my life away,
Sniff my strife away,
Cocked and shoot.
A Courteeners track on loop[37] in pyjamas eating waffles and spaghetti hoops.
No posters on my wall anymore, try to mitigate that via the four to the floor,
Ten quid bottle better pour out some more,
Feeling unsure so you go and score.[38]
Being 21 goes...

It breaks hearts: a mid-twenties lad seeing a skatepark.
From the time when we thought what mattered was to take part,
I recount it in boozers over mates and darts.
Stare up and ceiling,
That reality check leaves you reeling.
That inferior feeling, eyes water, skin peeling, the glass ceiling's revealing.
Like my mate, ski mask on and he's stealing,
School teacher on the side he's dealing,
Because on his wages you know he's dreaming if he thinks he can even get a studio flat in Ealing.
We're fully grown boys, you know us you sure do.
Girls' hair smelling of fags and perfume.
Battered sausages and burned food.
Comedowns, lungs brown, the worst mood.
Being 21 goes...

Adulthood came without you knowing and robbed your optimism and it's showing,
So now your bitterness is flowing.
The doubts of men plant seeds that've been growing.
I've got no first-class seat on a Boeing
So I'm wondering where my life has been going,

Saying 'Check my nose when I go in
and rack this up without the doorman knowing'.
My mate got a bait tattoo of a Smith and Wesson,[39]
Dream that you're smoking spliffs in the non-smoking section of a Best Western,
I'm jesting;
Politicking à la Peston.[40]
Maybe it's time to move to a city that I don't know and work my fingers to the bone,
And get rewarded with a mattress on the floor of a glorified walk in wardrobe?
Being 21 goes...

Notes

1. Wonga was a payday loan company favoured by one of my mates when times were tight.
2. Benson and Hedges are a British cigarette company.
3. Glen's vodka is one of the cheapest brands of vodka in the UK.
4. 'Blazing' meaning smoking weed/cannabis (see Fletcher et al., 2009: 246).
5. This is because in Norwich most of the bars and clubs had door policies which meant that you could not get in wearing trainers, a phenomenon seen in other cities in the UK too (see Hollands and Chatterton (2002: 303) for this in Newcastle). Some of the bars in Norwich would even list specific brands which, if you were wearing them, would mean you were not allowed to enter. As such, we often went out wearing the same shoes we had worn to school a few years earlier.
6. Reference to the game Goldeneye on the Nintendo 64 console. For my generation, this was a really seminal videogame, with its multiplayer function being (for me at least) a method of social interaction for someone who, as a young person, struggled to make friends.
7. This was a reference to the character DJ Eyeball Paul (played by Rhys Ifans) from the film *Kevin and Perry Go Large* (2000) who earned his nickname by taking shots of vodka through his eye.
8. Bose are a brand of speakers.
9. This was a show on MTV which ran between 2000 and 2010 where celebrities would offer tours of their homes (see Smith and Beal (2007) for more).
10. Billing was a slang term used by a mate of mine from London who lived in Norwich meaning to roll a joint.
11. The Pyramid stage is the main stage where the headliners play at Glastonbury Festival.
12. White Lightning was a brand of cheap and strong cider (Alcohol Concern, 2011).
13. 'Dispatches' is an investigative current affairs programme on Channel 4 in the UK.
14. Taking obvious inspiration from 'The Human League' song 'Don't You Want Me' (Virgin, 1981) which begins with the lyric: 'you were working as a waitress in a cocktail bar when I met you'.
15. 'Meow meow' (or Mcat, or mephedrone) is a stimulant similar to amphetamine which used to be legal.

16 Jarndyce vs Jarndyce is a long-running fictional legal case in Charles Dickens' novel *Bleak House*.
17 Dolce & Gabbana are an Italian designer brand.
18 This relates to one of the ways you could identity the kinds of lads you probably did not want to fight at the time, which was that they tucked their tracksuit bottoms into their socks, so displaying the logo.
19 This is a track by American rappers Rick Ross and Drake (Maybach/Def Jam, 2009).
20 Ounces (of drugs).
21 This ages the music, but older SMS text messaging used to have a feature called 'predictive text' which would anticipate the word you were putting in the message, and if you wrote the word 'Smirnoff' it would correct it to the word 'poisoned', which I always loved.
22 Festa was what we used to call my mate Ben's red Ford Fiesta.
23 This is a Norfolk phrase meaning mate/friend which is a bit like the term 'butt' in Wales.
24 Loose quote from the 1987 movie *Withnail and I* directed by Bruce Robinson.
25 My brother used to call a 20 pack of Camel Blue cigarettes 'a twenty deck'.
26 Ketamine is a tranquilliser which comes as a liquid, which when cooked turns into a crystalline that can be ground up into a powder and used as an illegal recreational drug.
27 Ketamine.
28 This is a skateboard trick.
29 Lean was a slang term used by a mate of mine from London meaning stoned. The word links here to the way Michael Jackson leaned forwards in a dance sequence in the music video for his track 'Smooth Criminal'.
30 Slang term for cocaine.
31 Line taken originally from Ovid's 'Amore' and later Christopher Marlowe's play 'Doctor Faustus' and refers to the horses which pull the chariot of time, i.e. wanting time to slow down (Stapleton, 2016).
32 Reference to the Spanish painter Francisco Goya who suffered an illness in his forties causing him to lose his sight (along with hearing and other ailments) but he continued to paint (Pérez-Trullén et al., 2018).
33 A French singer and actress (1927-2020) associated with the post-war bohemianism of the 'Left Bank' in Paris and themes of existentialism in her lyrics (Appignanesi, 2005: 83). I became aware of her from seeing elegant black and white photos of her dressed in all black and smoking cigarettes, and I thought she looked amazing.
34 Meaning shoes that cost over £100.
35 Slang term you might use to describe something positively. Describing someone as a 'problem' would be akin to saying: 'wow, this person is so good they are going to cause a problem for other people'.
36 The Camelot Group is the operator of the UK National Lottery.
37 The Courteeners are an English rock band who had a single called 'Not Nineteen Forever' (Polydor, 2008) which inspired this track. I ended up actually re-writing much of it and re-recording it with the phrase 'Being 19 Goes' as it flowed a bit better.
38 Meaning score drugs, i.e. buy drugs.
39 Smith and Wesson are an American manufacturer of firearms. A friend of mine – Andy – has two guns tattooed on his chest.
40 'Politicking' is a slang term used in American rap which means something akin to debating. Robert Peston is a British political journalist.

6

Dreaming from the Margins

What do these lyrics tell us about the experience of growing up in places like Tuxford, Louth, Fetcham, and more specifically Norwich? That is, what might they reveal about a side of England I have characterised as an England that no one cares about, and to what extent can they offer insights around key thematic areas of sociological enquiry? As Barron (2013: 540-541) writes in his work on the ethnographic nature of grime, rap music can facilitate and reflect what he describes as 'the emergence of new nodal points in the sonic landscape such as labour, masculinity, work, leisure and collectivity'. In order to explore the 'nodal points' in my own music, many of which overlap with those identified by Barron, I made the decision, informed by Atkinson's (1997) injunction to handle stories with methodological precision, to treat the stories in my lyrics as I would treat any other dataset in my scholarly work, and thematically coded them. To do this, I adopted a method I use regularly when interpreting interview transcriptions in my empirical studies of musicians' working lives (e.g. Musgrave, 2022, 2023a): grounded theory. Informed by the approach of sociologist Barney Glaser (1978, 1992), this technique has been extensively delineated elsewhere – see Willig (2008) for a particularly helpful example – and involves progressively identifying themes (or categories) from a dataset; in this case, lyrics. Shared events or commonalities which exist at a level of abstraction, and which to an extent come from and are produced by the researcher themselves, are coded together in thematic clusters to highlight patterns, e.g. every time friendships are mentioned, or every time family is mentioned, or every time money is mentioned, etc. Through a process known as 'constant comparative analysis' these categories then grow and shrink as they become subsumed together (e.g. friendship and family might be amalgamated into a single category as being about 'relationships'), until a point of theoretical saturation is reached. Following this methodological approach, the themes identified below emerged as areas I propose the lyrics offer the most meaningful insight towards. I have also included snippets of other rhymes from tracks I wrote and released over the years which did not chime explicitly with the themes in this book, or those from my very early career which I did not feel were of sufficient quality to transcribe and print in their entirety, but where specific rhymes were identified as having interest or salience. In undertaking this I identified four themes which will frame the analysis below: possibility and ambition, work and the future, masculinity and violence, and recognition and remembrance.

Possibility and Ambition

When I was eighteen years old, on my first day working at Norwich Union, I sat next to a friendly older guy – I would guess at the time in his late forties – who asked me how long I was planning to stay at the company. I shrugged with a kind of teenage, arsy uncertainty, and I will never forget how he said: 'I thought the same thing when I arrived here when I was seventeen, and I'm still here today'. This exchange highlights a concept which would come to preoccupy much of my thinking throughout my time in Norwich and which is omnipotent in the lyrics; a preoccupation derived in no small part from my own upbringing, the relentless striving of my Mum, and my family narrative – ambition. It comes up again and again, from 'ambition's an affliction and losing's not a class feeling' ('Long Way from Nowhere'), to 'where I come from there's one major employer, failure's our social paranoia. I've got blind vision I can't brush off à la Goya' ('I Can't Kickflip Anymore').

Some of these feelings of ambitiousness manifest in much the same way that other lyrical depictions of suburbia have: a frustration at being limited by my immediate geography and a rejection of, and pushing back against, the perceived repetitiveness and dullness of the surroundings. For example, the track '20Something' begins with repeated reference to the word 'same' in the extract: 'I'm in the same spot, and my pocket's got all the same rocks that I got in the same squat, the same scotch bottle, in the same shop' ('20Something'). Likewise, this technique is mirrored in the track 'Afghan Letters' with the lyric: 'this city never changes, same clubs, same drinks, same bed filled with different strangers'. These instances are similar to an excerpt from another band from the suburbs – Blur, from suburban Essex – who in their 1995 track 'Ernold Same' mockingly derided the repetitive drudgery of suburban commuting. There is also a reflexive acknowledgement of the contradictions of this kind of repetition in the track 'Small Town Lad Sentiments' which reflected the fact that so many of the weeks me and my mates shared seemed to follow the same pattern: spending the week complaining endlessly about our jobs, worried about where we would be by the time we were thirty, getting as intoxicated as possible on Friday and Saturday nights, spending all day Sunday telling ourselves that next week would be different, but nothing ever changing, feeling hemmed in by the possibilities of where we lived: 'I say that I'll change on Monday: day-dreaming past my bedtime'.

Norwich is sometimes – perhaps unfairly, perhaps not – referred to as 'the graveyard of ambition' (Williams et al., 2006: 27), or perhaps less commonly as a 'fur-lined rut';[1] a place which in its kindness and unpretentiousness, modesty and humility, combined with its geographical isolation and infrastructural insufficiency, renders it somewhere that it becomes easy to live, but by extension easy to sail and coast. Indeed, a report for *The Work Foundation*, published while I was working at Norwich Union, identified the absence of a culture of aspiration in the city (ibid.), and work by Norwich-based media theorist Martin Scott (2014: 17) too, drawing on the aforementioned work of Rogaly and Taylor on the residents of the housing estates which encircle the city, highlights 'one of the key drivers of deprivation and social exclusion in the [NELM estates] is often claimed to be a lack of aspiration'. Of course, it's important to contextualise what this really *means*; aspiration for whom and to do what? The normative or even moral question of what people *should* aspire to is beyond something I could reasonably comment on. Likewise, it is important, drawing on the work of educational sociologists like Garth Stahl (2015) or Louise Archer and colleagues (2010) that middle-class conceptions of ambition are not imposed on others. That being said, music offers a fascinating prism through which to explore this debate. For example, Scott also draws attention to the fact that 'Future Radio', a community-based radio station launched in Norwich in 2004, was located between the deprived areas of Mile Cross and Catton Grove precisely to 'tackle this perceived "sub-culture"'[1] [of apparent unambitiousness] (Scott, 2014). This decision illustrates the fascinating assumed connection between deprivation (both economic and in terms of outlook and perception) and cultural/creative work.

> *How old are you now?*
> *Oh yeah? How's that working out?*
> *Are you where you thought you'd be? 21 guns sound for your dreams in the ground*
> — 'Dreams Don't Live Here Anymore', Context (2015)

Dreaming What You Can't See?

During my years in Norwich, and reflected in these lyrics, I came to find the notion of what you might call a horizon deprivation, not captured by quantitative metrics of deprivation on government websites or colour-coded graphs showing 'Lower Layer Super Output Areas' – for instance – fascinating; that is, what we imagine is or is not possible based on what we consciously and unconsciously see as achievable in front of us every day, particularly in relation to creative work. This notion has been explored empirically in work by education researchers Kim Allen and Sumi Hollingworth (2013) which examined the aspirations fourteen- to sixteen-year-olds in various parts of England had to work in the more broadly defined knowledge economy (of which music forms part). In exploratory and biographical interviews, this research asked young people in three areas of deindustrialisation and social and economic deprivation (and thus framed as being somewhat similar) – a northern district of Stoke on Trent, inner-city Nottingham and East London – to reflect on images showing scenes depicting occupations in the creative industries in order to examine how place and place-based identities came to constitute geographies of aspiration and perceived possibilities. Informed, as per my own thinking, by Bourdieu's concept of habitus, the authors note the often overlooked geographic component in the emergence of what Beverley Skeggs (2004) calls 'plausibility structures', i.e. that 'habitus can be understood to relate not simply to class-based dispositional understandings of what is thinkable for "people like me" but *also* for "people from round here"' (Allen and Hollingworth, 2013: 501).

In this study the young people from Nottingham and London were able to articulate what the researchers – drawing on the work of Tim Butler

(2002), Butler and Robson (2003) and geodemographer Richard Webber (2007) – call a 'metropolitan habitus' or 'cosmopolitan sensibilities' (Nava, 2007), defined as being 'outward looking, associated with modernity, engagement with difference and a revolt against the traditional' (Allen and Hollingworth, 2013: 501). In this context, work in the creative industries was positioned by these young people as 'possible and desirable' as well as credible (ibid.: 508) rooted in factors such as (perceived) proximity to London, media and technology facilities in schools and colleges, and industry connections. The latter was particularly true in the London school where workshops and visits from current professionals provided both inspiration and legitimation. For the students in Stoke on Trent however, this was not found to be the case. Here, 'the invisibility of a local creative sector' (ibid.: 506) alongside other factors meant the images of creative occupations were treated with feelings of dismissal, mockery, disinterest and/or apathy. This work highlights wonderfully the emergence of what the researchers call a place-specific habitus, where aspirations vis-à-vis what is considered achievable is significantly (although of course not exclusively) moulded and mediated spatially, so that even in areas which might appear quantitatively to be similarly deprived, the qualitative, narrative experiences of the young people are enormously different in terms of creative ambition.

These differences in understandings of possibility are perhaps akin to what psychologists might think of as the capacity to imagine a different possible self or 'possible identity' (Oyserman and James, 2011). I can only speak honestly in the context of musical ambition as it is what I know best, but my personal sense is that in Norwich – and certainly in Tuxford or Louth – we don't see the kinds of major artistic, cultural and educational institutions just a few miles from our homes that Londoners do. We don't experience the visible lives of competition, excess, wealth and localised stories of global success; the plurality, diversity and cultural richness of having generation-defining culture being produced by people who share the same accent as you when you hear them on the radio, or who come from the same place as you. Nor do we experience the imperceptible pace of change, hustle, and social connectivity alongside affordable geographical mobility in the same way that, say, young people of all backgrounds – even within similarly deprived LSOAs to those in Norwich or Tuxford or Louth – growing up in London do. The lives of artistic opportunity in London feel a million miles away from the England no one cares about. Not far from where I used to live in the town of Wymondham in Norfolk there is an eighteenth-century, white, inscribed milestone (which looks not dissimilar to a tombstone) along an ancient stretch of road outside a supermarket which reads: 'London 101 Miles'. Often, this felt as though it might as well have said '1,001 Miles', or '10,001 Miles', or '1,000,001 Miles'. It was this I was trying to capture in the lyric: 'I've got a Mayfair [cigarette] and a Glens [vodka], I'm a million miles from Mayfair and a [Mercedes] Benz' ('Stretch').

This is not to minimise the deprivation experienced by many growing up in London: in London, deprivation of course means restrictions, challenges, forms of oppression, ferocious competition with wealthier newcomers rich in various form of capital, resentment at the startling inequality, and, in many cases, entirely different, or at least more immediate, *threats*, particularly for certain groups. London can be a brutal and unforgiving place. That is, many in London likely feel 'a million miles from Mayfair and a Benz' too. Even so, the symbols of artistic dreaming are in front of their eyes, and, as shown by Allen and Hollingworth (2013), the 'metropolitan habitus' is far closer. I note that even at the time of writing this book, a new Cultural Quarter named 'East Bank' was opening in East London around the site of the Queen Elizabeth Olympic Park which the Mayor of London at the time – Sadiq Khan – suggested would 'inspire a new generation of Londoners to pursue their creative ambitions' (Mayor of London, 2019). This is of course laudable, but what do 'creative ambitions' look like in Norwich, or Worsbrough, or Louth, or Tuxford? We often don't even know what creative ambitions look like, can be, or where they can go. Creative ambitions are hopes and dreams, but can you dream about something you have never seen? Empirical work on this subject is fascinating: for example, the 'continuation hypothesis of dreaming' suggests that dreams broadly reflect experiences we have already had (Schredl and Hofmann, 2003; Vallat et al., 2018), and in this sense our ability to dream is dependent on what we see, which then determines what we can imagine. I tried to capture this in the track 'This Is Us' with the lyric: 'sobriety bores us, so pour us something enormous, wonder what more is there for us? Middle England Pyramid stage performance? Dream on', where I was wondering out loud what more there was than what I could see, and if someone rapping about the mundanity of 'middle England' would ever end up headlining the Pyramid Stage at Glastonbury, and deciding it was not likely.

Certainly, these horizons are significantly mediated by class and one cannot oversimplify. Indeed, work by Lisa Mckenzie (2016, 2017) in fact draws parallels in the experiences of political marginalisation and social exclusion in both Nottinghamshire ex-mining villages (not far from Tuxford) and East London, suggesting working-class residents in both places share many perspectives relating to disillusionment and resentment; of 'abandonment, financial struggle and political remoteness' (Mckenzie, 2017: 276). Likewise, London is a big place and the experiences of young people in outer easterly boroughs like Redbridge or Barking and Dagenham are likely different to those of similar young people in inner boroughs like Westminster or Camden, say. Additionally, I was geographically isolated but had reserves of cultural capital from my upbringing which provided me with important advantages – not least my Mum's capacity to imagine me going to Cambridge as a child and an incredibly supportive and loving family – and therefore the picture is not a simple one. However, speaking personally, even as someone who is middle class by any metric, even I didn't know what creative ambition *could* be growing up in the isolated parts of England I did. I remember leaving one of my first meetings with my new manager after I moved to London in late 2011 where he asked me which major label or publisher I wanted to sign to. I had never even dreamed that was possible, nor did I know what a music publisher was. I did not even know what a publisher did. In a moment which was entirely surreal, I remember that I exited the tube station on a sunny and chilly December afternoon and saw a huge billboard outside Hammersmith Broadway for the make-up brand Garnier which read 'Believe in Miracles'. I remember stopping and taking a photograph of it as it felt so strange (I still have the picture on my phone, taken on 7th December 2011 at 14.44). Two years later I would be signed to Sony. I have absolutely no doubt that this would never have happened had I stayed in Norwich.

Work and the Future

'Geographies of Employment'

This uncertain relationship between the England no one cares about and creative work as outlined above, is reflected lyrically in uncertainties around *other* kinds of work too. In its bleakest manifestation I tried to articulate this vicariously relating to the strains of unemployment and the challenges of securing any kind of job at all. For a number of years this was the experience of my closest mate from school – Ben – whose struggle with unemployment and subsequent downward spiral I sought to reflect with the lyric: 'my mate's signing on saying "I'm more than a box to tick, I'm not a prick. Fuck this, I'll take their cash and get off my tits". It's a toxic mix; lost kids in a mosh pit, crushed rocks sniffed to escape feeling boxed in' ('Stretch'). Indeed, it was Ben I was referring to in the lyric: 'You go from getting stoned in your old room, to freezing your nuts off out in the dole queue' ('Small Town Lad Sentiments'). However, whilst his experience was extreme among my peer group it was not entirely unique; for many of us, looking for work in Norwich meant the relentless tedium of obsessing over the formatting and wording of CVs, making retail work or the six months spent as a barman in the local pub sound 'professional' with apparently transferrable skills and the buzzwords of reflexive 'self-description lexicography' (Cremin, 2003: 109) – meaning describing yourself as things like a 'self-starter' and a 'team player' – sending these CVs to recruiters like 'Office Angels' or off for jobs which sounded, frankly, miserable, and often never even hearing back. In this way, CVs became a document to pour and preoccupy over, with outcomes often being poor. When I wrote: 'Recently I've had a vicious inkling that my ship is sinking, in a place where typing out a CV is wishful thinking' ('Small Town Lad Sentiments'), I meant it.

However, eventually Ben and all my mates found work, but throughout the lyrics you can see a palpable frustration at the kind of work available, and more broadly at the scope of the career trajectories on offer in places like Norwich, or indeed Tuxford and Louth, which feel incredibly narrow in terms of both the absolute number of jobs and equally the *type* of jobs. The first way this is seen in the lyrics concerns the perceived mismatches between educational qualifications and the work these could secure. This tension, then, is captured in the line: 'We're feeling depressed, because we got told "stay in school, that's your secret to success", but fill a CV out, put it on their desk, are they fuck impressed' ('Small Town Lad Sentiments'). We can situate this feeling sociopolitically. My generation were entering a labour market marked by a rapid expansion of graduates in the wake of former British Prime Minister Tony Blair's famous statement in his 1999 Labour Party Conference speech that his government had 'set a target of fifty per cent of young adults going into Higher Education in the next century' (BBC, 1999). My peer group finished school, by which I mean finished sixth form and completed our A levels (which most of my friends did, itself a population which I understand is not entirely representative) in 2005, and were the final cohort to avoid the 'top up' tuition fees of £3,000 per year introduced in 2006.[2] Already at this point a national conversation was well underway regarding whether or not there were 'too many graduates' in the UK (Bowers-Brown and Harvey, 2004). That is, politicians, policy makers and wider society were, even before we began university, confronting questions relating to graduate employability and potential skills shortages in a context where 43% of eighteen- to thirty-year-olds were entering or had been through higher education in 2003 (DfES, 2003).[3]

These arguments had a number of dimensions, but central was what scholars of education Tamsin Bowers-Brown and Lee Harvey (2004) referred to as the 'elitist' argument, i.e. that the number of young people attending university should be reduced (Lea, 2002) owing to, at least in part, what they described at the time as 'the issue of over-qualification' (Bowers-Brown and Harvey, 2004: 245). Bowers-Brown and Harvey brought together data from sociologist Peter Brown and colleagues (2003) highlighting that back in 2001 there were already twenty times more graduates than 'elite' jobs (however defined), that 37% of the workforce were overqualified (Keep, 2002: 466) – that is, held qualifications higher than that required by their current role – and that this therefore demonstrated, according to some, that 'as the number of graduates increases, the benefit offered by a degree diminishes' (Kivinen and Ahola, 1999: 197). Whilst the authors gave this idea rather short shrift at the time, data from a decade later showed that 26% of all jobs nationally now required a university degree, an increase from 15% in 1997 (Felstead et al., 2013), and simultaneously, 47% of UK university leavers were working in non-graduate jobs (ONS, 2013), a phenomenon seen to correlate with job dissatisfaction (Green and Zhu, 2010) – although evidence is somewhat mixed in this area (see Steffy (2017) for more).

I wanted the references to CVs in particular in the track 'Small Town Lad Sentiments' to reflect the feeling among me and my peer group that the kind of 'education as a golden ticket' rhetoric we were told by our parents and teachers – and which we broadly accepted – was, for many, not playing out in the way we had hoped. I remember starting work for Norwich Union after I finished school but before starting university and being shocked and disheartened at the number of graduates working on my 'team' handling overseas car insurance claims. It felt hard to be ambitious or indeed optimistic about my own future. Even after graduating, the kinds of jobs some of my friends had in coffee shops or sandwich bars or Argos, or even returning back to Norwich Union, struck me as incredibly depressing. One of my friends once captured this by saying that they could maybe get a job in Norwich, but couldn't get a career (or at least not a career he wanted). Of course, careers in these parts of England do exist, but they were not what we wanted (assuming we even knew what we wanted). For example, when writing this book I looked up my former line manager from my time at Norwich Union – a lovely bloke, himself from Norwich. He is still working there, and has been there now for twenty-one years. Perhaps he loves it? Perhaps he hates it as much as we all did? All I know is that my mates were terrified at the idea of spending our lives burning 'hot rocks [of hash], locked in the stock room of Argos until your heart stops' ('Long Way from Nowhere'). Indeed, we can see statistically the kinds of graduate careers available to you in the England no one cares about. In 2022 the Office for Students (OfS) produced an interactive map and corresponding report entitled *A Geography of Employment* (OfS, 2022) showing the distribution of graduates occupying what they describe as 'highly skilled jobs'.[4] These findings were informed by data from the Graduate Outcomes (GO) survey and were broken down into five quintiles, with Q5 being the highest proportion of graduates in highly skilled jobs or further study, and Q1 being the lowest. Again, for each of the places I have lived, I have presented the data below, and the numbers reflect my sentiments:

Tuxford (OfS area 'Retford and Worksop E30000291'): Quintile 1 (68.4%)
Louth (OfS area 'Scunthorpe and Louth E30000264'): Quintile 1 (63.4%)
Fetcham (OfS area 'Crawley E30000196'): Quintile 2 (70.5%)[5]
Norwich (OfS area 'Norwich E30000248'): Quintile 2 (71.8%)

Make It Make Sense

Not only were my educational cohort confronting the issues of securing work in the context of increasing numbers of graduates – and therefore competition – and doing so within geographic areas of the country with low levels of highly skilled employment, but we also graduated into a depressed labour market. The majority of my peer group finished undergraduate education in the summer of either 2008 or 2009, immediately in the wake of the global financial crisis. Data from the Office for National Statistics shows that between the first quarter of 2008 and the second quarter of 2009, the United Kingdom's gross domestic product shrank by more than 6% and did not recover until the third quarter of 2013 (ONS, 2018). Alongside this, levels of unemployment did not recover until 2015, and real earnings have barely risen even to this day. A range of studies by economists analysing data from the United States and Canada highlight that college leavers who graduate during a recession suffer marked earnings reductions (Wozniak, 2010; Oreopoulos et al., 2012), with data showing this effect lasting a considerable length of time (Oyer, 2006), even up to fifteen years (Kahn, 2010). In the context of the UK, research economist Imran Tahir at the Institute for Fiscal Studies delivered a lecture in 2021 highlighting many of these issues, describing what he called 'the *curse* of graduating during a recession' (Tahir, 2021, emphasis added), with one of these issues being poor incomes.

This challenge for my cohort was also taking place alongside the fact that we were living through an era of rampant house price inflation where the average affordability ratio had moved nationally from approximately 3.5 in 1997 to 9.1 in 2021 (ONS, 2022). This process was, as I wrote these lyrics, taking a key marker of status and progress for my peer group and millions of other young people (Filandri and Bertolini, 2016) seemingly further out of reach: home ownership. Against this backdrop, the final report of the Intergenerational Commission in 2018 suggested that generational progress – the idea that subsequent generations enjoyed an unwritten social promise that they might hope to improve on the position of those who came before them – was 'a promise under threat' (Resolution Foundation, 2018: 25). Anxieties over the collapse of this 'promise' can be heard, for example, when I rapped about a mate of mine from London whom we had all met in Norwich, and the conversations we used to have concerning the fact that he felt no matter what he did or how much he saved up, he would never be able to afford any kind of property and the kind of bleak nihilism and risk-taking behaviour this engendered: 'ski mask on and he's stealing, school teacher on the side he's dealing, because on his wages you know he's dreaming if he thinks he can even get a studio flat in Ealing' ('Being 21 Goes').

However, the anxieties we had over work often transcended solely fiscal concerns and came to be reflected in broader anxieties around identity and fulfilment. For example, the lyric which begins the track 'Small Town Lad Sentiments' – 'Welcome to the breadline' – was said by my mate Ben and I remember the exact moment I wrote it in my phone in May 2011: I walked into his flat on Silver Road in Norwich and remember him having three overdue bills in front of him, making stacks of £1 out of coppers and pennies. He looked up at me, held out his arms and said: 'Welcome to the breadline'. Uttering these words with his typical self-deprecating yet insightful and unnerving humour, he seemed to be encapsulating so much of his frustration at the trajectory of his life: an incredibly smart guy, kicked out of school during sixth form, smoking lots of weed and developing anxiety, working in a tedious office job, skint and bored. The moment seemed to capture so much of how many of us felt our lives were unfolding, trapped in a cycle of fear, dullness and mundanity in jobs which felt utterly meaningless and which we would leave in a second to do something which we felt was worthwhile (whether we knew what that was or not). For a while, me and Ben both worked at Norwich Union; the work was so tedious that we would either take extended smoking breaks until they mandated that you had to clock out to smoke and then clock back in which scuppered this trick, or go and sit on the toilet for as long as possible without triggering suspicion. So, when I wrote the lyric 'at your desk job, trapped with no power. I used to try and make the days go faster with fag breaks for half an hour' ('Small Town Lad Sentiments') – this was a daily reality. Experiences such as these engendered a deep sense of dread about what our futures might look like. As I wrote in 'I Can't Kickflip Anymore': 'Run slowly horses of the night, we're fucked off because our life's not working out in the type of way that we thought it might'.

For many of my friends, and indeed other young people growing up in the England no one cares about, a longer-term relationship with this kind of labour market was something one needed to escape geographically, which for me and most of my mates meant moving to London. These labour market migration patterns in England are longstanding and well known, referred to by a report for the Centre for Cities (Swinney and

Williams, 2016) as *The Great British Brain Drain* where, faced with the kinds of figures from the aforementioned Office for Students report on employment outcomes in places like Tuxford, Louth or Norwich, moving is the only option. This was a move I resisted for a long time (partly out of fear of a city which felt big and frankly terrifying, partly out of cost), but which eventually became inevitable, where, echoing the term brain drain (which I don't actually love as it seems to suggest those that 'stay' have lesser brains somehow), I wrote, referring to the weed-induced stupor me and my friends were often in: 'I'm scared that I'll waste away and I'll stay until my brain degrades, and I'll be that old pisshead saying: "I could have made it mate"' ('Small Town Lad Sentiments'). Thus, I, like many, left; as I wrote at the end of 'Being 21 Goes': 'Maybe it's time to move to a city that I don't know and work my fingers to the bone, and get rewarded with a mattress on the floor of a glorified walk in wardrobe?'. Again, this vignette was true: my friend moved to Ladbroke Grove when he first came to London and slept in a room which was the wardrobe of a larger bedroom and he didn't own a bed, sleeping with his clothes piled up on the floor at the foot of his mattress.

However, there was another option exercised by one of my mates to opt out of Norwich's poor job market – joining the army. One of the loveliest blokes I know did this. We all went to his 'Passing Out' parade after he completed his basic training and in 2010 he was sent on a tour of Afghanistan (stationed in Kandahar). The track 'Afghan Letters' was based on real letters me and my girlfriend wrote to him which we bundled up with 'morale parcels' containing photos and CDs of rap tunes me and Ben were recording at the time. The section in the final verse of that tune again is true; I recall that on the night he came home we went drinking in a pub in Norwich and a firework went off making him tense up. He told us he had been bombed in his sleep so loud noises now startled him. On the one hand then, the army let him escape Norwich, but in that moment it was hard to work out if the place he had escaped to was better or worse.

Just drop [pills], rave and make racket,
The depraved way, pissing away your pay packet.
That's day to day for my age bracket, a trend:
Getting fucked on your army leave for weekends.

- 'Frantic', Context (2008)

A Quarter Life Crisis

Connecting all of these themes of work together – from unemployment to office-based mundanity, the emptiness of CVs, and those who opted out and joined the army – are questions around the future, and the kind of future it was possible to imagine when you're from these areas of England. When I read back these lyrics today, I can see how they are drenched with an existential questioning about where our lives would end up and the type of lives we would end up being able to have (and indeed provide for others, something I want to examine in the next section of this chapter). These anxieties can be seen throughout the lyrics where I refer to the lengthy and drawn out legal case at the centre of Charles Dickens's novel *Bleak House*, suggesting that this mirrored the fact that my friends and I seemed to spend forever 'waiting for our lives to start like Jarndyce' ('Long Way from Nowhere'). The track 'Being 21 Goes' in particular highlights these feelings of crisis, where I articulated not yet entering formal adulthood – 'Still say "When I grow up I want to be..." Is that an adult in front of me? Tell me "grow up", fuck that' ('Being 21 Goes') – as well as bleaker feelings about what being an 'adult' really meant: 'Adulthood came without you knowing and robbed your optimism and its showing, so now your bitterness is flowing. The doubts of men plant seeds that've been growing. I've got no first-class seat on a Boeing so I'm wondering where my life has been going' ('Being 21 Goes').

Conceptually, much of the angst in these lyrics chimes with one line of mine in the track 'Choose Lager', a track which plays on the opening scene from the movie *Trainspotting* (PolyGram, 1996) – based on the novel by Irvine Welsh – where Mark 'Rent Boy' Renton (played by Ewan McGregor) lists a series of choices society wants people to make before sardonically and mockingly saying 'choose life'. In my version of this, I had a line where I said: 'choose quarter life crisis' ('Choose Lager'). This term was popularised in the work *Quarterlife Crisis* by journalists Alexandra Robbins and Abby Wilner (2001) and is rooted in the subjective experience of what psychologist Jeffrey Arnett coined 'emerging adulthood'. For Arnett (2000: 471), this is a period of time between approximately the ages of eighteen and twenty-five during which: 'Emerging adults do not see themselves as adolescents, but many of them also do not see themselves entirely as adults' – a concept seen in the track 'Being 21 Goes' where

I describe myself and my peer group as 'fully grown boys', or in 'I Can't Kickflip Anymore' describing myself as 'a man seeing a boy trapped in a mirror'. Indeed, throughout the lyrics I was struck at regular allusions to childhood, e.g. 'it's changed from playing Goldeneye' ('20Something'), or 'we fall asleep on the sofa and wake up on the same sofa. That's indicative that our childhood is over' ('I Can't Kickflip Anymore'), or the fact that now seeing a skatepark breaks my heart because I can no longer kickflip as I once could and that this represented 'a poignant metaphor of something special that's slipped away' ('I Can't Kickflip Anymore').

During emerging adulthood, individuals undertake identity work focused on areas such as love, work and worldviews where they seek identifiers of a successful transition to adulthood, namely independence (both financially and in decision-making) and accepting responsibility (Arnett, 1997, 1998). Arnett highlights how these periods of exploration are 'not always experienced as enjoyable [for example] exploration in work sometimes results in…an inability to find work that is satisfying or fulfilling' (Arnett, 2000: 474). This transition from emerging adulthood into early adulthood has been theorised in scholarly work by Oliver Robinson (Robinson and Smith, 2010; Robinson et al., 2013), a psychologist specialising in identity, wellbeing and mental health during stages of life transitions, as the precise time of the quarter life crisis: 'a major developmental crisis [which] commonly occurs after 25 but before 35' (Robinson, 2015: 22) whereby the individual (in one formulation at least) struggles to move from one stage of development to the next. Methodologically explored via the 'adult crisis retrospective self-assessment tool' (ACERSAT), a form of 'locked-out' quarter life crisis has been highlighted where 'the person feels unable to gain access to the desired roles of adult life' (ibid.: 25), and which can be accompanied by 'anxiety about future uncertainty [and feeling] consumed by coping with the stress of change and the emotion that comes with it' (ibid.: 23). This has been seen to occur after leaving university specifically (Robinson, 2019).

In one very real way, my experience of a quarter life crisis as understood in the literature was distinct insofar as I made my romantic commitment to my girlfriend when we were sixteen and we have stayed together ever since, living together throughout university, getting married in our late twenties and having children in our thirties. In this sense, the central challenge faced by many in emerging adulthood of romantic attachment was never a concern of mine. However, both together and with our group of friends from school, me and my wife shared many of the concerns about where our lives were going. Looking back at my songs, I read one particular lyric with a smile on my face: 'Smudged stamps on my hand, smudged make-up on your face: we're each other's, displaced' ('A Long Way from Nowhere'). I remember writing this lyric as I loved the imagery of waking up on a Sunday morning after a big night out and seeing a smudged stamp on the back of my hand from the club the night before and the smudged make-up on her face after we had returned home and both fallen asleep still in our clothes. I felt these visual smudges were somehow representative of the lack of clarity over the direction of our lives; the blurred lines, imprecision and anxiety of 'emerging adulthood' in which: 'My mate said it'll all change one day but I'm wondering when. Just say you're cool – pretend' ('Stretch').

Masculinity and Violence

A third theme which emerges in these lyrics, and indeed in the lyrics of other rappers in contexts all over the world – from young Palestinian men in refugee camps (Skinner, 2022), the political nationalism of Irish rappers (hír and Strange, 2021), to homosociality and Black masculinity within gangsta rap (Oware, 2011) – is masculinity. Throughout the lyrics one can see a sketching of one side of the experience of growing up as a young man in the England no one cares about, and how tensions and expectations are negotiated. It can be seen, for example, in 'Afghan Letters' when my mate replies to my letter saying 'I know it's a bit weird for lads to write' because it felt like an odd thing for men to do, or where I express my worry at not being able to provide my girlfriend with the type of life I thought I should be expected to provide when I wrote 'I just wanted to give you more so that we could breathe more easily' ('Long Way From Nowhere'). This final point I remember being a crippling concern of mine in my mid-twenties: that I would not be able to give my girlfriend (now wife) the type of life I thought she deserved, a concern which on reflection seems odd for someone who was brought up in a household where my Mum was very much the 'breadwinner'. When we eventually moved to London, I recall that this represented such a central break in our lives that I wrote the lyric 'are we leaving here, or are you leaving me?' ('Long Way from Nowhere'), reflecting my worry that in leaving Norwich, my girlfriend might end up leaving me. Before we moved, I had the same dream three or four times that we went sky-diving together but I forgot to attach parachutes to us and we both fell to the ground. I don't think one requires a course of Freudian psychoanalysis to ascertain the meaning of this dream.

In these and many other lyrics written during this time in my life, I can see now a reflection of a relatively narrow experience of masculinity and masculine norms rooted in rigid parameters of acceptability, conformity and heteronormative expectations. Some of this has been seen to be widespread (such as in work by Mahalik et al. (2003) on the 'Conformity to Masculine Norms Inventory'), but it might also be geographically located too. I can recall examples which reflect this. For instance, after I moved to London, I remember that one weekend I came back to Norwich to visit some friends and we were in a bar celebrating something and we were drinking champagne out of coupes. A group of lads sat at a table a few feet away were laughing and said loudly 'you look gay'. I remember how relieved I felt that I no longer lived in the kind of place where this kind of narrow-mindedness was so common[6] – or at least where the plurality of voices, mass of population, and diversity of opinion meant that the louder, aforementioned 'cosmopolitan habitus' more effectively drowned out narrow-mindedness like this.

Prince of Wales Road

Perhaps the most obvious way masculinity is represented in the lyrics, however, is through the references to violence, and in particular its relationship to drinking. For a number of years me and my friends were certainly participating in what is understood as a binge drinking culture – that is, drinking excessively, as cheaply as possible (which inevitably meant buying Glen's vodka), and drinking to get drunk – with all the well understood correlations to experiences of aggression and violence (Rossow, 1996; Swahn and Donovan, 2005; Wells et al., 2005; Hughes et al., 2008). This was a culture of deciding to 'put on your school shoes, go out and get leathered in a Wetherspoons' ('20Something'). Certainly this happens all over England, but it was only when I left Norwich and moved to

London that I realised the kind of casual – even nonsensical – violence I saw on an almost weekly basis on nights out was unusual. Of course, there is awful violence in all places – youthfulness and maleness as determinants of violence are well known (Gilligan, 2000: 229) – and my life was not a violent life; it often only existed for a few minutes or hours at the weekend. However, the violence of my lived experience in Norwich felt as though it stemmed from a parochial boredom and angst where getting as drunk as possible, and punching someone as hard as possible, was normalised to the point of being part of the rhythm of the weekend. I tried to capture this sentiment by making reference to the opening line of J.G. Ballard's novel *Kingdom Come* (2006) with the line: 'the suburbs dream of violence, to be disturbing this silence' ('This Is Us'). This was a similar sentiment to that expressed by Mike Skinner years earlier when he had rapped: 'Geezers need excitement. If their lives don't provide them this they incite violence. Common sense' ('Geezers Need Excitement', Original Pirate Material, 2002). I saw some of this lashing out as being connected to the previous thematic area above, i.e. a response to the boredom and frustration of working at places like Norwich Union. As I suggest in one of the lyrics: 'This place really takes the piss, caged in a desk job and you're making it. Why do you think that my mates get shit faced and smack you in the face for the sake of it?' ('This Is Us').

Fiona Measham, a criminologist with an interest in transgressive leisure, and colleague Kevin Brain (2005: 262) highlight these practices as a 'culture of intoxication' in Britain, typified by 'binge and brawl'. Norwich is not a violent or unsafe place – far from it. The vast majority of the violence I saw and experienced was centred around just one street – Prince of Wales Road: a strip of bars, clubs, pubs and kebab shops which slopes downwards from the base of Norwich Castle to the train station. Roads like these exist in towns and cities all over England,[7] but its cultural place in my life was, for a number of years, significant; the first rap song I ever wrote in 2005 alongside my mate Ben (who called himself Phlite) was entitled 'Prince of Wales Road'. The reputation of this street reached national attention when, in 2015, Labour MP Liam Byrne suggested that the top four most dangerous places for drinkers in the United Kingdom based on hospital admissions following nights out were Blackpool, Stoke, Sunderland and Norwich (Byrne, 2015). Our local newspaper, the *Eastern*

Daily Press, was regularly full of incidents from this 500-yard stretch of nightlife and indeed continues to be to this day, including regular fights (Galea-Pace, 2022b; Sennitt, 2022; Walsh, 2022), and even, on occasion, deaths (Grimmer, 2011). A well-known feature of the street is the presence of the volunteer-run 'SOS Bus' on Friday and Saturday nights to look after anyone who is injured or vulnerable, reflecting the omnipresence of threats and feelings of insecurity, and its reputation was further entrenched in March 2017 when the controversial talk show host Jeremy Kyle made Norwich (with a focus on Prince of Wales Road) the focus of an episode entitled 'Dangers of a Night Out' as part of his series *The Kyle Files* on ITV.

Me and my mates would go drinking almost every weekend in our early twenties on this road and would inevitably witness people 'start' on other people, or us – meaning, start fights – and less commonly us starting on other people, often for the most minor reasons. Examples abound which combine the absurd and the callous. A funny memory was that a lad once screamed in my face and threatened to attack me because I didn't have a designer logo on my polo shirt. Many of the memories are rather less funny. When I wrote the lyrics, 'getting doner meat, drown it in garlic sauce, then throw in his face for no reason' ('I Can't Kickflip Anymore'), this was true: I was once stood outside a takeaway on Prince of Wales Road opposite the nightclub 'Mercy' with someone I knew from school, and I watched him throw a kebab covered in garlic sauce in a man's face, punch him to the ground and then stamp on the bloke's girlfriend's foot for absolutely no reason other than he thought it was funny. Likewise, the depictions of violence in the track '1.4 at 12' are also all true, including the mention of driving by 'Mr. Pizza, see[ing] some loony with a bleeding face, a paramedic's screaming please she needs some space' ('1.4 at 12'); I remember watching this, going past in a taxi as medical personnel attended to a man lying in a pool of blood. Whilst it didn't happen often, it was also not entirely unusual to see men hit women on nights out too, so when I wrote the line 'see a bloke in the street twat his bird' ('1.4 at 12'), this again was true. Every time this happened it always triggered a wave of violence where other men (usually bouncers from nearby venues) would rush over and viciously attack the man in question. I remember once seeing a man punch a woman outside a bar, and someone ran across the street with a bike chain (no idea where from) and beat the man to the ground with it. A final story is that a friend of mine at school who is Black and had grown up in London, was once walking past a pub when a man sat at a table shouted, with clearly racist intent, 'why are you walking like you're from London?'. He then walked over and smashed his pint glass into my mate's face, sending him to hospital. Cruel and needless violence like this on Prince of Wales Road between midnight and 4am was entirely ordinary.

> *They're laughing as they cave your head in,*
> *Violence is in their psyche, just like glass is in my mates' skin*
> — 'Prince of Wales Road', Context and Phlite (2005)

Jog On, You Mug

You can hear a more subtle and pervasive anxiety around violence in the lyrics too, beyond the night-time economy and midnight drunken brawls. For example, in the track '20Something' there is the line 'are we worthless mugs fussed about buying new shirts and drugs?... Buy you a tequila, swap for a tug' – a tongue-in-cheek reference to the film *The Football Factory* directed by Nick Love which came out in 2004 and which was quite influential among me and my friends at the time. The film is a portrayal of football hooligans and depicts the bitter rivalry between the Chelsea 'Firm' (played by Danny Dyer, Frank Harper, Tony Denham and others) and the Millwall 'Firm' (played by Tamer Hassan and others). The film was something of a controversial cult classic, engendering a media-led moral panic upon release with its social realist take on hooliganism described by one critic as irresponsible, 'yob tourism' (Williams, 2004). The mixture of revulsion and extolment the film received was informed partly by the film's use of genuine 'Firm' members as extras, and its apparent glorification of a subculture wherein it was critiqued for 'refusing to condemn the violent amorality of its characters' (Redhead, 2007: 91). Me and my friends, particularly Ben, loved it. It introduced a new lexicon into our vocabulary as we would tell people to 'jog on' (meaning, walk away) or call other people – or even ourselves as per the lyric above – 'mugs' (essentially, idiots). I remember watching it and buying lots of the brands worn in the film – Henri Lloyd, Hackett and Stone Island. The majority of these were fakes from eBay because we couldn't afford the full-price garments.

I can recall that this happened around the time we had been started on a few times by some fairly scary lads when we were just walking down the street in the middle of the day minding our own business – the kind of rare but somewhat terrifying encounters reflected in the lyric: 'Rudeboys staring; be wary of them' ('Stretch'). Me and Ben felt, at the time, that a good approach might be to dress as if we were, basically, hard as nails and that this might scare lads like this away; the logic being that certain brands acted as symbols of intent whereby if we wore a Burberry cap and looked as if we might, for example, headbutt someone if they tried to rob us, they might believe we would actually do it (when in fact we would be too afraid to do it) and thus leave us alone. These are the kinds of choices many young men have to make in response to the (perceived) spectre of violence in their lives. I look back now and think it's quite sad we felt this way, and sad that we emulated the behaviour of some of the portrayals in the movie.

Recognition and Remembrance

Ending Up Unremarkable
A final powerful theme clearly identifiable in the transcribed tracks concerns the desire to be recognised and remembered, encapsulated in the lyric that I feel in some ways sums up so much of what the stories in these songs were about: 'These are tales of lads who fear ending up unremarkable' ('20Something'). This lyric captures the fear that in feeling geographically and culturally peripheral, our lives would be rendered inconsequential and somehow meaningless; as 'dispirited' and 'characterless' as the suburban housing in Fetcham described earlier by Nairn and Pevsner (2002: 244). To an extent, much of this concern derives from the conventions of the kind of commercialised rap music I grew up listening to whereby the genre came to be associated principally, though not exclusively, with themes of ambition and material success (Lena, 2006) and where 'aggressive competition [is] essential to the aesthetic of [the genre]' (Shusterman, 1991: 630). However, I can also see how this anxiety stems from my upbringing. The lyrical looking elsewhere, a frustrating unsatisfaction with the immediate, a relentless desire to push forwards and higher and beyond to the next thing which might be bigger, louder, faster, better paid, etc., mirrors precisely what my Mum spent all her life doing,

and which my constant house moves and school moves were a reflection of. If the story I was brought up to internalise was that my grandparents were trapped by their circumstances, my parents pushed forwards, and now I had to go on further still, I suppose the question was: where was I going to? In particular, where was I going to after having achieved my family's dream of the University of Cambridge; was this supposed to be the end goal, or the beginning, and what would these achievements come to *mean* in an extended narrative that faced *forwards* after and beyond me instead of only *backwards* into my history? Perhaps this is part of what engendered my eventual disdain for the restrictions that I felt the England no one cares about placed on me and who I might be or become, and which of course is common in other representations of the suburbs too (Medhurst, 1997). Listening back to older tracks of mine too, I was moved by an excerpt I heard which reflected my sadness at the fact that when I attended my grandparents' funerals as a teenager, me, my parents and my siblings were the only ones in the room. On the one hand, of course, why should a small group of close loved ones at a funeral be upsetting? But I remember not being able to shake the feeling of hurt. I wrote: 'I'll leave your speakers kissed with bliss, get your quick lift from biffs,[8] my first grips a list of goals to achieve before this Earth I leave, praying a legion exist to grieve, and I'm not left like my priors, funerals barely packed, chairs stacked, I seethed' ('Frantic').

Against this backdrop, we can see constant references in the tracks to wanting to be recognised and remembered, particularly in the track 'This Is Us'. This can be seen with an amusing reference to someone I knew who robbed a shop and my suggestion that this was a good (and perhaps his only) route to infamy – 'rob the off-licence just to get your name in the paper' – to perhaps my shallow anxiety that I would not achieve what Wikipedia describe as 'notability' (a contentious concept addressed in the work of Taraborelli and Ciampaglia (2010), and Tripodi (2021) among others) to have my own entry on the online encyclopaedia: 'honestly, I'm feeling afraid that at this rate, I'll leave a non-existent Wikipedia page'. In the same track, this desire for some kind of legacy is suggested as being at least part of the reason for the regular allusions to drinking and drug taking: 'There's no mystery why we get in the type of state that we get, I maybe on some level do it to forget that I'm in my mid-twenties and no-one's heard of me yet'. Finally, the track ends with the clearest and most explicit reference to the longing which I explored in chapter three concerning my desire to tell the story of my life (and the lives of my peer group) so that we might be documented, making reference to the Channel 4 investigative journalism programme 'Dispatches' and how I hoped my music would be 'our' Dispatches: 'I'm a White Lightning kid, Nikes and spliffs, you know what I'm writing is tales of lads who spend their nights fighting pissed: a "Dispatches" you might have missed'.

Scholarly literature which has explored our human desires for meaning and significance in our lives helps us to make sense of these lyrical ideas in a broader sense, which I want to then go on to add a geographic component to in order that I might highlight the spatial dimension of these feelings. Prominent in this body of work is the notion of terror management theory (reviewed in the work of Greenberg et al., 2014): the idea that mortality awareness and existential anxieties concerning death can lead us to adopt ideas and practices which provide purpose and meaning to our lives, and in doing so ensure a legacy. This theory reflects what psychiatrist Robert Jay Lifton and philosopher Eric Olson (1974: 59) refer to as 'man's search for meaning and the effort to express it'. This search can take a variety of forms, but one of those which has been explored is the symbolic immortality (ibid.) that can come from acts of creativity (see also Rank, 1968). In this context, research has explored the fascinating connection between creativity and legacy (see Perach and Wisman (2019) for a comprehensive review), with works of art being seen as mechanisms for achieving personal symbolic immortality, i.e. one's name being remembered (Shneidman, 1973), or collective symbolic immortality, i.e. songs which will endure (Lifton, 1973). Psychologists Brett Waggoner, Jesse Bering and Jamin Halberstadt (2023: 3, emphasis added) define this kind of immortality as 'the timelessness or eternal fame gained from performative work (e.g., art, invention, brand, teaching, science, construction, etc.) *connecting the self to others past, present, and future*'.

Underpinning this desire, as suggested by the italicised element of the quote above, is the concept of a form of 'ethical capital' which is 'biographical in nature, transmitted informally by the lessons one's life teaches and the life stories one narrates' (Williams et al., 2010: 893). In other words, the development of the kind of symbolic immortality suggested in the lyrics above is a process which is, implicitly, achieved intergenerationally (Wade-Benzoni and Tost, 2009), 'with our attitudes and behaviors influencing, and being influenced by, our descendants and ancestors, respectively' (Waggoner et al., 2023: 4). In other words, part of what drives human beings' desire to leave a legacy is the articulation of a fulfilling vision of the self and an identity which provides us with a source of wellbeing, and which is negotiated in response to, and in anticipation of, our histories. Given the narrative of my upbringing sketched out in chapter two, it is clear to me now why this feeling was so powerful in my life and so prominent in my lyrics. Being remembered, then, is connected to the stories we tell; through art we can seek to tell stories so that we might be remembered, but we also craft these stories through our acts of narrative identity construction rooted in remembering. These are processes which get to the heart of questions around purpose and meaning, and which can be seen explored in the lyrics of the songs I wrote as I grappled with these issues, and which centralise the role of storytelling not only in my upbringing and its framing as a journey starting with my grandparents, but also in my songwriting as a form of identity-exploring, particularly in the context of peripheral parts of England. However, this connection between existential ideas of meaning and their realisation through narratives of the self, I would find encapsulated most clearly with reference to a small lyrical snippet and a movie I had loved when I was at school.

The First Rule of Fight Club Is...

In the process of writing this book I listened to all of the tracks I had ever recorded (some of which were released, most of which were not), and revisited all those I had written but never recorded. One of those I didn't include in the previous chapter was a track called 'The Harrier' – the first track I ever got played on BBC Radio 1 in 2008 by the DJ Huw Stephens, a moment I will always remember as Ben was driving at the time and he rang me up screaming with excitement that I had just come on the radio in his car. I was struck listening to it by how I had described myself as a character from a film which came out when I was at school, *Fight Club*, referring to myself as: 'rap's Tyler Durden' ('The Harrier'). I had forgotten this reference, but it occurs to me now that this film, with its existential take on the soullessness and mundanity of an apparently feminised and materialistic corporate America being rectified via a reformulation of violent masculinity to allow the men to find meaning and purpose in their lives, connects many of the findings from this chapter together. The film, like my own lyrics, can be seen to reflect notions of possibility and dreaming, work and the future, masculinity and violence, and the desire for recognition. In one of the most often-cited monologues from the movie, Tyler Durden, played by Brad Pitt, addresses a room full of men who have come to fight, saying: 'An entire generation pumping gas, waiting tables: slaves with white collars.... We've all been raised on television to believe that one day we'd all be millionaires and movie gods and rock stars. But we won't. And we're slowly learning that fact. And we're very, very pissed off'.

We see in this quote what sociologist Omar Lizardo (2007: 237) calls 'the great cultural contradiction of the post-industrial society': that is, the experience of being trapped in the purposelessness of 'bullshit jobs' in the service sector (Graeber, 2013, 2018) and the incompatibility of this sociostructural reality with contemporary ideas of self-understanding or self-actualisation through consumerism and/or its ultimate ambition of achieving celebrity-status, and thus realising our dreams of stardom: in other words, the kind of angst reflected in the palpable sense of anger and dismissal heard in the lyric which begins the track 'Long Way from Nowhere' – 'You work in a bar, I'm working in a call centre, babe *can you taste the resentment?*'. In both the film and the novel (Palahniuk, 1996), the solution – fighting – has been framed as a 'muscular existentialism' (Ng, 2005) not unlike the way I perceived some of the violence on Prince of Wales Road, defined by Lizardo (2007: 235) as: 'a cathartic release from all of the pent-up frustration that accrues from the countless everyday humiliations and subsequent requirement to engage in socio-emotional self-control on the part of the service worker'. In Tyler Durden's monologue, and indeed throughout the film, existentialist notions are clear and have been well-documented in scholarly works of media studies (Grønstad, 2003; Edger and Helsel, 2012; Baker, 2014) which highlight the film's 'explorations of suffering, death, nothingness, and absurdity' (Bennett, 2005: 71). This has led some to position *Fight Club* as a work of existentialist literature, and it was clearly one which chimed with me and which can be heard echoing in the lyrical articulations of challenges relating to work and identity, masculinity and escape, and a desire to be remembered.

The reference in the monologue to our desire to be 'gods' as Tyler Durden calls them, is fascinatingly mirrored in the fact that one of my closest mates – Andy – when we were in our early twenties had the word 'deity' in capital letters tattooed across his stomach,[9] in the same place that the rapper Tupac Shakur famously had the phrase 'Thug Life' adorned. This tattoo actually came about because Andy came into the pub I was working in one day and said 'tell me a cool five letter word', to which I said 'deity' – I remember he didn't know what it meant at the time – and a few days later he came back with it tattooed on him. This emblem seemed to speak, without us even knowing it, of our participation in, as the founding father of sociology Emile Durkheim wrote in 1898, a 'society that instituted [the cult of the individual] and made of man the god whose servant it is' (2009: 9). Me and Ben even wrote a track when we first started making rap music, called 'Drift', which contained the line: 'we produce the Bible, with "deity" tattoos displayed on disciples'. Perhaps the clearest place I can see the themes of Durden's monologue is in the track 'This Is Us' which has the following extract, eerily similar to that from *Fight Club* which perhaps I must have unknowingly internalised:

> *We're the kids dreaming in school uniforms and trainers.*
> *Thinking that we'll be huge and that's why our nothingness pains us.*
> *We were just watching [MTV] Cribs all day at home and so, mate, can you blame us?*
> *I'm thinking that living in a small town like this we'll just grow to be strangers.*
> *Light pipes for your pipe dream of growing up to be famous*
> — 'This Is Us', Context (n.d.)

Much like the words of Tyler Durden here, I seemed to be reflecting how a childhood spent watching TV shows like *Cribs* on MTV – a programme described by sociologists of sport Maureen Smith and Becky Beal (2007: 103) as representing 'a fantasy commodity of successful manhood' – had engendered feelings of 'nothingness' (itself an unknowing chiming with existentialist Jean-Paul Sartre's 1956 classic *Being and Nothingness*) as we sat in our pocket of suburban England, lighting glass pipes filled with weed, hoping to make sense of where our lives were going and who we were. It is here, again, that stories and their relationship to the self act as the pivot around which so many of the ideas in this book oscillate. That is, what the lyrics in this fourth conceptual section seem to be reflecting is a desire to construct a version of my identity, the identity of my peer group, and the identity of the geographies with which I identified, which had some temporal significance; in other words, the hope that this story was a story that was worth telling, and that in telling it I could simultaneously reveal *and* construct a presentation of myself and *our*selves which would be remembered from places which often felt forgotten in cultural conversations. This relationship between stories and selves is also core to what *Fight Club* is about, i.e. 'the constitutive relationship between identity and narrative history' (Friday, 2003, n.p.). For *Fight Club*, however, this endeavour is ultimately only vanity. In perhaps the most famous line from the film which went on to be weaponised against an entire generation (Alyeksyeyeva, 2017; Murray, 2018) – broadly, my millennial generation – Tyler Durden tells the men that want to join him: 'You are not a beautiful and unique snowflake'. In this respect, perhaps my cries from the suburbs about feeling isolated and wanting to be remembered and canonised though the musical stories I was telling was simply a narcissism: a clarion call which wanted to tell a story to make sense of who we are (or the people we think we are, or the people we want other people to think we are) with a story which has a beginning (my family and the parts of England no one cares about), a middle (the songs I was writing), but a palpable fear about what the ending might be.[10]

Narrative and Meaning

For some thinkers these lyrical themes of wanting to be remembered, perhaps even being thought of as special, are indeed a reflection of the narcissism of my millennial generation. Personality psychologists Jean Twenge and William Campbell suggested in 2009 that people of my age were growing up in an age of entitlement afflicted with what they called *The Narcissism Epidemic*. A large number of empirical studies are helpfully collected together in a short commentary piece by the same authors in the journal *Personality Disorders* (2014). They present data from work using the Narcissist Personality Inventory (itself much criticised, e.g. Cain et al., 2008) showing an explosion in narcissistic personality disorder, and, indicatively, that the number of teenagers seen to agree with the statement 'I am an important person' has increased from 12% in 1952 to 80%

in 1989 (Newsom et al., 2003). To an extent, I wonder if deciding to write a book about my own lyrics in itself represents an inflated sense of self and importance, and is thus a narcissistic act? That is, I considered these songs good enough and of sufficient merit to write them out in their entirety, thematically analyse them, and then then spend thousands of words interpreting them. Fascinatingly, social psychologist Nathan DeWall and colleagues (2011) analysed the lyrics of popular songs released between 1980 and 2007 and found increases in lyrics relating to anti-social behaviour and self-focused pronouns (indicative of narcissism), reflecting findings from Twenge and Foster (2010) showing similar increases in individualistic traits in the United States between 1982 and 2009. In this sense, perhaps my endeavour in this book captures and reflects the self-obsessed nature of my generation perfectly.

On the other hand, as has been suggested, the desire to be remembered and the expression of this via enduring creative works is long-standing (Becker, 1973; Yalom, 1980). Certainly the quest for status alone as a product of creative practice has been suggested to be narcissistic (Mahadevan et al., 2019) but this is not the *sole* purpose of my own endeavour which – as explored throughout this book – has been driven by a commitment to narrative and methods of self-understanding and negotiating questions of identity and meaning. Here, again, the work of Brett Waggoner and colleagues (2023) is insightful and prescient in bringing together key contributions in this debate. The psychologists highlight work on what is referred to as the meaning maintenance model which suggests that 'humans are inexhaustible meaning makers' (Heine et al., 2006: 91) and that this meaning-making occurs socially and relationally. For philosopher Frank Martela and psychologist specialising in meaning Michael Steger (2016), human beings achieve this by seeking three key features in their lives: coherence, purpose and significance. Central to this process is the role of narrative, and, as explored in chapter three, stories articulated by families are crucial in this regard. Work examining the way that parents tell stories to their children as mechanisms of providing narrative coherence[11] has shown this to correlate with higher psychological wellbeing (Adler et al., 2016; Vanaken et al., 2022), and, of particular interest in the context of my own lyrics and the analysis undertaken here, has identified emerging adulthood as a key moment in the development of this coherence (Waters and Fivush, 2015). In other words, stories can provide coherence in a context where coherence is constructed (Berger, 1984), and coherence is a source of meaning.[12]

For the French philosopher Albert Camus (1955: 3–49), this establishment of coherence was the ambition of *all* artistic practices; the articulation by the artist of coherence in a life of incoherence. However, what I want to suggest here is that while there is something (in Camus's and others' orientation at least) universal about these existential themes in my lyrics, they are also both representative of the power of stories, as I have wanted to attest to throughout this book, and revealing of the England no one cares about too. In the first sense, the foregrounding of musical narrative as a form of meaning-making is, it strikes me, very much a product of my family and the narrative they told (and which I am telling now). My lyrical preoccupation with these existential themes where music acts as a technology of the self, is derived from and informed by my *intergenerational* self – the narrative of my upbringing and the salience in my life of these questions of trajectory, attaining, purpose, and the negotiation of class identity, which are themselves perhaps driven by a kind of (lower-)middle-class inferiority complex of needing to improve and be better. But these narratives are also, crucially, geographically constituted. That is: the self-efficacy of my Mum told me, growing up, that I could do anything; the restrictions of my geography, once I had grown up, made me fear I might be nothing.

Notes

1 See work by Beauregard et al. (2018) on the use of this term as regards its implications for ambition.
2 In 2023 at the time of writing, this figure now stands at £9,250 per year for undergraduate study in England.
3 The slightly reformulated Higher Education Initial Participation Rate (HEIPR) – 'an estimate of the likelihood of a young person participating in Higher Education by age 30, based on current participation rates' (DfE, 2019) – crossed Tony Blair's threshold in the academic year 2017/18 when the figure reached 50.2%.
4 This definition draws on the Standard Occupation Classification (SOC2020) and relates to SOC major groups 1–3, i.e. professional and managerial roles.
5 It is worth highlighting, however, that this area (Crawley E30000196) sits right up alongside 'London E30000234' in Quintile 4 where outcomes are far better.

6 It is also important to add here for balance that while the wider county of Norfolk is a highly conservative place in attitude which is reflected in voting patterns, and indeed growing up I recall hearing truly despicable views – e.g. a farmer in the pub I once worked in was laughing with his friends about a Nigerian who had moved into the area and who needed to 'go back up a tree in Bongo Bongo Land' – the Norwich South constituency (which contains the University of East Anglia) is far more progressive, even radical (see the publication 'The Norwich Radical' or the work of Alan Finlayson (2016) for example).
7 See work by Bromley and Nelson (2002) for a spatial analysis of crime and disorder in another small UK city – Worcester – and the central challenges of night-time leisure zones as sites of violence, harassment and disorder.
8 Ben used to often refer to joints (of cannabis) as 'biftas'.
9 This tattoo can be seen in the final scenes of the music video I filmed for the track 'Off With Their Heads'.
10 Interestingly, musicians have been shown to suffer from losing control of their own narratives of their death, as the work of Alice Masterson (2022) on Janis Joplin's posthumous career highlights.
11 The Family Narratives Lab (Emory University, Department of Psychology) directed by Robyn Fivush is perhaps the pre-eminent source of scholarship on this subject.
12 Writer Bruce Feiler's wonderful 2013 article for the *New York Times* entitled 'The Family Stories That Bind Us' is also worth highlighting here.

7

Based on a True Story

'Represent, Represent'

I suggested in the introduction that this book had two central ambitions: to use the lyrics I wrote as a young man to better understand both a place (which I have characterised throughout as the England no one cares about), and a person (me). I want to conclude, therefore, by interrogating the representation of place(s) and personhood contained in my lyrics in this book and their subsequent analysis, and to furthermore engage with broader questions around how and whether we can, methodologically, understand entities (such as places like these) with complex identities. As I argued in chapter three, many types of lyrics have, I would suggest, the potential to act as data given their capacity to offer insights into the author, communicating things which other traditional forms of data collection often cannot. Likewise, *rap* lyrics often have a particularly ethnographic dimension given their microsociological spatial observations which when combined with the injunction on the author to 'keep it real' (as is the case in rap music), means that questions of authenticity and, once again, truth are brought to the fore as key terms to catechise and apply analytical nuance. What does it mean, then, to *be* or to *keep it* 'real',[1] in the way that the term is terminologically employed in rap music? Additionally, what does an understanding of 'keeping it real' mean for the way listeners can or should understand the lyrics of mine contained in this book, and indeed of other rappers? Many of the stories in my lyrics are, as explained throughout, stories of non-fiction and thus real in the sense that they are factual; these incidents were real incidents that really happened to me and/or my peer group. Likewise, the way I felt about the England no one cares about in Tuxford, in Louth, in Fetcham, and in Norwich and the way those feelings were lyrically expressed was a real feeling at the time too. However, does this apparent realness – realness here being used in the same way it might be employed colloquially, i.e. to be broadly synonymous with terms like authentic or accurate – make my representation of this England 'real' – 'real' here relating to the 'realness' of hip hop? In other words, is it possible that I kept it 'real', but presented an image which was not real? Or was I not, in fact, keeping it 'real' but presenting a real representation? Is it possible for a representation to be 'real' given that it reflects subjectivities, and indeed, who is defining what being 'real' means in rap music? As Morpheus played by Laurence Fishburne famously asks of Neo (Keanu Reeves) in the 1999 movie *The Matrix*: 'What is real? How do you define real?'; a reference which would later be picked up by philosopher Slavoj Žižek in his 2002 work which interrogates notions of another kind of real – the Lacanian Real – entitled *Welcome to the Desert of the Real!* Unpacking these terms and the multiple entangled and overlapping definitions of real and 'real' as applied to these lyrics will therefore be the task of this first section of my concluding thoughts.

Performing the 'Real'
The classic hip-hop album *Illmatic* (1994, Columbia) by NaS features a track where the chorus echoes and repeats one of the core mantras of rap music: 'represent represent, represent represent'. What is meant by this term in this context and how can we connect it to the representation of places, persons, and questions of 'realness'? Author and hip-hop scholar Murray Forman (2000: 89) in his work on this subject defines 'representing'[2] as: 'employing multiple communicative modes and cultural practices to define and articulate individual or posse identities, spatial locales grounded in the 'hood, and other aspects of individual and collective significance'. In other words, the term is seen to encompass concepts of value relating to both the person *and* the place – which for Murray was, in his words, 'the 'hood',[3] but which of course for me was, to mirror the terminology, 'the 'burbs'. For now, I want to focus on the geographic component; that is, the practice of rap musicians 'representing' – showing respect to and for – where they are from. This can occur on varying levels, from the broader city (Los Angeles, New York, London), specific zones and areas within that city (South Central, Queens, East London), to specific areas

within that zone (Compton, Queensbridge, Bow), to even more specific streets or street corners (Crenshaw, 41st Side of 12th Street, or Roman Road); or, in my case, the England no one cares about, Norwich, and Prince of Wales Road. This compressed articulation of the immediate – what Forman (2000: 76) refers to as 'spatialised themes of intense locality' – of named streets or alleyways or tower blocks, 'suggests that "reality", authenticity and reduced spatial scales are conceptually linked' (ibid.: 77). In other words, choosing to identify with these areas is a method through which rap music articulates issues of meaning, identity and selfhood in the lives of those making the music.

This then highlights an interesting question: if geographical 'representing' is, as suggested by Forman, connected to questions of reality and/or 'realness', what do we mean when we talk about being 'real' in rap music; after all, of course, these places are real in that they exist, but what does it mean to 'represent' them (if this is different from *representing* them) and be 'real'? 'Realness' is a long-discussed term amongst scholars writing about hip hop. For many, the concept of 'realness' is inextricably connected to race, in particular to Blackness and the articulation and negotiation of a specific kind of apparently authentic Black identity (Gilroy, 1997; Clay, 2003). Writers about global hip-hop cultures outside of the United States, particularly those with many non-Black artists such as Korea for example (Hare and Baker, 2017) have emphasised that 'realness' can also mean other forms of negotiation, e.g. around language and localism (Mitchell, 2001; Pennycook, 2007). Certainly these two positions on race and language overlap to an extent. For example, the rapper Iggy Azalea – a White, Australian woman – raps (but does not talk) in what has been referred to as African American English (AAE) while simultaneously claiming in her lyrics 'First things first, I'm the realist' on the track 'Fancy' (Def Jam/Virgin EMI, 2014). This has been suggested by linguists Maeve Eberhardt and Kara Freeman (2015) to be a form of linguistic appropriation. The discussion around definitions of keeping it 'real' have been well unravelled and critiqued by scholars more adept at doing so than myself (e.g. Kopano, 2002; Stanford, 2011). However, what unifies many of these understandings is that 'realness' is *not* a simple synonym for authenticity; it is a specific, culturally coded form of authenticity about what is *and is not* considered 'real' and by extension, what is *and is not* being true to oneself within the paradigm of hip-hop 'realness'. For example, Bronwen Low and colleagues (2013) highlight how, theoretically, a gay rapper rapping about their specific Queer identity would be being true to themselves and authentic, but this would fall outside the definition of being 'real' as understood in the narrow prism of hip-hop culture – although work by artist and scholar of Black popular culture Shanté Smalls (2018) on this topic has done much to advance our understanding of how this simplistic binary is in fact more subtle in the history of hip-hop culture.

However, to once again hint at the work of Erving Goffman (1956), there is also a performative element to 'realness' that requires one to adhere to that performance, and which in doing so complicates notions of authenticity. In other words, when thinking about being 'real', how do we understand a *performance* (which has dramaturgical implications) which is simultaneously *authentic*? This has perhaps been most fascinatingly articulated in an article which examines the concept of being 'real', employing Lacanian psychoanalysis as the conceptual lens to understand 'realness' in the life of the murdered US rap star Tupac Shakur, and in doing so highlight 'the complicated relations of lived experience, the hip-hop real, and the Lacanian Real'[4] (Kane, 2002: 653). Kane cites the example of a 1995 deposition by the rapper connected to an unlawful death lawsuit which had been filed following the murder of a Texas state trooper during a traffic stop. It was suggested that the rapper's lyrics had incited the murder given that the defendant had a copy of the rapper's album *2Pacalypse Now* in the cassette player of his vehicle. Kane (2002: 655) explains in the extended extract below:

Tupac was fairly ruthless or 'profoundly utilitarian' in including elements from actual events that, more often than not, happened to people he knew. But his comments to Vibe [Magazine], made while he was incarcerated, are telling: 'When you do rap albums, you got to train yourself. You got to constantly be in character'. Not only are the postures learned, they end up becoming the reality; the code ends up superceding the message. In that interview, given while he was in prison for sexual assault, Tupac goes on to renounce his violent persona: 'You used to see rappers talking all that hard shit, and then you see them in suits and shit at the American Music Awards…I wanted to keep it real, and that's what I thought I was doing. But…let someone else represent it. I represented it too much. I was thug life'. This is a perfect example of the dynamic of the real, and specifically of Tupac's definition and exploitation of the real. He says that he assumed the character of a violent person, and then, in order to keep it real, he didn't compromise his class position by putting on a suit or selling out. We can see that just as putting on a suit is not real, Tupac implies that he has put on the costume of the real. The hip-hop real seems to be a suit that Tupac, in this interview, is tired of wearing.

Thus, rappers *choose* to 'represent' that which is understood as 'real', but this representation must (generally) at the same time also occur from a place of actual realness in order to be understood as 'real'. In other words, lyrical representations are 'highly selective and are drawn from a range of mundane, less controversial and less marketable urban experiences' (Forman, 2000: 77), but must also be understood to be a genuine part of the rappers' lived experience. This is the kind of reasoning which explains why the US rapper Rick Ross, whose lyrics often portray a materialistic criminal lifestyle (indeed, he is named after convicted drug trafficker 'Freeway' Ricky Ross), had to so carefully negotiate his reputation after it emerged he had worked years earlier as a correctional officer (Roks, 2020). In this sense there is a subtle difference between truth and 'realness'. By this I mean, none of my lyrics, for example, refer to me going to the University of Cambridge, which was *true* but not, I felt at the time, 'real'; or, perhaps more accurately, not acceptable within the parameters of a culturally specific form of acceptability within a genre which had, as suggested, grown in its inclusivity (Harrison, 2009: 100), but not so much as to absorb an emblem of the dominant culture such as an elite university. Likewise, my references to sitting in greasy spoon cafes 'mopping up my bean juice with my chips' ('20Something'), drinking Glen's vodka, fighting, fear about my future, a rejection of suburbia, and seeing my mates struggle with unemployment, were both true *and* 'real'. In essence, the nature of my class position meant that I was able to inhabit both of these worlds and negotiate between them, but to try and do so at least from a place of openness; for example, whilst I never mentioned life at university in my lyrics I did not hide it in press interviews nor did I change my lyrics to conceal the cultural references which came (at least in part) from this university experience, such as, for example, Ovid, Christopher Marlowe and Goya in 'I Can't Kickflip Anymore', or Charles Dickens in 'Long Way From Nowhere', or the political journalist Robert Peston in 'Being 21 Goes'.

This tension between what is 'real' and what is real – and what is being 'represented' and what is represented – can be seen in the case of Mike Skinner too. That is, we can think of some of his lyrics as sharing features with the genre of autofiction i.e. representative of 'quasi-real autobiographical narratives in which authors "toy" with the truth, that is to say allow themselves to drift away from a strict account of facts in order to give a testimony of their imaginative lives as much as their factual ones' (Schmitt, 2010: 125). In one of Mike Skinner's tracks entitled 'Streets Score' (*All Got Our Runnins*, Vice Records, 2001) he raps: 'I wear Nike a lot, my hoodie's a tight Schott, but does my life sound as interesting as a fight in a chip shop? I think not, the hype's not to be believed... Let's get back to the story...' This is an incredibly rare moment of sincerity from a rap artist. What does it reveal? Firstly, that whilst we can take the anthropological insights of rap seriously, simultaneously they represent *a truth*, and not *the truth*. This is what Stoia et al. (2018: 355) mean when they refer to the existence of rap tropes: lyrics which are, and are not, part of the lexical cannon of rap and which rappers perceive (whether correctly or not) as being what the listener would find interesting and want to hear.

Yet, the picture of authenticity, realness/'realness' and truth is more complex still. Living in geographical locales which lacked cultural aliveness (at least from my perspective) meant that I grew up absorbed in and engaged with mediated representations of actual realness through forms of media; that is, through the rap music I was listening to – as explored here – but also through films. It is interesting that *Fight Club* formed part of my analysis above given my lyrical reference to being 'rap's Tyler Durden' ('The Harrier'), when the narrator in the film and novel in fact *projects* Durden as his emblem of masculine idealism and then cannot work out if he is a real person or not. Likewise, my analysis in the previous chapter made reference to the movie *The Football Factory* and its media reception as being indicative of a form of brutal, realistic representation of football hooliganism. However, as cultural scholar Steve Redhead (2007: 102) suggests, the apparent realism of this film is, as per all forms of social realist media, 'a construction rather than any simple, straightforward representation or reflection of "reality"'. Taken together, the media me and others in my generation grew up consuming did perhaps represent what Jean Baudrillard (1997: 12) understood as the artistic imagination signifying a *negation* of or escape from the real via the assertion of truth, but where in fact artistic images have become 'no longer the mirror of reality, they are living in the heart of reality…transformed…into hyperreality'.[5]

Places, People and Identities

The second question I want to ask is: in this context of needing to be 'real', how can we understand both the spatial and the personal components of representing, i.e. the place and the identity of a place, and the person and the identity of a person. In other words, how real is the 'real' of places and people rooted in 'representing'? With reference to places, of course, places do not have single identities. In Doreen Massey's classic 1991 essay 'A global sense of place' which examines the concept of spatial identity in her North London neighbourhood, she explains: 'If it is now recognised that people have multiple identities then the same point can be made in relation to places' (Massey, 1991: 28). In other words, geographical locales are places of discrepancy and disjuncture, experienced and understood differently by different actors based on their different positions within that space. Succinctly, then, Massey (ibid.: 29) notes: 'places do not have single, unique "identities"; they are full of internal conflicts'. This simple point captures that to which I alluded earlier when examining the map of Norwich and Norfolk and the shading of Lower Layer Super Output Areas; methodological variety is the mechanism through which we might seek to understand how places are experienced by those within them – the ethnographic, the statistical, the autoethnographic, the historical, and, as per the argumentation in this book, the artistic. Together, they offer the potential to highlight the experiential richness of spatial experience, and in this book I have sought to offer music and lyrics, and, crucially, the stories these lyrics can tell, as one part of this methodological puzzle.

However, it is important to acknowledge, as I have tried to undertake here with reference to my own lyrics, that methodological approaches come with their own epistemologies. In other words, they are not neutral and scientific,[6] and this is certainly the case with reference to my lyrics. However, does this negate my argument that rap lyrics have ethnographic insight? I would suggest not, because ethnographies are not objective either (Hegelund, 2005). The story I have told about the England no one cares about through my music was a story told *via* and *through* my life story; a subjective spatial representation *of* an intergenerational, narrative subjectivity. It must be seen and understood in this way; a story of narrative construction layered *on top of* a story about narrative construction told within the parameters of genre-specific storytelling and parameters of 'realness'. They were lyrics based on a true story informed by a life based on a true story. This is what Žižek (1989: 59) captures when he writes that exercises in identity construction of this kind often 'overlook the way our act is already part of the state of things we are looking at'. This does not mean that any of these things I wrote about my experiences of this facet of England were untrue. They were *all true*. However, as Forman (2000: 83) so astutely notes when writing about the way rappers 'represented' places such as Compton in South Central Los Angeles, these representations are: 'simultaneously real, imaginary, symbolic and mythical'. He suggests the most central question is not whether the representations are true and accurate, but *why* these representations have been chosen and what these representations represent in the lives of those undertaking the 'representing'. In thinking about this subject at great length as has been afforded to me in undertaking the journey in this book, I think I now better understand the answer to this question in my own life. In other words, I began this book by exploring how the suburbs have been represented; my own music has shown how they have been 'represented'. In my case, then, the England that I feel no one cares about was, to an extent, represented as *particularly* limiting partly because issues of progress were so prominent and emphasised in the construction of my intergenerational self. It was, to an extent, represented as being *particularly* unable to be a place which could provide me with the meaning I was looking for partly because questions of narrative meaning-making were always framed to me as being rooted in moving 'beyond' the immediate. It was, to an extent, represented as *particularly* violent and angst-ridden partly because these were themes which had 'realness' and salience within the genre. These are the things that preoccupied me, and the stories of my music were a product of both my genre and my subjectivities which drove my preoccupations: the *parameters* of my genre, the *narrative* of my family, the *challenges* of my geography, and the *insecurities* of my class.

In this way, to understand the lyrics, you need to understand the person. In his aforementioned deposition, the rapper Tupac Shakur, when defending himself against the claims that his lyrics had inspired murder, said: 'Before you can understand what I mean, you have to know how I lived or how the people I'm talking to live' (Bruck, 1997). He is saying, in essence, to understand the stories I have told in my lyrics, you need to understand *my* story; to use the phraseology of my Dad, you need to understand *my* flames on the ceiling. Indeed, Tupac's story is a fascinating one. His parents (Afeni Shakur and Billy Garland) were both members of the Black Panther Party (see Bloom and Martin (2016) for a wonderful history). His mother Afeni was a member of Panther 21: a group of twenty-one Black Panther members arrested, of which thirteen stood trial, charged with attempting to blow up police stations (Zimroth, 1974). All were acquitted, and at the time of her acquittal Afeni was eight months pregnant with Tupac. His stepfather Mutulu Shakur was a member of the Black Liberation Army and Black nationalist and Black separatist organisations such as the Republic of New Afrika (see Onaci, 2020). As Kane (2002: 644, emphasis added) so presciently notes: 'raised in the midst of men and *myths* like Huey Newton and Geronimo Pratt, Tupac *felt the force of his genealogy*'. I profoundly agree. In addition, I would suggest that this sentiment is true not only with reference to Tupac but more broadly too; genealogy indeed exerts a narrative force which informs our construction of identity. It did in my life: my name, my family, Yorkshire, mining, progress, ambition, frustration, negotiation, suburbia, class, meaning, and so on. These are chapters and component parts in the reason I saw and continue to see the world in the way I do, and why my music expressed the things it did. Perhaps I would say this as a qualitative researcher of social and cultural life, but for me, quantitative markers of identity or narrow labels ascribed based on characteristics are, I would contend, entirely insufficient. There are longer temporalities and complexities at play which the kind of social science I am most interested in reading can reveal, and why rich, 'thick', qualitative, *narrative accounts* which understand the central importance of stories really matter.

A Vignette on Peripherality

In essence this book has been, I would argue, a deep and extended vignette on one person's subjective experience of peripherality. Certainly, peripherality is primarily understood to be a geographic phenomenon indicating rurality and a physical removal from centres of power and/or decision-making – which is certainly the case in each of the regions of England I grew up in (except perhaps Surrey given its proximity to London). Peripherality also exists as a relational term – i.e. being an outsider – and certainly in Surrey this was very much my experience in school. However, work exploring peripherality in Western Ireland has advanced the conceptualisation of 'aspatial' peripherality' (McDonagh, 2002: 100); that is, a more subjective understanding of the lived experience of *feeling* on the periphery. The ambiguous definitions of peripherality have often overlapped and intersected with definitions of marginality too, i.e. being on the margins. Certainly, marginalisation has a crucial political dimension – racial, ethnic, religious, sexual, etc. – but work by Lucia Máliková and colleagues (2016: 96), also in rural Ireland, helpfully delineates how marginality can be understood through a variety of different objective and subjective prisms. The authors' typology of marginality encompasses the geometric, ecological, economic, social, political and, drawing on Margarita Schmidt (1998), *perceptual* – an internal form of marginality where a region is 'perceived to be marginal by its inhabitants'. To an extent, my experience of peripherality or marginality is, I would argue, both geographic and perceptual: an objective spatial distancing in North Nottinghamshire, Lincolnshire and Norfolk, in particular from cultural production and decision-making in London, but also a subjective perceptual exclusion from both cultural and artistic development *and* a broader national conversation where the 'other' kinds of England (the verdant countryside, the bustling metropolis, and the politically left behind) warranted greater attention, from someone who was simultaneously sitting on the periphery of class negotiations. My lyrics, then, reflect the subjectivities of someone who felt for a long time that I was speaking about my peer group who 'can't think outside the box, we live there: ostracised' ('This Is Us').

In a musical context, two scholars are worth highlighting in advancing our understandings of the development of music careers in peripheral locations such as those I grew up in. Australian music scholar Christina Ballico (2017: 361) has published extensively on what she describes as 'relational geographies of peripherality and isolation'. In both her work in Perth in Western Australia (Ballico, 2018, 2019), and a recent edited collection on peripheral music scenes around the world from Iceland and Papua New Guinea to perhaps less obvious examples like Dublin and Austin, Texas (Ballico, 2021), her work has emphasised the contradictory nature of developing musical identities and careers in places such as these. That is, on the one hand, as my own lyrics highlight, peripherality goes hand-in-hand with feelings of exclusion and frustration. As Ballico (2021: 197) notes: 'such locales are at risk of being overlooked in the enduring histories of well-known bands who originate from these otherwise peripheral scenes'. In the context of the discussion in the previous chapter on legacies and remembrance, it is clear why feelings such as these might be a source of angst. On the other hand, however, peripherality is understood as having many benefits and has been suggested as a key leverage in creativity (Grabher, 2018). Indeed, speaking personally, the mundanity, the sameness, the frustration, and the angst I experienced growing up and living in these places was the source of my inspiration and what I wrote best about, from a place which in many ways I loved but also felt trapped by. As I said in the track 'Being 21 Goes': 'I love this city, it's my home but I mean, I've been out shitfaced in the same bars every week since I turned 18'. However, when I left, much of my inspiration was gone.

There are other benefits of peripherality highlighted in the literature which also chime with me personally too. For example, Ballico (2021: 7) denotes the capacity of artists from these places to 'embrace the discourse of "otherness"', and indeed I can see this reflected linguistically in some of my own lyrics via the use of local words which might be seen as part of a desire for a linguistic reclaiming of marginality. For example, in 2013 I was interviewed by the online magazine *Vice* and was, somewhat unusually, asked to compose a haiku. In it, I proudly described myself as the posh student from Cambridge had once described me: 'a parochial lout, scribbling imagery rap forgot about' (*Vice*, 2013). In the songs too, there are Norfolk-specific phrases like 'pass the lighter b'or' ('1.4 at 12'), or the use of the Norfolk phrase 'what's occurring' in the lyric: 'you need to keep en garde, what's occurring is deep' ('20Something'). In 'Afghan Letters' too I describe an incident where 'five lads rocked up and I doubt he was going to get wrong'; this is another Norfolk phrase (*I don't want to get wrong with you*) which would be akin to saying 'I don't want to get on the wrong side of you'. These are examples of East Anglian English (Fisiak and Trudgill, 2001), a kind of marginalised accent you will rarely hear on television or film (Bishop, 2022), and certainly not in rap music. However, whilst I did not rap in a Norfolk accent (given that I don't speak with one), and did at the same time often slightly exaggerate other words and accents (terms like 'twatting' someone, or 'geezer'), I was conscious of embracing and representing where I came from – much like the practices of divergency enacted by West Country rappers in the work of Adam de Paor-Evans (2020a). Thus, peripherality is understood as a duality (see also McDonagh, 2022); as being both restricting but also providing a sense of pride. Along with this, the music scene in Norwich is an unmistakably friendly and supportive place. The opportunities I had there to perform in local venues with supportive promoters, supportive crowds, supportive institutions (like the local *BBC Introducing in Norfolk* initiative, for example), and a small-scale, homegrown, supportive hip-hop scene was undeniable, cannot be overstated, and I will always be grateful for them.

However, whilst Norwich was (and is) friendly and supportive, it undoubtedly musically exists outside of the major centres of cultural intermediation, resulting in its cultural marginalisation with very real impacts. Ballico (2021: 201) suggests that geographical isolation and peripherality 'affords many benefits and opportunities which far outweigh the drawbacks and challenges'. I am not confident that I agree with this optimistic conclusion. Here, I want to highlight the work of the second scholar of interest in this discussion – economic geographer Allan Watson – who has done much to explore the development of regional music scenes outside of the major cultural centres in the UK, notably the 'global music city' (Watson, 2008) of London. Whilst his work (like that of Ballico) highlights that 'not all roads to London', with many well-developed alternative scenes in places like the North West of England, for instance, his work also illustrates that these scenes are experienced by some who live and work there as places of insularity and disconnectedness. This is emphasised further in a policy-making sense in non-urban contexts given the 'particular (metropolitan) geographical biases [in] policy' (Watson, 2020: 1577) relating to the creative industries, informed by theses of agglomeration and clustering such as the 'creative class' in the creative city (Florida, 2002), which serve to exclude the contributions made by those outside of major cities (Chapain and Comunian, 2010). In his work, Watson (2020: 1575) reveals 'the complex socio-spatial strategies that local creative actors develop to cope with their disconnected status [from] London, an obligatory point of symbolic validation'. Here, he notes that many within these regional music economies feel part of a 'music *scene*' rooted in a system of collective support, but not part of the 'music *industry*' which is located within the hegemonic power of London. Whilst some musicians and music professionals were happy to simply ignore London, for others this othering engendered a perception of isolation. When reading Watson's insightful work on Manchester and Liverpool – two large cities in Northern England – I could not help but think that if this was how people in these cities felt, how do you think those of us living in Tuxford, Louth or Norwich feel?

Writing the Narrative Self

Much of the writing in this book has been deeply personal; both chapter two on the telling of my family narrative and chapter five containing my lyrics are autobiographical in nature, with the analysis in chapter six being often autoethnographic. Central to the act of writing this book has been the application of reflexivity to my life, my upbringing, and my views; why I thought and think the way I do and the intersections between these perceptions and practices, and my geographies and family, with the power of stories being the central theme throughout. I suggested in the introduction that whilst I wanted to use my lyrics to interrogate the England no one cares about, and perhaps in doing so give this book a modicum of broader appeal outside of my own life, I also wanted to use the practice of writing this book – inspired by texts of autofiction and others – to better understand myself too. In other words, part of the ambition of this text has been, as noted by Celia Hunt (2000: 185), an author with expertise on the relationship between fiction, autobiography and the self, to reflect the purpose of writing, shifting 'from creating a literary project to providing a mechanism for psychological insight'. This section will briefly reflect on how I feel about these aims at the conclusion of the endeavour.

Music and Wellbeing

I suggested at the beginning of this book that I was not confident that this text – which I wrote purely as a passion project – explicitly chimed with the dominant thread of my scholarly work on mental health, wellbeing and music. However, as I reach the end of *this* story, I have come to re-evaluate this. That is, in writing autobiographically about my music, and understanding this writing as a partly therapeutic exercise, I have come to use my own music and its analysis as a form of, I suppose, poetry, and thinking about the connections between music and my life as a mechanism for thinking about my *own* wellbeing. As poet Gillie Bolton (1999: 119) notes, Apollo was the God of both poetry and medicine, and in this sense it is perhaps not unusual to think of these two elements – creative writing and wellbeing – as being connected. Indeed, scholarly reviews of literature into the therapeutic and wellbeing effects of writing have highlighted a range of studies demonstrating writing's positive impact on wellbeing (Wright and Chung, 2001; Hussain, 2010). Studies have taken place in quantitative, clinical experiments, many conducted by social psychologist James Pennebaker (e.g. Pennebaker and Evans, 2014; Pennebaker, 2018), whilst others have presented insights from qualitative work into creative writing rooted in methodologies such as psychodynamic theory (Hunt, 2000) or poetry workshops (Bolton, 1999). Whilst the precise *mechanism* through which these wellbeing impacts via writing are achieved is debated and the subject of theoretical positioning, the impacts *are* well-evidenced, and indeed, I would suggest my own experience in writing this book can act as a further case study in this body of work.

For example, travelling back to see where I was born and grew up in Tuxford was strangely moving. Knowing that I was seeing it around the same age my parents would have been when they moved there, and having my own young children at the same age they would have, reaffirmed to me that they always did what they thought was right and what they thought was best for us as kids, just as me and my wife are doing now for our kids. Likewise, confronting the pain of what happened to me in Surrey was hugely beneficial. In a way, going back there and seeing it for the scruffy, mundane place it is made me reflect more deeply on the value I had ascribed to it growing up. Seeing the mundanity made me feel somehow better. Visiting Surrey also allowed me to confront why I fell in love with this genre of music and why the stories in this music spoke so powerfully to me, and in doing so address the question I asked at the beginning of this book about why I valued rap. Historian Robin Kelley (2004: 130) describes the interest shown by some White suburban audiences in Black cultural production as indicative of a 'voyeurism' driven by a staged authenticity of Black expression from the inner city; 'a place of adventure, unbridled violence, erotic fantasy and/or an imaginary alternative to suburban boredom'. It is hard to entirely reject everything about this thesis; however, for me, I was reminded that I found this music during a time in my life, living in suburban Surrey, when I felt very much maligned for simply being who I was: struggling to make friends or fit in at school, and being relationally entirely peripheral and alone a lot. It occurs to me that it is unsurprising that the voices of the men I heard in rap music like Tupac Shakur (the first rap album I ever owned was his album *Thug Life* after I stole a cassette tape from my cooler older cousin who lived in Manchester), Wu-Tang Clan, Jay-Z, and others, spoke to me as emblems of a person (whether 'real'/real or not) I could perhaps try and be via rap: authoritative, unashamed, assertive, respected, as well as complicated, insightful and intelligent, instead of being how I actually was: fearful, embarrassed, uncertain, and geeky. Whilst my existing research to date has focused on the contradictory ways music careers impact wellbeing both positively and negatively (Gross and Musgrave, 2020), delving reflexively into the role music-making (and career musicianship) played in my own life has added a new, personal dimension to this body of work. That is, whilst life as a musician certainly brought me a great deal of angst, of worry, of uncertainty and frustration – allowing me to empathise with those I interview about wellbeing, for example – music *also* acted as form of identity construction, the development (or perhaps projection) of confidence and self-esteem where I certainly lacked it, and a method through which to negotiate, and try and make sense of, the trajectory of my life and of my family's lives.

Writing this book has also helped me to confront many of the issues around why I stopped making music. That is, the expressions of feeling I channelled in my music have, broadly, left my life. I am no longer parochial and anxious; broadly, I am more cosmopolitan and happy. Perhaps these two characteristics caused music-making to lose salience in my life. However, listening to the songs and reading back the lyrics made me profoundly miss musicianship. Yet, I think more than that, I miss many of the experiences in my music – the times with my friends in emerging adulthood now that my life has changed, and so have their lives. At the same time, I don't want to go back, but I do miss it. In a way, so much of rap is like this. As Kane (2002: 647–648) argues, specific forms of the genre engage with that which does not exist – e.g. projections of wealth yet to come as in the case of the American rapper Shyne – and when it does arrive, fame (particularly, Kane argues, for Black celebrities) engenders an ostracising from the very place one 'represented' and thus subsequently creates a longing for 'a return to the authenticity of poverty'. Certain forms of rap music, such as my own, exist therefore within, as Kane highlights, the circularity of the 'future anterior' (Pease, 2000: 19), where a coherent and valorised form of 'realness' in one's immediate past and in one's immediate present is connected to a desired future, and where that past is a prerequisite for status in that future. The issue is, however, that the musical present *and* this future are both dependent on the keeping alive *of* that past; a past which is, inevitably, moving further away so that the successful imagined future in fact renders that past invisible. In a practical sense, how could I continue to write rap music laced with angst rooted in perceptions of geographic limitation and relational forms of negotiated youthfulness, when I no longer felt or lived those things; once I lived in London with a job which paid me relatively well, living with my wife and family and having breakfast in Gail's? How could Mobb Deep keep writing about life in the 'projects' once they became millionaires? How could Dizzee Rascal write about grit in Bow with such profound ethnographic insight and such viscerality once he had earned enough to move out to suburban Chislehurst in Bromley. Of course, he could not: he had to write 'Dance With Me' with Calvin Harris or 'Bonkers' with Armand Van Helden. It is not and cannot be the same. This is the fleeting and ephemeral trap, and indeed the magic, of this kind of rap.

Another personal benefit of writing this book – and hopefully a benefit from the perspective of a reader too – has been my engagement with such a varied range of scholarship and, I hope, my interdisciplinary bringing together of these works. That is, there exists today an injunction upon academics to become specialists within particular disciplines – of which musicians' psychosocial lives, and mental health and the music industry, is mine – which when combined with broader structural challenges around the quantification of academic careers via metrics and evaluation exercises means that, according to Juan Pablo Pardo-Guerra (2022) and to employ Foucauldian phraseology, disciplines become disciplined, and in doing so become increasingly conservative and homogeneous. In this respect, there is less time and scope within academic workloads, alongside the pace of modern life, to carve out time and space to explore areas of interest outside of these places of objectified measurement and discipline-specific focus. However, for this book, I was able to temporarily step outside of this and engage with broader ideas in sociology and psychology (both of which I see myself as part of – perhaps the former more than the latter), as well as other areas of academic writing which have always fascinated me but where I honestly had not had the time to read many of the things I wanted to. I could for this project explore music by engaging with psychogeography, psychoanalysis, narrative psychology, existentialism, the sociology of class, the psychology of identity, transgressive leisure, criminal proceedings relating to lyrics, methodological debates about the validity of stories, hip hop therapy, public health data, ethnographies of pit villages by Lisa Mckenzie (2016) or Black lives in East London by Joy White (2020), and do all of this alongside using this exercise as an excuse to re-read the classic texts of Bourdieu and Foucault. For this book, I made the time to do it, and I am so thankful that I did, to discover texts as magnificent and varied as Michael Sheringham's spellbinding (2006) exploration of *Everyday Life* using French critical theory, to re-engage with George Orwell's *Road to Wigan Pier*, and listen to Asakaa drill music from Ghana. The interdisciplinary variety afforded to me via the scope of my work is a source of immense personal enjoyment.

Finally, the journey of this book (both the writing of it and the travelling around the England no one cares about) has confirmed one thing to me: I don't like the suburbs. Tracey Thorn of the groups Everything But The Girl and Massive Attack wrote in her memoir *Another Planet: A Teenager in Suburbia* that the suburbs were, contradictorily, in her 'bones' and yet had been left behind as she, like me, sought out a different kind of life in the city. She wrote: 'I feel terribly at home here, and terribly out of place' (Thorn, 2020: 204). I, on the other hand, don't feel at home in the suburbs. When I spent time in the suburbs again for this book, I hated it. In this sense, I felt that I chimed with the insights of Peter Williams (1986) in his work which articulated those whom Richard Webber (2007: 183) describes as being typified by a 'rejection of suburbia as a lifestyle choice'. I have certainly chosen to reject the suburbs in my own life, and indeed in my children's lives, and whilst I miss much of the time I spent there growing up, and miss the times with my friends, I am glad I no longer feel trapped, nor do I want my children to feel peripheral, although perhaps they will grow up to lament living in a big city and dream of the tranquillity of another kind of England.

George & Camille

I recall that when I pitched this book, an anonymous peer reviewer suggested that it had the capacity to be meaningful and insightful but only if I was prepared to be brave but most of all honest; unflinchingly, uncompromisingly, brutally honest. I hope, at least by this metric, I have been successful, or at least as successful as you feel narratives of this kind have the capacity to be, understood in the metric of truth and accuracy (Fivush and Grysman, 2022). Writing this book has been an intense experience. When I was asked by the research institutes I work in which theme or area of research this work speaks to, I told them that I didn't know and I did not really care; I was writing it because I wanted to and because it felt important even if only to me. It has been liberating and to an extent unsettling to write in this way insofar as it is unfamiliar; I have never cried, for instance, whilst writing academic work in the past. When writing this book, and indeed when re-reading and re-drafting, I cried a lot.

In the end, whilst I hope that this books contributes, even in just a small way, towards a variety of areas of disciplinary interest, offering a modest case study through which to explore concepts such as lyrics and placemaking, rap as ethnography, subjectivities of peripherality, and the power of narratives in our lives, it has perhaps been of greatest merit to me and my own family. That is, writing this book has afforded me the very rare and special privilege to be able to stitch together stories from three phases of my life: the formative intergenerational narratives told to me by my parents during my childhood and adolescence, the musical narratives of suburban life constructed on my iPhone in my early adulthood, and the scholastic architecture and theoretical frameworks encountered via my professional work as an academic in the latest stage of my life. In doing so, I have had the chance afforded to very few to chart the stories of my life, whether told around a dinner table by my Mum or in a recording studio over rap beats by me, in the hope that now my children have something which perhaps one day they might read when they too are constructing their own identities. The stories in this book, then, are for my inspirational daughter Camille, and my treasured son, born as I was completing this book, who is now the fourth generation in a row to hold the name which has embedded within it the stories of our family: George.

Notes

1. Throughout this chapter I will use the term 'real', written in this way, to denote the use of the term in rap music, whilst the term real (written without apostrophes) indicates the more everyday use of the term.
2. Again, I use the term 'representing' in apostrophes to denote the use the term within the paradigm of hip-hop culture, and the term representing (without apostrophes) to indicate the more everyday use of the term.
3. The work of Kelley (1996) unpacks this term in more detail.
4. It felt to me rather like too profound a conceptual detour to delineate Lacan's concept of 'the Real' in detail here. See philosopher Tom Eyers's 2012 book *Lacan and the Concept of the 'Real'* for one of the more accessible explanations of this concept.
5. See Roks (2020) for more on rap music as being '(hyper)real'.
6. See Phillips (1993) and Hegelund (2005) for more on the objectivity/subjectivity in social science research debate.

Bibliography

Abebe, T. (2021) Storytelling through popular music: Social memory, reconciliation, and intergenerational healing in Oromia/Ethiopia, *Humanities*, 10(2), p. 70.

Adetunji, J. (2017) The end of Eddy – and why writing about life can be a dangerous game, *The Conversation*. Available online: https://theconversation.com/the-end-of-eddy-and-why-writing-about-life-can-be-a-dangerous-game-72211.

Adler, J.M., Lodi-Smith, J., Phillipe, F.L., & Houle, I. (2016) The incremental validity of narrative identity in predicting well-being: A review of the field and recommendations for the future, *Personality and Social Psychology Review*, 20(2), pp. 142–175.

Aidi, H. (2004) 'Verily, there is only one hip-hop Umma': Islam, cultural protest and Urban marginality, *Socialism and Democracy*, 18(2), pp. 107–126.

Akande, A. (2013) Code-switching in Nigerian hip-hop lyrics, *Language Matters: Studies in the Languages of Africa*, 44(1), pp. 39–57.

Alcohol Concern (2011) White Cider and street drinkers: Recommendations to reduce harm, Alcohol Concern. Available online: https://rebuildingshatteredlives.org/wp-content/uploads/2013/01/White_Cider_and_Street_Drinkers_report_April_2011.pdf.

Allen, K., & Hollingworth, S. (2013) 'Sticky subjects' or 'cosmopolitan creatives'? Social class, place and urban young people's aspirations for work in the knowledge economy, *Urban Studies*, 50(3), pp. 499–517.

Alyeksyeyeva, I.O. (2017) Defining snowflake in British post-Brexit and US post-election public discourse, *Science and Education a New Dimension. Philology*, 39(143), pp. 7–10. Available online: https://seanewdim.com/wp-content/uploads/2021/04/Defining-snowflake-in-British-post-Brexit-and-US-post-election-public-discourse-I.-O.-Alyeksyeyeva.pdf.

Anderson, L. (2006) Analytic autoethnography, *Journal of Contemporary Ethnography*, 35(4), pp. 373–395.

Andrews, K. (2018) 'Urban' sounds: It's time to stop using this hackneyed term for black music, *The Guardian* (14th August 2018). Available online: www.theguardian.com/music/shortcuts/2018/aug/14/urban-time-stop-hackneyed-term-black-music.

Ansdell, G. (2005) Being who you aren't; doing what you can't: Community music therapy and the paradoxes of performance, *Voices: A World Forum for Music Therapy*, 5(3).

Appignanesi, L. (2005) *Simon de Beauvoir*, Haus Publishing.

Archer, G. (2018) Why do the elites despise the 'aspidistra class'? *UnHerd*. Available online: https://unherd.com/2018/10/elites-despise-aspidistra-class/.

Archer, L., Hollingworth, S., & Mendick, H. (2010) *Urban Youth and Schooling*, McGraw-Hill Education.

Arnett, J.J. (1997) Young people's conceptions of the transition to adulthood, *Youth & Society*, 29, pp. 1-23.

Arnett, J.J. (1998) Learning to stand alone: The contemporary American transition to adulthood in cultural and historical context, *Human Development*, 41, pp. 295-315.

Arnett, J.J. (2000) Emerging adulthood: A theory of development from the late teens through the twenties, *American Psychologist*, 55(5), pp. 469-480.

Ashon, W. (2018) *Chamber Music: About the Wu-Tang (in 36 Pieces)*, Granta Books.

Atkinson, P. (1997) Narrative turn or blind alley? *Qualitative Health Research*, 7(3), pp. 325-344.

Aktinson, P. (1999) Review essay: Voiced and unvoiced, *Sociology*, 33(1), pp. 191-197.

Atkinson, P. (2005) Qualitative research – unity and diversity, *Forum: Qualitative Social Research*, 6(3).

Atkinson, P. (2015) *For Ethnography*, SAGE.

Atkinson, P., & Silverman, D. (1997) Kundrea's *Immortality*: The interview society and the invention of the self, *Qualitative Inquiry*, 3, pp. 304-325.

Azzi, M.S. (1996) Multicultural tango: The impact and the contribution of the Italian immigration to the tango in Argentina, *International Journal of Musicology*, 5, pp. 437-453.

Back, L. (2023) What sociologists learn from music: Identity, music-making, and the sociological imagination, *Identities*. Online first: https://www.tandfonline.com/doi/full/10.1080/1070289X.2023.2268969.

Back, L., & Puwar, N. (eds.) (2013) *Live Methods*, Wiley-Blackwell.

Baker, K.G., & Gippenreiter, J.B. (1998) Stalin's purge and its impact on Russian families, in Danieli, Y. (ed.) *International Handbook of Multigenerational Legacies of Trauma*, Plenum Press, pp. 403-434.

Baker, R.E. (2014) Chuck Palahniuck's *Fight Club* apropos of Sartre's bad faith and Camus's calculated culpability, *Global Journal of Human-Social Science*, 14(1), pp. 1-9.

Baker, T.C. (2022) *Reading My Mother Back: A Memoir in Childhood Animal Stories*, Goldsmiths Press.

Ballard, J.G. (2006) *Kingdom Come*, Fourth Estate.

Ballico, C. (2017) Another typical day in this typical town: Place as inspiration for music creation and creative expression, *Australian Geographer*, 48(3), pp. 349-363.

Ballico, C. (2018) Everyone wants a festival: The growth and development of Western Australia's contemporary live music festival sector, *Event Management*, 22, pp. 111-121.

Ballico, C. (2019) 'It allowed me to deliver the biggest show of their national tour': An examination of contemporary live music festivals in peripheral and geographically isolated locales, in Walters, T., & Jepson, A.S. (eds.) *Marginalisation and Events*, Routledge, pp. 208-221.

Ballico, C. (2021) *Geographically Isolated and Peripheral Music Scenes: Global Insights and Perspectives*, Palgrave Macmillan.

Bandura, A. (1977) Self-efficacy: Toward a unifying theory of behavioural change, *Psychological Review*, 84(2), pp. 191–215.

Bandura, A. (1994) Self-efficacy, in Ramachaudran, V.S. (ed.) *Encyclopaedia of Human Behavior*, Vol. 4, Academic Press, pp. 71–81.

Bandura, A. (1997) *Self-Efficacy: The Exercise of Control*, W.H. Freeman.

Barron, L. (2013) The sound of street corner society: UK grime music as ethnography, *European Journal of Cultural Studies*, 16(5), pp. 531–547.

Bartleet, B.L. (2009) Behind the baton: Exploring autoethnographic writing in a musical context, *Journal of Contemporary Ethnography*, 38(6), pp. 713–733.

Bartleet, B.L., & Ellis, C. (2009) *Music Autoethnographies: Making Autoethnography Sing / Making Music Personal*, Australian Academic Press.

Baudrillard, J. (1997) *Art and Artefact* (ed. Zurbrugg, N.), SAGE.

Baumann, G. (1995) Managing a polyethnic milieu: Kinship and interaction in a London suburb, *The Journal of the Royal Anthropological Institute*, 1(4), pp. 725–741.

Baumeister, R.F. (2010) The Self, in Baumeister, R.F., & Finkel, E.J. (eds.) *Advanced Social Psychology: The State of the Science*, Oxford University Press, pp. 139–175.

Baumgartner, M.P. (1988) *The Moral Order of a Suburb*, Oxford University Press.

BBC (1999) UK politics – Tony Blair's speech in full, *BBC News* (28th September 1999). Available online: http://news.bbc.co.uk/1/hi/uk_politics/460009.stm.

BBC (2002) 'This generation is being wiped out', *BBC News* (18th October 2002). Available online: http://news.bbc.co.uk/1/hi/england/2339141.stm.

BBC (2022) Drill music artist B-Levelz jailed for drug dealing, *BBC Essex Online* (25th January 2022). Available online: www.bbc.co.uk/news/uk-england-essex-60118850.

Beauregard, T.A., Basile, K.A., & Canonico, E. (2018) 'The fur-lined rut': Telework and career ambition, in Kelliher, C., & Richardson, J. (eds.) *Work, Working and Work Relationships in a Changing World*, Routledge, pp. 17–36.

Beavis, A.S.W., Hojjati, A., Kassam, A., Choudhury, D., Fraser, M., Masching, R., & Nixon, S.A. (2015) What all students in healthcare training programs should learn to increase health equity: Perspectives on postcolonialism and the health of Aboriginal Peoples in Canada, *BMC Medical Education*, 15(155).

Becker, E. (1973) *The Denial of Death*, Free Press.

Beer, D. (2014) Hip-hop as urban and regional research: Encountering an insider's ethnography of city life, *International Journal of Urban and Regional Research*, 38(2), pp. 677–685.

Bender, K., Barman-Adhikari, A., DeChants, J., Haffejee, B., Anyon, Y., Begun, S., Portillo, A., & Dunn, K. (2017) Asking for change: Feasibility, acceptability, and preliminary outcomes of a manualized photovoice intervention with youth experiencing homelessness, *Children and Youth Services Review*, 81, pp. 379–389.

Bennett, D., & Burnard, P. (2016) Human capital career creativities for creative industries work: lessons underpinned by Bourdieu's tools for thinking, in Comunian, R., & Gilmore, A. (eds.) *Higher Education and the Creative Economy: Beyond the Campus*, Routledge, pp. 123–142.

Bennett, R. (2005) The death of Sisyphus: Existentialist literature and the cultural logic of Chuck Palahniuk's *Fight Club*, *Stirrings Still*, 2(2), pp. 65–80.

Berger, J. (1984) *And Our Faces, My Heart, Brief as Photos*, Bloomsbury.

Berlant, L. (2011) *Cruel Optimism*, Duke University Press.

Bertolani, B., Bonfanti, S., & Boccagni, P. (2021) At home in the gurdwara? Religious space and the resonance with domesticity in a London suburb, *Religion*, 51(3), pp. 423–442.

Betjeman, J. (2005) *Faith and Doubt of John Betjeman: An Anthology of His Religious Verse*, Bloomsbury.

Bhattacharya, K. (2009) Othering research, researching the other: De/colonizing approaches to qualitative inquiry, in Smart, J. (ed.) *Higher Education: Handbook of Theory and Research*, Vol. 24, Springer, pp. 105–150.

Bilston, S. (2013) 'Your vile suburbs can offer nothing but the deadness of the grave': The stereotyping of early Victorian suburbia, *Victorian Literature and Culture*, 41(4), pp. 621–642.

Bird, A.E., & McAndrew, F.T. (2019) Does namesaking a child influence attachment style, *North American Journal of Psychology*, 21(13), pp. 39–44.

Bishop, D. (2022) Tha's a rummun ent it: Why does the East Anglian accent get overlooked, *Eastern Daily Press* (7th January 2022). Available online: www.edp24.co.uk/news/20635145.thas-rummun-ent-east-anglian-accent-get-overlooked/.

Bloom, J., & Martin, W.E. (2016) *Black against Empire: The History and Politics of the Black Panther Party*, University of California Press.

Blumenfeld, S. (1986) *Jew Boy*, Lawrence & Wishart Ltd [originally published by Cape in 1935].

Bochner, A. (2001) Narrative's virtues, *Qualitative Inquiry*, 7(2), pp. 131–157.

Bochner, A. (2002) Perspectives on inquiry III: The moral of stories, in Knapp, M.L., & Daly, J.A. (eds.) *Handbook of Interpersonal Communication* (3rd edition), SAGE, pp. 73–101.

Bochner, A., & Ellis, C. (2016) *Evocative Ethnography: Writing Lives and Telling Stories*, Routledge.

Bohanek, J.G., Fivush, R., Zaman, W., Lepore, C.E., Merchant, S., & Duke, M.P. (2009) Narrative interaction in family dinnertime conversations, *Merrill-Palmer Quarterly*, 55(4), pp. 488–515.

Bolton, G. (1999) 'Every poem breaks a silence that had to be overcome': The therapeutic power of poetry writing, *Feminist Review*, 62, pp. 118–132.

Bonde, L.O., Ruud, E., Skanlånd, M.S., & Trondalen, G. (2013) (eds.) *Musical Life Stories: Narratives on Health Musicking*, Norwegian Academy of Music.

Borasi, R., Sheedy, J.R., & Siegel, M. (1990) The power of stories in learning mathematics, *Language Arts*, 67(2), pp. 174–189.

Bossard, J.H.S., & Boll, E.S. (1955) Personality roles in the large family, *Child Development*, 26(1), pp. 71–78.

Boulton, J. (1987) *Neighbourhood and Society: A London Suburb in the Seventeenth Century*, Cambridge University Press.

Bourdieu, P. (1977) *Outline of a Theory of Practice*, Cambridge University Press.

Bourdieu, P. (1979) *La distinction: Critique sociale du jugement*, Les Editions de Minuit.

Bourdieu, P. (1981) Men and machines, in Knorr-Cetina, K., & Cicourel, A.V. (eds.) *Advances in Social Theory and Methodology: Toward an Integration of Micro- and Macro-Sociologies*, Routledge and Kegan Paul, pp. 304–317.

Bourdieu. P. (1987) What makes a social class? On the theoretical and practical existence of groups, *Berkeley Journal of Sociology*, 32, pp. 1–17.

Bourdieu, P. (2014) *On the state: Lectures at the Collège de France, 1989–1992* (ed. Champagne, P., Lenoir, R., Poupeau, F., & Rivière, M.C.), Polity.

Bourdieu, P., & Wacquant, L. (1992) The purpose of reflexive sociology (The Chicago Workshop), in Bourdieu, P., & Wacquant, L. *An Invitation to Reflexive Sociology*, Polity, pp. 61–216.

Bourgeois, M.R. (2019) Artistic Resistance in the Holy Land: '48 Palestinian Fiction and Hip-Hop, unpublished PhD thesis (Ohio State University).

Bowers-Brown, T., & Harvey, L. (2004) Are there too many graduates in the UK? A literature review and analysis of graduate employability, *Industry & Higher Education*, 18(4), pp. 243–254.

Bradley, A. (2009) *Book of Rhymes: The Poetics of Hip Hop*, Basic Books.

Bramwell, R. (2015) *UK Hip-Hop, Grime and the City: The Aesthetics and Ethics of London's Rap Scenes*, Routledge.

Bramwell, R., & Butterworth, J. (2019) 'I feel English as fuck': Translocality and the performance of alternative identities through rap, *Ethnic and Racial Studies*, 42(14), pp. 2510-2527.

Bramwell, R., & Butterworth, J. (2020) Beyond the street: The institutional life of rap, *Popular Music*, 39(2), pp. 169-186.

Brar, D.S. (2021) *Teklife, Ghettoville, Eski: The Sonic Ecologies of Black Music in the Early 21st Century*, Goldsmiths Press/MIT Press.

Brinton, B., & Fujiki, M. (2017) The power of stories: Facilitating social communication in children with limited language abilities, *Social Psychology International*, 38(5), pp. 523-540.

Bromley, R.D.F., & Nelson, A.L. (2002) Alcohol-related crime and disorder across urban space and time: Evidence from a British city, *Geoforum*, 33(2), pp. 239-254.

Bronfenbrenner, U. (1979) *The Ecology of Human Development: Experiments by Nature and Design*, Harvard University Press.

Brook, O., Miles, A., O'Brien, D., & Taylor, M. (2022) Social mobility and 'openness' in creative occupations since the 1970s, *Sociology*, OnlineFirst. doi: 10.1177/00380385221129953.

Brooks, P. (1984) *Reading for the Plot: Design and Intention in Narrative*, A.A. Knopf.

Brooks, P. (2022) *Seduced by Story: The Use and Abuse of Narrative*, New York Review Books.

Brooks, S. (2019) Brexit and the politics of the rural, *Sociologica Ruralis: Journal of the European Society for Rural Sociology*, 60(4), pp. 790-809.

Broun, J.L. (2020) Place, identity and social conflict in post-industrial England: Cases from South Lincolnshire in the 1980s, *Contemporary British History*, 34(3), pp. 331-357.

Brown, P., Hesketh, A., & Williams, S. (2003) Employability in a knowledge-driven economy, *Journal of Education & Work*, 16(2), pp. 107-120.

Bruck, C. (1997) The takedown of Tupac, *The New Yorker* (29th June 1997). Available online: www.newyorker.com/magazine/1997/07/07/the-takedown-of-tupac.

Bruner, J. (1990) *Acts of Meaning*, Harvard University Press.

Bruner, J. (1991) The narrative construction of reality, *Critical Inquiry*, 18, pp. 1-21.

Bulley, J., & Sahin, Ö. (2021) *Practice Research*, PRAG-UK.

Butler, T. (2002) Thinking global but acting local: The middle classes in the city, *Sociological Research Online*, 7(3), pp. 50-68.

Butler, T., & Robson, G. (2003) *London Calling: The Middle Classes and the Re-making of Inner London*, Berg.

Byrne, L. (2015) Shocking new figures reveal worst 50 places in UK for alcohol misuse, Liam Byrne MP. Available online: https://liambyrnemp.co.uk/shocking-new-figures-reveal-worst-50-places-in-uk-for-alcohol-misuse.

Cain, N.M., Pincus, A.L., & Ansell, E.B. (2008) Narcissism at the crossroads: Phenotypic description of pathological narcissism across clinical theory, social/personality psychology, and psychiatric diagnosis, *Clinical Psychology Review*, 28(4), pp. 638–656.

Camus, A. (1955) *An Absurd Reasoning: The Myth of Sisyphus and Other Essays*, Vintage.

Caramanica, J. (2020) The long, complicated history of 'urban' music, *The New York Times* (15th June 2020). Available online: www.nytimes.com/2020/06/15/arts/music/popcast-urban-music.html.

Carey, H., Florisson, R., O'Brien, D., & Lee, N. (2020) Getting in and getting on: Class, participation and job quality in the UK Creative Industries, PEC Policy Review Series: Class in the Creative Industries – Paper No. 01. Available online: https://pec.ac.uk/research-reports/getting-in-and-getting-on-class-participation-and-job-quality-in-the-uks-creative-industries.

Caruso, D.B. (2006) Lyrics used against rappers in court, *The Seattle Times* (21st December 2006). Available online: www.seattletimes.com/nation-world/lyrics-used-against-rappers-in-court/.

Castillo-Garsow, M., & Nichols, J. (2016) *La Verdad: An International Dialogue on Hip Hop Latinidades*, Ohio State University Press.

Chapain, C., & Comunian, R. (2010) Enabling and inhibiting the creative economy: The role of the local and regional dimensions in England, *Regional Studies*, 44(6), pp. 717–734.

Charmaz, K. (2016) The power of stories and the potential of theorizing for social justice studies, in Denzin, N., & Giardina, M. (eds.) *Qualitative Inquiry through a Critical Lens*, Routledge, pp. 39–55.

Clay, A. (2003) Keepin' it real: Black youth, hip-hop culture, and Black identity, *American Behavioral Scientist*, 46(10), pp. 1346–1358.

Cobain, I. (2018) London drill rapper killed in knife attack admitted music's effect on crime, *The Guardian* (2nd August 2018). Available online: www.theguardian.com/uk-news/2018/aug/02/london-drill-rapper-killed-in-knife-attack-admitted-musics-effect-on.

Coleman, J. (2014) *Global English Slang: Methodologies and Perspectives*, Routledge.

Collins, H. (2005) We're not just moody hood-rats, *The Guardian* (23rd May 2005). Available online: www.theguardian.com/music/2005/may/23/popandrock.britishidentity.

Comunian, R., & Gilmore, A. (eds.), *Higher Education and the Creative Economy: Beyond the Campus*, Routledge, pp. 123–142.

Cook, J. (2000) Culture, class and taste, in Munt, S. (ed.) *Cultural Studies and the Working Class*, A&C Black, pp. 97–112.

Cornwell, J. (1984) *Hard-Earned Lives: Accounts of Health and Illness from East London*, Tavistock.

Cowan, J.K. (1990) *Dance and the Body Politic in Northern Greece*, Princeton University Press.

Cowley, J. (2022) *Who Are We Now? Stories of Modern England*, Picador.

Cragg, M. (2013) Context – Small Town Lad Sentiments (Mike Skinner remix): New music, *The Guardian* (18th September 2013). Available online: www.theguardian.com/music/musicblog/2013/sep/18/context-small-town-lad-sentiments-mike-skinner-remix.

Crane, H. (2007) Swimmers objected to servicemen using the pool, *Sutton and Croydon Guardian* (28th November 2007). Available online: www.yourlocalguardian.co.uk/news/1863898.swimmers-objected-to-servicemen-using-pool/.

Cremin, C.S. (2003) Self-starters, can-doers and mobile phoneys: Situations vacant columns and the personality culture in employment, *The Sociological Review*, 51(1), pp. 109–128.

Cullen, B.T., & Pretes, M. (2000) The meaning of marginality: Interpretations and perceptions in social science, *The Social Science Journal*, 37(2), pp. 215–229.

Cunningham, G. (2004) Houses in between: Navigating suburbia in late Victorian writing, *Victorian Literature and Culture*, 32(2), pp. 421–434.

Cutler, C. (2003) 'Keepin' it real': White hip-hoppers' discourses of language, race and authenticity, *Journal of Linguistic Anthropology*, 13(2), pp. 211–233.

Dalton, T.A., & Krout, R.E. (2006) The grief song-writing process with bereaved adolescents: An integrated grief model and music therapy protocol, *Music Therapy Perspectives*, 24, pp. 94–107.

Davies, K. (2014) Siblings, stories and the self: The sociological significance of young people's sibling relationships, *Sociology*, 49(4), pp. 679–695.

Davis, F. (1959) The cabdriver and his fare: Facets of a fleeting relationship, *American Journal of Sociology*, 65(2), pp. 158–165.

Davis, S. (1985) Pop lyrics: A mirror and molder of society, *ETC: A Review of General Semantics*, 42(2), pp. 167–169.

Dawes, R.M. (1999) A message from psychologists to economists: Mere predictability doesn't matter like it should (without a good story appended to it), *Journal of Economic Behavior & Organization*, 39, pp. 29–40.

Dekel, R., & Goldblatt, H. (2008) Is there intergenerational transmission of trauma? The case of combat veterans' children, *American Journal of Orthopsychiatry*, 78(3), pp. 281–289.

de Lacey, A. (2023) *Level Up: Live Performance and Creative Process in Grime Music*, Routledge.

Dennis, A. (2007) Poetic (in)justice? Rap music lyrics as art, life and criminal evidence, *Columbia Journal of Law & the Arts*, 31(1), pp. 1–42.

DeNora, T. (1999) Music as a technology of the self, *Poetics*, 27, pp. 31–56.

Department for Education (DfE) (2019) Participation rates in higher education: Academic years 2006/2007–2017/2018 (Provisional), DfE. Available online: https://assets.publishing.service.gov.uk/government/uploads/system/uploads/attachment_data/file/843542/Publication_HEIPR1718.pdf.

Department for Education and Skills (DfES) (2003) The future of higher education, DfES, The Stationery Office.

DeVito, S. (2013) The power of stories and images in law school teaching, *Washburn Law Journal*, 53(1), pp. 51–70.

DeWall, C.N., Pond Jr, R.S., Campbell, W.K., & Twenge, J.M. (2011) Tuning in to psychological change: Linguistic markers of personality traits and emotions over time in popular US song lyrics, *Psychology of Aesthetics, Creativity and the Arts*, 5(3), pp. 200–207.

Donoghue, J. (2010) *Anti-Social Behaviour Orders: A Culture of Control?*, Springer.

Dorst, J.D. (1989) *The Written Suburb: An American Site, An Ethnographic Dilemma*, University of Pennsylvania Press.

Downing, J. (2020) Rapping French cities in the 1990s: Blurring Marseille and brightening Paris in contested processes of boundary marking, *French Politics, Culture & Society*, 38(3), pp. 136–154.

Dražanová, L. (2014) National identity and the interplay between national pride and ethnic exclusionism: The exceptional case of the Czech Republic, *Ethnopolitics*, 14(3), pp. 235–255.

DrillaSE (2023) UK drill rappers currently in jail (2023), *YouTube*. Available online: https://www.youtube.com/watch?v=wpgvZLOYEeo&ab_channel=DrillaSE.

Dukes, R.L., Bisel, T.M., Borega, K.N., Lobato, E.A., & Owens, M.D. (2003) Expressions of love, sex and hurt in popular songs: A content analysis of all-time greatest hits, *The Social Science Journal*, 40, pp. 643–650.

Duneier, M., Kasinitz, P., & Murphy, A. (2014) *The Urban Ethnography Reader*, Oxford University Press.

Durand, A-P. (2002) *Black, Blanc, Beur: Rap Music and Hip-Hop Culture in the Francophone World*, Scarecrow Press.

Durkheim, E. (2009) *Sociology and Philosophy 1898*, Routledge.

Ebbatson, R. (2005) *An Imaginary England: Nation, Landscape and Literature, 1840–1920*, Routledge.

Eberhardt, N., & Freeman, K. (2015) 'First things first, I'm the realest': Linguistic appropriation, white privilege, and the hip-hop persona of Iggy Azalea, *Journal of Sociolinguistics*, 19(3), pp. 303–327.

Edger, K., & Helsel, S. (2012) Constructivist education with media: Using *Fight Club* to teach existential counselling theory, *Education and General Studies*, 1(2), pp. 48–53.

Ekpoudom, A. (2024) *Where We Come From: Rap, Home & Hope in Modern Britain*, Faber & Faber.

Elligan, D. (2004) *Rap Therapy: A Practical Guide for Communicating with Youth and Young Adults through Rap Music*, Dafina Books.

Elliott, B. (2017) *Coal Mine Disasters in the Modern Era c. 1900–1980*, Pen & Sword History.

Ellis, C., Adams, T.E., & Bochner, A.P. (2011) Autoethnography: An overview, *Forum Qualitative Sozialforschung*, 12(1), Art. 10.

Erikson, E.H. (1963) *Childhood and Society*, Norton Press.

Erikson, E.H. (1968) *Identity: Youth and Crisis*, Norton Press.

Evans, G., & Mellon, J. (2016) Identity, awareness and political attitudes: Why are we still working-class? *British Social Attitudes*, 33, pp. 4–22.

Evans, J.M., & Baym, N.K. (2022) The audacity of clout (chasing): Digital strategies of Black youth in Chicago DIY hip-hop, *International Journal of Communication*, 16, pp. 2669–2687.

Ewence, H. (2022) Moving 'out' to be 'in': The suburbanization of London Jewry, 1900–1939, *Urban History*, pp. 1–18.

Eyers, T. (2012) *Lacan and the Concept of the 'Real'*, Springer.

Fatsis, L. (2019) Policing the beats: The criminalisation of UK drill and grime music by the London Metropolitan Police, *The Sociological Review*, 67(6), pp. 1300–1316.

Feiler, B. (2013) The family stories that bind us – This life, *The New York Times* (17th March 2013). Available online: www.nytimes.com/2013/03/17/fashion/the-family-stories-that-bind-us-this-life.html.

Felstead, A., Gallie, D., Green, F., & Inanc, H. (2013) *Skills at Work in Britain: First Findings from the Skills and Employment Survey 2012* [project report], Centre for Learning and Life Chances in Knowledge Economies and Societies, Institute of Education. Available online: https://orca.cardiff.ac.uk/id/eprint/67983/1/1.%20Skills%20at%20Work%20in%20Britain%20-%20mini-report.pdf.

Filandri, M., & Bertolini, S. (2016) Young people and home ownership in Europe, *International Journal of Housing Policy*, 16(2), pp. 144–164.

Finlayson, A. (2016) 'The new economics' in Norwich: A revival of radical left-wing economic thinking? *Renewal: A Journal of Social Democracy*. Available online: https://renewal.org.uk/the-new-economics-in-norwich-a-revival-of-radical-left-wing-economic-thinking/.

Fisiak, J., & Trudgill, P. (2001) *East Anglian English*, Boydell & Brewer.

Fivush, R., & Grysman, A. (2022) Accuracy and reconstruction in autobiographical memory: (Re)consolidating neuroscience and sociocultural developmental approaches, *Wiley Interdisciplinary Reviews: Cognitive Science*, e1620.

Fivush, R., Habermas, T., Waters, T.E.A., & Zaman, W. (2011) The making of autobiographical memory: Intersections of culture, narratives, and identity, *International Journal of Psychology*, 46(5), pp. 321–345.

Fleming, D. (2001) Narrative leadership: Using the power of stories, *Strategy and Leadership*, 29(4). doi: 10.1108/sl.2001.26129dab.002.

Fletcher, A., Bonell, C., Sorhaindo, A., & Rhodes, T. (2009) Cannabis use and 'safe' identities in an inner-city school risk environment, *International Journal of Drug Policy*, 20, pp. 244–250.

Florida, R. (2002) *The Rise of the Creative Class*, Basic Books.

Foot Whyte, W. (1943) *Street Corner Society: The Social Structure of an Italian Slum*, University of Chicago Press.

Forman, M. (2000) 'Represent': Race, space and place in rap music, *Popular Music*, 19(1), pp. 65–90.

Forman, M. (2002) *The 'Hood Comes First: Race, Space and Place in Rap and Hip-Hop*, Wesleyan University Press.

Foster, H. (1995) The artist as ethnographer?, in Marcus, G.E., & Myers, F.R. (eds.) *The Traffic in Culture: Refiguring Art and Anthropology*, University of California Press, pp. 302–309.

Foster, V. (2015) *Collaborative Arts-Based Research for Social Justice*, Routledge.

Foucault, M. (1966) *Les Mots et Les Choses: Une Archeologie des Sciences Humaines*, Editions Gallimard.

Foucault, M. (1988) Technologies of the Self, in Martin, L.H., Gutman, H., & Hutton, P.H. (eds.) *Technologies of the Self: A Seminar with Michel Foucault*, University of Massachusetts Press, pp. 16–49.

Foucault, M. (1997) *Ethics: Subjectivity and Truth*, New Press.

Frank, A.W. (2000) The standpoint of storyteller, *Qualitative Health Research*, 10, pp. 354–365.

Frank, A.W. (2002) Why study people's stories? The dialogical ethics of narrative analysis, *International Journal of Qualitative Methods*, 1(1), Article 6.

Frankel, N. (2012) *Oscar Wilde: The Uncensored Picture of Dorian Gray*, Harvard University Press.

Franozi, R. (1998) Narrative Analysis – Or why (and how) sociologists should be interested in narrative, *Annual Review of Sociology*, 24, pp. 517–554.

Freud, S., & Breuer, J. (2004) *Studies in Hysteria* (trans. Luckhurst, N.), Penguin.

Friday, K. (2003) 'A generation of men without history': *Fight Club*, masculinity, and the historical symptom, *Postmodern Culture*, 13(3). Available online: https://muse.jhu.edu/article/44976.

Friedman, S. (2016) Habitus clivé and the emotional imprint of social mobility, *The Sociological Review*, 64(1), pp. 129–147.

Friedman, S., & Laurison, D. (2020) *The Class Ceiling: Why It Pays to Be Privileged*, Bristol University Press.

Friedman, S., O'Brien, D., & Laurison, D (2016) 'Like skydiving without a parachute': How class origin shapes occupational trajectories in British acting, *Sociology*, 51(5), pp. 992–1010.

Friedman, S., O'Brien, D., & McDonald, I. (2021) Deflecting privilege: Class identity and the intergenerational self, *Sociology*, 55(4), pp. 716–733.

Frith, S. (1989) Why do songs have words?, *Contemporary Music Review*, 5(1), pp. 77–96.

Frith, S. (1997) The suburban sensibility of British rock and pop, in Silverstone, R. (ed.) *Visions of Suburbia*, Routledge, pp. 269–279.

Frost, D., & Phillips, R. (2011) *Liverpool '81: Remembering the Toxteth Riots*, Liverpool University Press.

Galea-Pace, S. (2022a) 'It was a mistake': Delia admits regret at famous Norwich City rally cry, *Norwich Evening News* (28th February 2022). Available online: https://www.eveningnews24.co.uk/news/22328945.it-mistake-delia-admits-regret-famous-norwich-city-rally-cry/.

Galea-Pace, S. (2022b) Norwich: Four men charged after Prince of Wales fight, *Eastern Daily Press* (2nd December 2022). Available online: www.edp24.co.uk/news/23167055.norwich-four-men-charged-prince-wales-road-fight/.

Garrisi, D. (2017) The Victorian press coverage of the 1842 report on child labour. The metamorphosis of images, *Early Popular Visual Culture*, 15(4), pp. 442–478.

Gasparini, P. (2004) *Est-il je? Roman autobiographique et autofiction*, Éditions du Seuil.

Gasteier, M. (2009) *Illmatic (33 1/3)*, Bloomsbury Publishing.

Geertz, C. (1988) *Works and Lives: The Anthropologist as Author*, Stanford University Press.

Giesen, C.A.B. (2021) *Coal Miner's Wives: Portraits of Endurance*, University Press of Kentucky.

Gilbert, D. (Forthcoming) The uncool hunt: Searching for the creative suburb, in van Damme, I., McManus, R., & Dehaene, M. (eds.), *Creativity from Suburban Nowheres: Rethinking Cultural and Creative Practices*, University of Toronto Press.

Gildart, K. (2013) *Images of England through Popular Music: Class, Youth and Rock 'n' Roll, 1955–1976*, Palgrave Macmillan.

Gilligan, J. (2000) *Violence: Reflections of Our Deadliest Epidemic*, Jessica Kingsley.

Gilroy, P. (1997) 'After the love has gone': Bio-politics and the etho-poetics in the Black public sphere, in McRobbie, A. (ed.) *Back to Reality? Social Experience and Cultural Studies*, Manchester University Press, pp. 83–115.

Ginsburg, F. (1991) Indigenous media: Faustian contract of global village?, *Cultural Anthropology*, 6(1), pp. 92–112.

Glaser, B.G. (1978) *Theoretical Sensitivity: Advances in Methodology of Grounded Theory*, Sociological Press.

Glaser, B.G. (1992) *Basics of Grounded Theory Analysis*, Sociological Press.

Goffman, E. (1956) *The Presentation of Self in Everyday Life*, University of Edinburgh Social Sciences Research Centre.

Gold, R. (1958) Roles in sociological field observations, *Social Forces*, 36, pp. 217–223.

Golden, T.L. (2020) Reframing photovoice: Building on the method to develop more equitable and responsive research practices, *Qualitative Health Research*, 30(6), pp. 960–972.

Golden, T.L., & Wendel, M.L. (2020) Public health's next step in advancing equity: Re-evaluating epistemological assumptions to move social determinants from theory to practice, *Frontiers in Public Health*, 8, Article 131, pp. 1–7.

Goldsmith, M. (2006) Reviewed work(s): Studies in hysteria by Sigmund Freud, Joseph Breuer, Rachel Bowlby and Nicola Luckhurst, *Modern Language Studies*, 36(1), pp. 84–88.

Goodwin, M.J., & Heath, O. (2016) The 2016 referendum, Brexit and the left behind: An aggregate-level analysis of the result, *The Political Quarterly*, 87(3), pp. 323–332.

Gottschall, J. (2012) *The Storytelling Animal: How Stories Make Us Human*, Houghton Mifflin.

Gottschall, J. (2021) *The Story Paradox: How Our Love of Storytelling Builds Societies and Tears Them Down*, Basic Books.

Grabher, G. (2018) Marginality as strategy: Leveraging peripherality for creativity, *Environment and Planning A: Economy and Space*, 50(8), pp. 1785–1794.

Graeber, D. (2013) On the phenomenon of bullshit jobs: A work rant, *Strike Magazine*, 3. Available online: https://strikemag.org/bullshit-jobs/.

Graeber, D. (2018) *Bullshit Jobs: A Theory*, Simon & Schuster.

Grealy, L. (2008) Negotiating cultural authenticity in hip-hop: Mimicry, whiteness and Eminem, *Continuum: Journal of Media & Cultural Studies*, 22(6), pp. 851–865.

Green, F., & Zhu, Y. (2010) Overqualification, job dissatisfaction, and increasing dispersion in the returns to graduate education, *Oxford Economic Papers*, 62(4), pp. 740–763.

Green, N. (2005) Songs from the Wood and sounds of the suburbs: A folk, rock and punk portrait of England, 1965–1977, *Built Environment*, 31(3), pp. 255–270.

Greenberg, J., Vail, K., & Pyszczynski, T. (2014) Terror management theory and research: How the desire for death transcendence drive out strivings for meaning and significance, in Elliot, A.J. (ed.) *Advances in Motivation Science*, Elsevier, pp. 85–134.

Grem, D.E. (2006) 'The South got something to say': Atlanta's Dirty South and the southernization of hip-hop America, *Southern Cultures*, 12(4), pp. 55–73.

Grimmer, D. (2011) Update: Man attacked in Norwich's Prince of Wales Road died from a bleed to the brain, *Eastern Daily Press* (14th August 2011). Available online: www.edp24.co.uk/news/crime/21135766.update-man-attacked-norwichs-prince-wales-road-died-bleed-brain/.

Grønstad, A. (2003) One-dimensional men: 'Fight Club' and the poetics of the body, *Film Criticism*, 28(1), pp. 1–23.

Gross, S., & Musgrave, G. (2020) *Can Music Make You Sick? Measuring the Price of Musical Ambition*, University of Westminster Press.

Grossmith, G., & Grossmith, W. (1919) *The Diary of a Nobody*, J.W. Arrowsmith Ltd.

Haddad, Y.Y., & Balz, M.J. (2006) The October riots in France: A failed immigration policy or The Empire Strikes Back, *International Migration*, 44(2), pp. 22-34.

Hall, P. (1996) Ealing, the queen of London's Victorian railway suburbs, *Urban Design Studies*, 2, pp. 31-44.

Hall, S. (1977) Culture, the media and the 'ideological effect', in Curran, J., Gurevitch, M., & Woollacott, J. (eds.) *Mass Communication and Society*, Edward Arnold, pp. 315-348.

Hammersley, M. (2016) An ideological dispute: Accusations of Marxist bias in the sociology of education during the 1970s, *Contemporary British History*, 30(2), pp. 242-259.

Hammersley, M. (2018) What is ethnography? Can it survive? Should it? *Ethnography and Education*, 13(1), pp. 1-17.

Hammersley, M., & Atkinson, P. (1997) *Ethnography: Principles in Practice*, Routledge.

Hammou, K. (2016) Mainstreaming French rap music. Commodification and artistic legitimation of othered cultural goods, *Poetics*, 59, pp. 67-81.

Hancox, D. (2013) *Stand Up Tall: Dizzee Rascal and the Birth of Grime*, Amazon Kindle.

Hancox, D. (2018) *Inner City Pressure: The Story of Grime*, HarperCollins.

Hanson, S. (2014) *Small Towns, Austere Times: The Dialectics of Deracinated Localism*, Zero Books.

Haralambos, M. (1974) *Right On: From Blues to Soul in Black America*, Eddison.

Harding, T., Cockcroft, L., & Carlin, B. (2007) Disabled veterans jeered at swimming pool, *The Telegraph* (22nd November 2007). Available online: www.telegraph.co.uk/news/uknews/1570130/Disabled-veterans-jeered-at-swimming-pool.html.

Hare, S., & Baker, A. (2017) Keepin' it real: Authenticity, commercialization, and the media in Korean hip hop, *SAGE Open* (April-June 2017), pp. 1-12.

Harkness, G. (2011) Backpackers and gangstas: Chicago's white rappers strive for authenticity, *American Behavioral Scientist*, 55(1), pp. 57-85.

Harris, J. (2010) The sound of the suburbs and literary tradition, *The Guardian* (3rd April 2010). Available online: www.theguardian.com/culture/2010/apr/03/suburbia-pop-betjeman-john-harris.

Harrison, A. (2017) What we can learn from The Streets's [sic] complex portraits of British masculinity, *The Fader* (23rd March 2017). Available online: www.thefader.com/2017/03/23/the-streets-original-pirate-british-masculinity-essay.

Harrison, A.K. (2009) *Hip Hop Underground: The Integrity and Ethics of Racial Identification*, Temple University Press.

Harrison, K., Jacobsen, K., & Sunderland, N. (2019) New skies above: Sense-bound and place-based songwriting as a trauma response for asylum seekers and refugees, *Journal of Applied Arts & Health*, 10(2), pp. 147-167.

Hegelund, A. (2005) Objectivity and subjectivity in the ethnographic method, *Qualitative Health Research*, 15 (5), pp. 647-668.

Heine, S.J., Proulx, T., & Vohs, K.D. (2006) The meaning maintenance model: On the coherence of social motivations, *Personality and Social Psychology Review*, 10(2), pp. 88-110.

Hesmondhalgh, D. (2013) *The Cultural Industries*, SAGE.

Hesmondhalgh, D., & Melville, C. (2001) Urban breakbeat culture: Repercussions of hip-hop in the United Kingdom, in Mitchell, T. (ed.) *Global Noise: Rap and Hip Hop outside the USA*, Wesleyan University Press, pp. 86-110.

Hess, M. (2005) Hip-hop realness and the white performer, *Critical Studies in Media Communication*, 22(5), pp. 372-389.

hÍr, L., & Strange, L. (2021) *Tiocfaidh Ár Lá, get the brits out, lad*: Masculinity and nationalism in Irish language rap videos, *Social Semiotics*, 31(3), pp. 466-488.

Hislop, I. (2022) In Suburbia, BBC Radio 4.

Hjørnevik, K., Waage, L., & Hansen, A.L. (2022) Musical life stories: Coherence through musicking in the prison setting, *Crime, Media, Culture*, pp. 1-21.

Hollands, R., & Chatterton, P. (2002) Changing time for an old industrial city: Hard times, hedonism and corporate power in Newcastle's nightlife, *City*, 6(3), pp. 291-315.

Hughes, D., Keith, S., Morrow, G., Evans, M., & Crowdy, D. (2013) What constitutes artist success in the Australian music industries?, *International Journal of Music Business Research*, 2(2), pp. 61-80.

Hughes, K., Anderson, Z., Morelo, M., & Bellis, M.A. (2008) Alcohol, nightlife and violence: The relative contributions of drinking before and during nights out to negative health and criminal justice outcomes, *Addiction*, 103(1), pp. 60-65.

Hundley, T. (2003) English towns battle heroin abuse, *The Chicago Tribune* (7th February 2003). Available online: www.chicagotribune.com/news/ct-xpm-2003-02-07-0302070414-story.html.

Hunt, C. (2000) *Therapeutic Dimensions of Autobiography in Creative Writing*, Jessica Kingsley.

Huq, R. (2008) The sound of the suburbs: The shaping of Englishness and the socio-cultural landscape after New Labour, in Perryman, M. (ed.) *Imagined Nation: England After Britain*, Lawrence and Wishart, pp. 49-62.

Huq, R. (2013) *Making Sense of Suburbia through Popular Culture*, Bloomsbury Academic.

Hussain, D. (2010) Healing through writing: Insights from research, *International Journal of Mental Health Promotion*, 12(2), pp. 19-23.

Hyder, R. (2014) Black music and cultural exchange in Bristol, in Stratton, J., & Zuberi, N. (eds.) *Black Popular Music in Britain Since 1945*, Routledge, pp. 78–94.

Ilan, J. (2012) 'The industry's the new road': Crime, commodification and street cultural tropes in UK urban music, *Crime, Media, Culture*, 8, pp. 39–55.

Ilan, J. (2020) Digital street culture decoded: Why criminalizing drill music is street illiterate and counterproductive, *British Journal of Criminology*, 60, pp. 994–1013.

Jay-Z (2010) *Decoded*, Virgin Books.

Johnson, T.H., DuPee, M., & Shaaker, W. (2017) *Taliban Narratives: The Use and Power of Stories in the Afghanistan Conflict*, Oxford University Press.

Jones, C.E. (2005) *The Black Panther Party (Reconsidered)*, Black Classic Press.

Jones, S. (1988) *Black Culture, White Youth: The Reggae Tradition from JA to UK*, Macmillan Education.

Joyce, J. (1916) *A Portrait of the Artist as a Young Man*, B.W. Huebsch.

Kahn, L. (2010) The long-term labor market consequences of graduating from college in a bad economy, *Labour Economics*, 17(2), pp. 303–316.

Kane, T. (2002) Bringing the real: Lacan and Tupac, *Prospects*, 27, pp. 641–663.

Kaplan, D.H. (2015) Immigration and the making of place in Paris, *Journal of Cultural Geography*, 32(1), pp. 23–39.

Keep, E. (2002) The English vocational education and training policy debate, *Journal of Education and Work*, 15(4), pp. 457–479.

Kelley, R.D.G. (1996) Kickin' reality, kickin' ballistics: 'Gangsta rap' and postindustrial Los Angeles, in Perkins, E. (ed.) *Droppin' Science: Critical Essays on Rap Music and Hip Hop Culture*, Temple University Press, pp. 117–157.

Kelley, R.D.G. (2004) Looking for the 'real' nigga: Social scientists construct the ghetto, in Forman, M., & Neal, M.A. (eds.) *That's The Join! The Hip-Hop Studies Reader*, Routledge, pp. 119–136.

Kernis, M.H., & Goldman, B.M. (2003) Stability and variability in self-concept and self-esteem, in Leary, M.R., & Tangney, J.P. (eds.) *Handbook of Self and Identity*, Guilford, pp. 106–127.

Key Changes (n.d.) About our work, Key Changes. Available online: www.keychanges.org.uk/about-our-work/.

Keyes, C.L. (2002) *Rap Music and Street Consciousness*, University of Illinois Press.

Kirk, T. (2019) Jailed rapper caught out by song lyrics revealing drug-dealing lifestyle, *Evening Standard* (4th March 2019). Available online: www.standard.co.uk/news/crime/jailed-rapper-caught-out-by-song-lyrics-revealing-drugdealing-lifestyle-a4081871.html.

Kivinen, O., & Ahola, S. (1999) Higher education as human risk capital: Reflections on changing labour market conditions, *Higher Education*, 38, pp. 191-208.

Kliman, J. (2010) Intersections of social privilege and marginalization: A visual teaching tool, in Ariel, J., Hernández-Wolfe, P., & Stearns, S.M. (eds.) *Expanding Our Social Justice Practices: Advances in Theory and Training*, American Family Therapy Academy, pp. 39-48.

Klokker, R.H., & Jæger, M.M. (2022) Family backgrounds and cultural lifestyles: Multigenerational associations, *Poetics*, 92(B), pp. 1-13.

Knowles, C. (2022) *Serious Money: Walking Plutocratic London*, Allen Lane.

Kobin, C., & Tyson, E. (2006) Thematic analysis of hip-hop music: Can hip-hop therapy facilitate empathic connections when working with clients in urban settings?, *The Arts in Psychotherapy*, 33(4), pp. 343-356.

Kohler Riessman, C. (1993) *Narrative Analysis*, SAGE.

Kopano, B.N. (2002) Rap music as an extension of the Black rhetorical tradition: 'Keepin' it real', *Western Journal of Black Studies*, 26(4), pp. 204-214.

Kotilainen, S. (2012) An inherited name as the foundation of a person's identity: How the memory of a dead person lived on in the names of his or her descendants, *Thanatos*, 1(1), pp. 1-24.

Krohn, F.B., & Suazo, F.L. (1995) Contemporary urban music: Controversial messages in hip-hop and rap lyrics, *ETC: A Review of General Semantics*, 52(2), pp. 139-154.

Kubrin, C.E. (2006) 'I see death around the corner': Nihilism in rap music, *Sociological Perspectives*, 48(4), pp. 433-459.

Kubrin, C.E., & Nielson, E. (2014) Rap on trial, *Race and Justice*, 4(3), pp. 185-211.

Kuhn, A. (1995) *Family Secrets: Acts of Memory and Imagination*, Verso.

Kulish, N. (2022) The power of stories, *Journal of the American Psychoanalytic Association*, 70(5), pp. 829-844.

Larkin, P. (2012) *Philip Larkin Poems, Selected by Martin Amis*, Faber & Faber.

Lawrence, D.H. (1913) *Sons and Lovers*, Gerald Duckworth and Company Ltd.

Lawrence, D.H. (1914) *The Prussian Officer and Other Stories*, Gerald Duckworth and Company Ltd.

Lea, R. (2002) *Education and Training: A Business Blueprint for Reform*, Institute of Directors Policy Unit.

Leggett, V. (2012) Retiring Norfolk headteacher speaks out over education issues, *Eastern Daily Press* (5th December 2012). Available online: www.edp24.co.uk/news/retiring-norfolk-headteacher-speaks-out-over-education-issues-541614.

Lena, J.C. (2006) Social context and musical content of rap music, 1979-1995, *Social Forces*, 85(1), pp. 479-495.

Leung, J.K.L., & Fong, P.S.W. (2011) The power of stories in the construction industry: Lessons from other domains, *VINE: The Journal of Information and Knowledge Management Systems*, 41(4), pp. 466-482.

Levy, I. (2012) Hip hop and spoken word therapy with urban youth, *Journal of Poetry Therapy*, 25(4), pp. 219-224.

Lien, N., & Chen, Y. (2013) Narrative ads: The effect of argument strength and story format, *Journal of Business Research*, 66(4), pp. 516-522.

Lifton, R.J. (1973) The sense of immortality: On death and continuity of life, *American Journal of Psychoanalysis*, 33, pp. 3-15.

Lifton, R.J., & Olson, E. (1974) *Living and Dying*, Wildwood House.

Lizardo, O. (2007) *Fight Club*, or the cultural contradictions of late capitalism, *Journal for Cultural Research*, 11(3), pp. 221-243.

Louis, E. (2014) *En Finir avec Eddy Bellegueule*, Editions du Seuil.

Loveday, V. (2014) 'Flat-capping it': Memory, nostalgia and value in retroactive male working-class identification, *European Journal of Cultural Studies*, 17(6), pp. 721-735.

Low, B., Tan, E., & Celemencki, K. (2013) The limits of 'keepin' it real': The challenges for critical hip-hop pedagogies of discourses of authenticity, in Hill, M.L., & Petchauer, E. (eds.) *Schooling Hip-Hop: Expanding Hip-Hop Based Education across the Curriculum*, Teachers College Press, pp. 118-136.

Lutz, F. (1981) Ethnography: The holistic approach to understanding schooling, in Green, J., & Wallat, C. (eds.) *Ethnography and Language in Educational Settings*, Ablex, pp. 51-63.

Lyddane, D. (2006) Understanding gangs and gang mentality: Acquiring evidence of the gang conspiracy, *The United States Attorney Bulletin on Gang Prosecutions*, 54(3), pp. 1-14.

MacKuen, M.B. (1983) Political drama, economic conditions, and the dynamics of presidential popularity, *American Journal of Political Science*, 27(2), pp. 165-192.

Madanikia, Y., & Bartholomew, K. (2014) Themes of lust and live in popular music lyrics from 1971 to 2011, *SAGE Open*. doi: 10.1177/2158244014547179.

Madden, R. (1999) Home-town anthropology, *The Australian Journal of Anthropology*, 10(3), pp. 259-270.

Madhavan, A., & Nair, S. (2016) *Lincolnshire Diversity in the Arts: Research and Development*, Arts Council England & University of Lincoln.

Mahadevan, N., Gregg, A.P., & Sedikides, C. (2019) Is self-regard a sociometer or a hierometer? Self-esteem tracks status and inclusion, narcissism tracks status, *Journal of Personality and Social Psychology*, 116(3), pp. 444-466.

Mahalik, J.R., Locke, B.D., Ludlow, L.H., Diemer, M.A., Scott, R.P.J., Gottfried, M., & Freitas, G. (2003) Development of the Conformity to Masculine Norms Inventory. *Psychology of Men & Masculinity*, 4(1), pp. 3–25.

Mailer, N. (1957) The White Negro, *Dissent*, 4, pp. 276–293.

Malik, K. (2023) *Not So Black and White: A History of Race from White Supremacy to Identity Politics*, Hurst Publishers.

Máliková, L., Farrell, M., & McDonagh, J. (2016) Perception of marginality and peripherality in an Irish rural context, *Quaestiones Geographicae*, 35(4), pp. 93–105.

Malinowski, B. (1922) *Argonauts of the Western Pacific: An Account of the Native Enterprise and Adventure in the Archipelagos of Melanesian New Guinea*, EP Dutton & Co.

Mann, R., & Fenton, S. (2017) English national identity, Resentment and the Leave vote, *Discover Society*, 45. Available online: https://archive.discoversociety.org/2017/06/06/english-national-identity-resentment-and-the-leave-vote.

Margaret, S. (1960) *Tradition and Change: A Study of Banbury*, Oxford University Press.

Markert, J. (2007) Sing a song of drug use-abuse: Four decades of drug lyrics in popular music – from the sixties through the nineties, *Sociological Inquiry*, 71(2), pp. 194–220.

Maronitis, K. (2021) The present is a foreign country: Brexit and the performance of victimhood, *British Politics*, 16, pp. 239–253.

Martela, F., & Steger, M.F. (2016) The three meaning of meaning in life: Distinguishing coherence, purpose and significance, *The Journal of Positive Psychology*, 11(5), pp. 531–545.

Martin, C. (2013) A bittersweet love letter to the London suburbs, *Vice* (6th November 2013). Available online: www.vice.com/en/article/mvnqen/a-bittersweet-love-letter-to-the-suburbs.

Massey, D. (1991) A global sense of place, *Marxism Today*, June 1991, pp. 24–29.

Masterson, A. (2022) 'A woman left lonely': Pariah femininity and the posthumous career of Janis Joplin, *Feminist Media Studies*. OnlineFirst. doi: 10.1080/14680777.2022.2110605.

Mauss, M. (1954) *The Gift: The Form and Reason for Exchange in Archaic Societies*, Cohen & West.

Mayor of London (2019) Mayor breaks ground to start construction on new culture powerhouse, Mayor of London/London Assembly. Available online: www.london.gov.uk/press-releases/mayoral/mayor-breaks-ground-to-start-construction.

McAdams, D.P. (1985) *Power, Intimacy, and the Life Story: Personological Inquiries into Identity*, Guilford Press.

McAdams, D.P. (1993) *The Stories We Live By: Personal Myths and the Making of the Self*, Guilford Press.

McAdams, D.P. (1996) Personality, modernity, and the storied self: A contemporary framework for studying persons, *Psychological Inquiry*, 7, pp. 295–321.

McAdams, D.P. (2001) The psychology of life stories, *Review of General Psychology*, 5(2), pp. 100–122.

McAndrew, F.T. (2022) The namesaking of children as an investment strategy for managing kin relations and bonding fathers to their children, *Evolutionary Behavioral Science*, 16(3), pp. 220–228.

McDonagh, J. (2002) Peripherality and the West of Ireland: The need for re-evaluation?, in McDonagh, J. (ed.) *Economy, Society, and Peripherality: Experiences from the West of Ireland*, Arlen House, pp. 97–112.

McFerran, K., Baker, F., Patton, G.C., & Sawyer, S.M. (2006) A retrospective lyrical analysis of songs written by adolescents with anorexia nervosa, *European Eating Disorders Review*, 14, pp. 397–403.

Mckenzie, L. (2012) Narratives from the inside: Re-studying St Anns in Nottingham, *Sociological Review*, 3, pp. 457–476.

Mckenzie, L. (2013) Foxtrotting the riot: The slow rioting in Britain's Inner City, *Sociological Research Online*, 18(4).

Mckenzie, L. (2016) 'It's not ideal': Reconsidering 'anger' and 'apathy' in the Brexit vote among an invisible working class, *Competition & Change*, 21(3), pp. 199–210.

Mckenzie, L. (2017) The class politics of prejudice: Brexit and the land of no-hope and glory, *The British Journal of Sociology*, 68(S1), pp. 265–280.

McLean, K.C., & Breen, A. (2014) Selves in a world of stories during emerging adulthood, in Arnett, J.J. (ed.) *The Oxford Handbook of Emerging Adulthood*, Oxford University Press, pp. 385–400.

McLean, K.C., Pasupathi, M., & Pals, J.L. (2007) Selves creating stories creating selves: A process model for self-development, *Personality and Social Psychology Review*, 11(3), pp. 262–278.

McLeod, K. (1999) Authenticity within hip-hop and other cultures threatened with assimilation, *Journal of Communication*, 49(4), pp. 134–150.

McNally, K. (2007) 'Where's the spinning wheel?' Frank Sinatra and working-class alienation in 'Young at Heart', *Journal of American Studies*, 41(1), pp. 115–133.

Measham, M., & Brain, K. (2005) 'Binge' drinking, British alcohol policy and the new culture of intoxication, *Crime, Media, Culture*, 1(3), pp. 262–283.

Medhurst, A. (1997) Visions of suburbia in British popular culture, in Silverstone, R. (ed.) *Visions of Suburbia*, Psychology Press, pp. 240–268.

Melville, C. (2004) Beats, rhymes and grime, *New Humanist*. Available online: https://newhumanist.org.uk/articles/822/beats-rhymes-and-grime.

Merrill, N., & Fivush, R. (2016) Intergenerational narratives and identity across development, *Developmental Review*, 40, pp. 72–92.

Meyers, F.R., & Marcus, G.E. (1995) *Traffic in Culture: Refiguring Art and Anthropology*, University of California Press.

Mishler, E.G. (2005) Patient stories, narratives of resistance and the ethics of humane care: A la recherché du temps perdu, *Health*, 9(4), pp. 431-451.

Mitchell, T. (2001) Introduction: Another root – Hip-hop outside the USA, in Mitchell, T. (ed.) *Global Noise: Rap and Hip-Hop outside the USA*, Wesleyan University Press, pp. 1-38.

Mohanty, S.P. (1993) The epistemic status of cultural identity: On 'Beloved' and the postcolonial condition, *Cultural Critique*, 24, pp. 41-80.

Mohanty, S.P. (2018) *Literary Theory and the Claims of History: Postmodernism, Objectivity, Multicultural Politics*, Cornell University Press.

Mole Valley District Council (2010) Built Up Areas Character Appraisal: Bookham and Fetcham, Mole Valley Local Development Framework, Mole Valley District Council. Available online: www.molevalley.gov.uk/sites/default/files/home/building-planning/local-plans/bookhambuacaaccess.pdf.

Moran, M. (2011) Opposing exclusion: The political significance of the riots in French suburbs (2005-2007), *Modern & Contemporary France*, 19(3), pp. 297-312.

Muir, H. (2006) Rapper who killed producer for 'disrespect' gets 30 years, *The Guardian* (3rd November 2006). Available online: www.theguardian.com/uk/2006/nov/03/ukguns.musicnews.

Murger, H. (1883) *The Bohemians of the Latin Quarter (Scènes de la vie de bohème)*, Vizetelly and Co.

Murray, A.H. (2018) Generation Snowflake? *RSA Journal*, 164(4), pp. 44-47.

Musgrave, G. (2014) Creativity, Capital and Entrepreneurship: The Contemporary Experience of UK Urban Music, unpublished PhD thesis (University of East Anglia).

Musgrave, G. (2017) Making sense of my creativity: Reflecting on digital autoethnography, *Journal of Artistic and Creative Education*, 13(1), pp. 1-11.

Musgrave, G. (2022) Losing work, losing purpose: Representations of musicians' mental health in the time of Covid-19, in Tschmuck, P., Morrow, G., & Nordgard, D. (eds.) *Rethinking the Music Business: Music Contexts, Rights, Data and Covid-19*, Springer International Publishing, pp. 11-28.

Musgrave, G. (2023a) Musicians, their relationships, and their wellbeing: Creative labour, relational work, *Poetics*, 96, 101792. doi: 10.1016/j.poetic.2023.101762.

Musgrave, G. (2023b) Music and wellbeing vs. musicians' wellbeing: Examining the paradox of music-making positively impacting wellbeing, but musicians suffering from poor mental health, *Cultural Trends*, 32(3), pp. 280-295.

Musgrave, G., Howard, C., Schofield, A., Silver, E., & Tibber, M.S. (2023) Mental health and the music industry: An evolving intervention landscape, *The Lancet Psychiatry*, 10(5), pp. 311–313.

Nairn, I., & Pevsner, N. (2002) *The Buildings of England: Surrey* (2nd edition, rev. Cherry, B.), Yale University Press.

Nasser, N. (2004) Southall's Kaleido-scape: A study in the changing morphology of a west London suburb, *Built Environment*, 30(1), pp. 76–103.

Nava, M. (2007) *Visceral Cosmopolitanism: Gender, Culture and the Normalisation of Difference*, Berg.

Nayak, A. (2006) Displaced masculinities: Chavs, youth and class in the post-industrial city, *Sociology*, 40(5), pp. 813–831.

Negus, K. (2011) *Producing Pop: Culture and Conflict in the Popular Music Industry*, Keith Negus. Available online: https://research.gold.ac.uk/5453/1/Producing_Pop.pdf.

Negus, K., & Sledmere, A. (2022) Postcolonial paths of pop: A suburban psychogeography of George Michael and Wham! *Popular Music*, 41(2), pp. 131–151.

Nelson, K., & Fivush, R. (2004) The emergence of autobiographical memory: A social cultural developmental theory, *Psychological Review*, 111(2), pp. 486–511.

Nelson, R. (ed.) (2013) *Practice as Research in the Arts: Principles, Protocols, Pedagogies, Resistances*, Palgrave Macmillan.

Newman, T.B. (2003) The power of stories over statistics, *British Medical Journal*, 327, 1424.

Newsom, C.R., Archer, R.P., Trumbetta, S., & Gottesman, I.I. (2003) Changes in adolescent response patterns on the MMPI/MMPI-A across four decades, *Journal of Personality Assessment*, 81(1), pp. 74–84.

Ng, A.H.S. (2005) Muscular existentialism in Chuck Palahniuk's *Fight Club*, *Stirrings Still*, 2(2), pp. 116–138.

Nicholson, G. (2009) *Justifying Our Existence: An Essay in Applied Phenomenology*, University of Toronto Press.

Nicolaides, B., & Wiese, A. (2007) *The Suburb Reader*, Routledge.

Nielson, E., & Dennis, A. (2019) *Rap on Trial: Race, Lyrics, and Guilt in America*, The New Press.

Noor, P. (2018) How can we reclaim the St George's Cross from the far right? *The Guardian* (12th September 2018). Available online: www.theguardian.com/lifeandstyle/2018/sep/12/how-can-we-reclaim-the-st-georges-cross-from-the-far-right.

Norman, P. (2004) *Shout! The True Story of the Beatles*, Pan.

Norwich City Council (2022) 100 facts about Norwich council housing. Available online: www.norwich.gov.uk/info/20384/a_century_of_norwich_council_housing/2458/100_facts_about_norwich_council_housing.

Oakley, L., Laurison, D., O'Brien, D., & Friedman, S. (2017) Cultural capital: Arts graduates, spatial inequality, and London's impact on cultural labor markets, *American Behavioral Scientist*, 61(12), pp. 1510–1531.

O'Callaghan, C., & Grocke, D. (2009) Lyric analysis research in music therapy: Rationales, methods and representations, *The Arts in Psychotherapy*, 36, pp. 320–328.

Office for National Statistics (ONS) (2013) Graduates in the UK labour market: 2013. Available online: www.ons.gov.uk/employmentandlabourmarket/peopleinwork/employmentandemployeetypes/articles/graduatesintheuklabourmarket/2013-11-19.

Office for National Statistics (ONS) (2018) The 2008 recession 10 years on, ONS. Available online: www.ons.gov.uk/economy/grossdomesticproductgdp/articles/the2008recession10yearson/2018-04-30.

Office for National Statistics (ONS) (2021) Housing affordability in England and Wales: 2021, ONS. Available online: www.ons.gov.uk/peoplepopulationandcommunity/housing/bulletins/housingaffordabilityinenglandandwales/2021.

Office for National Statistics (ONS) (2022) Ethnic group, England and Wales: Census 2021, ONS. Available online: www.ons.gov.uk/peoplepopulationandcommunity/culturalidentity/ethnicity/bulletins/ethnicgroupenglandandwales/census2021#how-ethnic-composition-varied-across-england-and-wales.

Office for Students (OfS) (2022) A geography of employment: Autumn 2022 – Updated official statistics classifying local variations in graduate opportunities, OfS. Available online: www.officeforstudents.org.uk/media/a9ff44f7-990e-4e27-8559-d59a0093db66/geography-of-employment-sept2022-final.pdf.

O'Hagan, S. (2022) 'Song are little dangerous bombs of truth': Nick Cave and Sean O'Hagan – an exclusive book extract, *The Guardian* (11th September 2022). Available online: www.theguardian.com/music/2022/sep/11/nick-cave-on-music-grief-and-spirituality-faith-hope-carnage.

Okirike, N. (2021) 9 must-hear songs from Ghana's buzzing drill scene, Okay Africa. Available online: www.okayafrica.com/ghana-drill-music-songs-asakaa/.

Onaci, E. (2020) *Free the Land: The Republic of New Afrika and the Pursuit of a Black Nation State*, University of North Carolina Press.

Optiz, J.M., Pavone, L., & Corsello, G. (2016) The power of stories in pediatrics and genetics, *Italian Journal of Pediatrics*, 42, 35. doi: 10.1186/s13052-016-0241-z.

O'Reilly, K. (2012) *Ethnographic Methods* (3rd edition), Routledge.

Oreopoulos, P., Von Wachter, T., & Heisz, A. (2012) The short and long-term career effects of graduating in a recession, *American Economic Journal: Applied Economics*, 4(1), pp. 1–29.

Orwell, G. (1934) *Keep the Aspidistra Flying*, Victor Gollancz Ltd.

Orwell, G. (2021) *The Road to Wigan Pier*, Oxford University Press.

Orwell, G., Orwell, S., & Angus, I. (1980) *My Country Right or Left 1940-1943 (The Collected Essays, Journalism and Letters of George Orwell Vol. 2)*, Harcourt.

Osumare, H. (2001) Beat streets in the global hood: Connective marginalities of the hip-hop globe, *The Journal of American Culture*, 24(1-2), pp. 171-181.

Oware, M. (2011) Brotherly love: Homosociality and Black masculinity in gangsta rap music, *Journal of African American Studies*, 15, pp. 22-39.

Oyer, P. (2006) Initial labor market conditions and long-term outcomes for economists, *Journal of Economic Perspective*, 20(3), pp. 143-160.

Oyserman, D., & James, L. (2011) Possible identities, in Schwartz, S.J., Luyckx, K., & Vignoles, V.L. (eds.) *Handbook of Identity Theory and Research*, Springer, pp. 117-145.

Palahniuk, C. (1996) *Fight Club*, W.W. Norton.

Palmer, R. (1975) *A Touch of the Times*, Penguin.

Paor-Evans, A. (2018) From Broken Glass to Ruf Diamonds: Manchester hip hop, in Mazierska, W. (ed.) *Sounds Northern: Popular Music, Culture and Place in England's North*, Equinox Publishing, pp. 155-173.

Paor-Evans, A. (2020a) *Provincial Headz: British Hip Hop and Critical Regionalism*, Equinox Publishing.

Paor-Evans, A. (2020b) Urban myths and rural legends: An alternative take on the regionalism of hip hop, *Popular Music and Society*, 43(4), pp. 414-425.

Pardo-Guerra, J.P. (2022) *The Quantified Scholar: How Research Evaluations Transformed the British Social Sciences*, Columbia University Press.

Patterson, J.P. (2012) Radar: Context, *NME* (30th May 2012). Available online: www.josephjppatterson.co.uk/2012/05/nme-radar-context.html.

Paxman, J. (2007) *The English*, Penguin.

Peacock, D.K. (1999) *Thatcher's Theatre: British Theatre and Drama in the Eighties*, Greenwood Publishing Group.

Pease, D. (2000) Doing justice to CLE James' Mariners, Renegades and Cast Aways, *Boundary 2*, 27(2), pp. 1-19.

Pennebaker, J.W. (2018) Expressive writing in psychological science, *Perspective on Psychological Science*, 13(2), pp. 226-229.

Pennebaker, J.W., & Evans, J.F. (2014) *Expressive Writing: Words That Heal*, Idyll Arbor.

Pennycook, A. (2007) Language, localization, and the real: Hip-hop and the global spread of authenticity, *Journal of Language, Identity & Education*, 6(2), pp. 101-115.

Perach, R., & Wisman, A. (2019) Can creativity beat death? A review and evidence on the existential anxiety buffering functions of creative achievement, *Journal of Creative Behavior*, 53(2), pp. 193-210.

Pérez-Trullén, J.M., Ascaso, F.J., & Auría, M. (2018) Did poor eyesight influence Goya's late works? Medicine and art history in search for an interpretation of Goya's late paintings, *Acta Ophthalmologica*, 96(6), pp. 652-654.

Peterson, R., & Berger, D. (1975) Cycles in symbolic production: The case of popular music, *American Sociological Review*, Vol. 40, pp. 97-107.

Pettijohn, T.F., & Sacco, D.F. (2009) The language of lyrics: An analysis of popular billboard songs across conditions of social and economic threat, *Journal of Language and Social Psychology*, 28(3), pp. 297-311.

Phillips, D.C. (1993) Subjectivity and objectivity: An objective inquiry, in Hammersley, M. (ed.) *Educational Research (Volume One): Current Issues*, SAGE, pp. 57-72.

Phillips, D., Davis, C., & Ratcliffe, P. (2007) British Asian narratives of urban space, *Transactions of the Institute of British Geographers*, 32(2), pp. 217-234.

Pratt, A. (1997) The cultural industries production system: A case study of employment changes in Britain, 1984-91, *Environment and Planning A*, 29(11), pp. 1953-1974.

Presser, L., & Sandberg, S. (2015) *Narrative Criminology: Understanding Stories of Crime*, New York University Press.

Prévos, A.J.M. (1998) Hip-hop, rap, and repression in France and in the United States, *Popular Music & Society*, 22(2), pp. 67-84.

Prévos, A.J.M. (2001) Postcolonial popular music in France: Rap music and hip-hop culture in the 1980s and 1990s, in Mitchell, T. (ed.) *Global Noise: Rap and Hip Hop outside the USA*, Wesleyan University Press, pp. 39-56.

Priestley, J.B. (1934) *English Journey*, Heinemann.

Psathas, G. (1980) Approaches to the study of the world of everyday life, *Human Studies*, 3(1), pp. 3-17.

Puchner, M. (2018) *The Written World: The Power of Stories to Shape People, History and Civilization*, Penguin Random House.

Putter, K.C., Krause, A.E., & North, A.C. (2021) Popular music lyrics and the COVID-19 pandemic, *Psychology of Music*, 50(4), pp. 1280-1295.

Qiu, L., Chan, S.H.M., Ito, K., & Sam, J.Y.T. (2021) Unemployment rate predicts anger in popular music lyrics: Evidence from top 10 songs in the United States and Germany from 1980 to 2017, *Psychology of Popular Media*, 10(2), pp. 256-266.

Ramsey, G.P. (2003) *Race Music: Black Cultures from Bebop to Hip-Hop*, University of California Press.

Rank, O. (1968) *Art and the Artist: Creative Urge and Personality Development*, W.W. Norton.

Reay, D. (2000) A useful extension of Bourdieu's conceptual framework? Emotional capital as a way of understanding mothers' involvement in children's schooling, *Sociological Review*, 48(4), pp. 568-585.

Reay, D. (2005) Beyond consciousness? The psychic landscape of social class, *Sociology*, 39(5), pp. 911–928.

Redhead, S. (2007) This sporting life: The realism of *The Football Factory*, *Soccer and Society*, 8(1), pp. 90–108.

Reichl, S. (2004) Flying the flag: The intricate semiotics of national identity, *European Journal of English Studies*, 8(2), pp. 205–217.

Reisner, L., & Rymajdo, K. (2022) The 0161 rap gap: The marginalisation of Black rap musicians in Manchester's live music scene, *Popular Music*, pp. 1–14.

Resolution Foundation (2018) A new generational contract: The final report of the Intergenerational Commission, Resolution Foundation/Intergenerational Commission. Available online: www.resolutionfoundation.org/app/uploads/2018/05/A-New-Generational-Contract-Full-PDF.pdf.

Robbins, A., & Wilner, A. (2001) *Quarterlife Crisis*, Bloomsbury.

Robinson, O.C. (2015) Emerging adulthood, early adulthood and quarter-life crisis: Updating Erikson for the twenty-first century, in Žukauskiene, R. (ed.) *Emerging Adulthood in a European Context*, Routledge, pp. 17–30.

Robinson, O.C. (2019) A longitudinal mixed-methods case study of quarter life crisis during the post-university transition: Locked-out and locked-in forms in combination, *Emerging Adulthood*, 7, pp. 167–179.

Robinson, O.C., & Smith, J.A. (2010) Investigating the form and dynamics of crisis episodes in early adulthood: The application of a composite qualitative method, *Qualitative Research in Psychology*, 7, pp. 170–191.

Robinson, O.C., Wright, G.R.T., & Smith, J.A. (2013) The holistic phase model of early adult crisis, *Journal of Adult Development*, 20, pp. 27–37.

Rodman, G.B. (2009) Race…and other four letter words: Eminem and the cultural politics of authenticity, *Popular Communication*, 4(2), pp. 95–121.

Rogaly, B., & Taylor, B. (2009a) *Moving Histories of Class and Community: Identity, Place and Belonging in Contemporary England*, Palgrave Macmillan.

Rogaly, B., & Taylor, B. (2009b) 'I don't want to be classed, but we are all classed': Making liveable lives across generations, in Wetherell, M. (ed.) *Identity in the 21st Century*, Palgrave Macmillan, pp. 41–58.

Rogers, J. (2022) *The Sound of Being Human: How Music Shapes Our Lives*, White Rabbit.

Roks, R.A. (2020) 'Keeping it (hyper)real': A musical history of rap's quest beyond authenticity, in Siegel, D., & Bovenkerk, F. (eds.) *Crime and Music*, Springer, pp. 271–285.

Rossow, I. (1996) Alcohol-related violence: The impact of drinking patters and drinking context, *Addiction*, 91, pp. 1651–1661.

Roy, D.F. (1959) Banana time: Job satisfaction and informal interaction, *Human Organization*, 18, pp. 158–168.

Rukeyser, M. (2006) *Collected Poems of Muriel Rukeyser* (ed. Kaufman, J.E., & Herzog, A.F.), University of Pittsburgh Press.

Rundell, M. (2017) Metropolitan elite' is a lazy misnomer, in Bozek, R. (ed.) *The Political Elite and Special Interest*, Greenhaven Publishing.

Ryan, E.B., Pearce, K.A., Anas, A.P., & Norris, J.E. (2004) Writing a connection: Intergenerational communication through stories, in Pratt, M.W., & Fiese, B.H. (eds.) *Family Stories and the Life Course*, Lawrence Erlbaum Associates, pp. 375-398.

Rza (2004) *The Wu-Tang Manual*, Riverhead.

Saeed, S. (2020) A history of denial: The problem with the term 'urban music', *The National News* (9th June 2020). Available online: www.thenationalnews.com/arts-culture/music/a-history-of-denial-the-problem-with-the-term-urban-music-1.1031206.

Sanders, S.R. (1997) The power of stories, *The Georgia Review*, 51(1), pp. 113-126.

Sangalang, C.C., & Vang, C. (2017) Intergenerational trauma in refugee families: A systematic review, *Journal of Immigrant and Minority Health*, 19, pp. 745-754.

Sartre, J.-P. (1956) *Being and Nothingness*, Philosophical Library.

Savage, J. (1992) *England's Dreaming: Sex Pistols and Punk Rock*, Faber & Faber.

Savage, M. (2011) *Identities and Social Change in Britain since 1940: The Politics of Method*, Oxford University Press.

Savage, M., Bagnall, G., & Longhurst, B. (2001) Ordinary, ambivalent and defensive: Class identities in the Northwest of England, *Sociology*, 35(4), pp. 875-892.

Savage, M., Devine, F., Cunningham, N., Taylor, M., Li, Y., Hjellbrekke, J., Le Roux, B., Friedman, S., & Miles, A. (2013) A new model of social class? Findings from the BBC's Great British Class Survey experiment, *Sociology*, 47(2), pp. 219-250.

Sayer, D. (2014) *Rank Hypocrisies: The Insult of the REF*, SAGE.

Schmidt, M.H. (1998) An integrated systemic approach to marginal regions: From definition to development politics, in Jussila, H., Leimgruber, W., & Majoral, R. (eds.) *Perception of Marginality: Theoretical Issues and Regional Perceptions of Marginality*, Ashgate, pp. 45-66.

Schmitt, A. (2010) Making the case for self-narration against autofiction, *a/b: Auto/Biography Studies*, 25(1), pp. 122-137.

Schmitt, A. (2017) *The Phenomenology of Autobiography: Making It Real*, Routledge.

Schofield, J. (2003) *Caphouse Colliery: A Brief History of Mining* (3rd edition), National Coal Mining Museum for England.

Schoonhoven, M. (2006) Looking for the Blue Door? De Representative van Londen in Notting Hill, unpublished Master's thesis (Rijksuniversiteit Groningen).

Schredl, M., & Hofmann, F. (2003) Continuity between waking activities and dream activities, *Consciousness and Cognition*, 12, pp. 298-308.

Scott, M. (2014) *Media and Development*, Bloomsbury Publishing.

Sennitt, O. (2022) Man knocked unconscious and jaw fractured in city assault, *Eastern Daily Press* (6th October 2022). Available online: www.edp24.co.uk/news/crime/23028759.man-knocked-unconscious-jaw-fractured-city-assault/.

Shapiro, J. (2014) *Lawyers, Liars and the Art of Storytelling: Using Stories to Advocate, Influence and Persuade*, American Bar Association.

Sheringham, M. (2006) *Everyday Life: Theories and Practices from Surrealism to the Present*, Oxford University Press.

Shin, J. (2016) Corpus-based analysis on gendered items in hip-hop and country song lyrics, *Corpus Linguistics Research*, 2, p. 41.

Shusterman, R. (1991) The fine art of rap, *New Literary History*, 22(3), pp. 613–632.

Sibley, D. (1995) *Geographies of Exclusion: Society and Difference in the West*, Routledge.

Sinclair, I. (2002) *London Orbital: A Walk Around the M25*, Granta Books.

Sindelar, N.W. (2016) A moveable feast, *The Hemingway Review*, 36(1), pp. 120–126.

Sintonen, T., & Auvinen, T. (2009) Who is leading, leader or story? The power of stories to lead, *Tamara Journal*, 8(2), pp. 95–109.

Skeggs, B. (2000) *Formations of Class and Gender*, SAGE.

Skeggs, B. (2004) *Class, Self, Culture*, Routledge.

Skinner, C. (2022) 'There was something inside of me I needed to let out': Occupied masculinities, emotional expression and rap music in a Palestinian refugee camp, *Men and Masculinities*, 25(2), pp. 292–309.

Sligte, D., Nijstad, B., & Dreu, C. (2013) Leaving a legacy neutralizes negative effects of death anxiety on creativity, *Personality and Social Psychology Bulletin*, 39(9), pp. 1152–1163.

Slingerland, G., Kooijman, J., Lukosch, S., Comes, T., & Brazier, F. (2021) The power of stories: A framework to orchestrate reflection in urban storytelling to form stronger communities, *Community Development*, 54(1), pp. 18–37.

Smalls, S.P. (2018) Queer hip hop: A brief historiography, in Maus, F.E., & Whiteley, S. (eds.) *The Oxford Handbook of Music and Queerness*, Oxford University Press, pp. 121–142.

Smith, D.R. (2023) *The Fall and Rise of the English Upper Class: Houses, Kinship and Capital Since 1945*, Manchester University Press.

Smith, G.D. (2014) Seeking 'success' in popular music, in Randles, C. (ed.) *Music Education: Navigating the Future*, Routledge, pp. 183–200.

Smith, M.M., & Beal, B. (2007) 'So you can see how the other half lives': MTV 'cribs' use of 'the other' in framing successful athletic masculinities, *Journal of Sport and Social Issues*, 31(2), pp. 103–127.

Smith, P. (1996) *The Coral Sea*, Norton and Company.

Smith, P. (1998) *Patti Smith Complete*, Doubleday.

Smith, S. (1972) *New Selected Poems*, New Directions Publishing.

Smyth, H. (2003) Running the gauntlet: *A compact city within a doughnut of decay*, in Burton, E., Jenks, M., & Williams, K. (eds.) *The Compact City: A Sustainable Urban Form?*, Routledge, pp. 87–97.

Shneidman, E.S. (1973) *Deaths of a Man*, Quadrangle.

Social Mobility Commission (2022) State of the Nation 2022 technical annex B: Technical details, 'How do we define socio-economic background'. Available online: www.gov.uk/government/publications/state-of-the-nation-2022-a-fresh-approach-to-social-mobility/technical-annex-b-technical-details#how-we-define-socio-economic-background.

Sociological Review (2019) Thinking on the Move: The Possibilities and Problems of Walking Sociologically [webpage linking to output of the 'Thinking on the Move' conference held 5th–6th September, 2019]. Available online: https://thesociologicalreview.org/announcements/events/past-events/thinking-on-the-move-the-possibilities-and-problems-of-walking-sociologically/.

Sonke, J., Golden, T., Francois, S., Hand, J., Chandra, A., Clemmons, L., Fakunie, D., Jackson, M.R., Magsamen, S., Rubin, V., Sams, K., & Springs, S. (2019) Creating healthy communities through cross-sector collaboration [White paper], University of Florida Center for Arts in Medicine / ArtPlace America.

Speers, L. (2017) *Hip-Hop Authenticity and the London Scene: Living Out Authenticity in Popular Music*, Routledge.

Spitulnik, D. (1993) Anthropology and mass media, *Annual Review of Anthropology*, 22, pp. 293–315.

Stahl, G. (2015) *Identity, Neoliberalism and Aspiration: Educating White Working-Class Boys*, Routledge.

Stanford, K.L. (2011) Keepin' it real in hip hop politics: A political perspective of Tupac Shakur, *Journal of Black Studies*, 41(1), pp. 3–22.

Stapleton, M.L. (2016) *Marlowe's Ovid: The Elegies in the Marlowe Canon*, Taylor & Francis.

Steffy, K. (2017) Wilful versus woeful underemployment: Perceived volition and social class background among overqualified college graduates, *Work and Occupations*, 44(4), pp. 467–511.

Stoia, N., Adam, K., & Drakulich, K. (2018) Rap lyrics as evidence: What can music theory tell us?, *Race and Justice*, 8(4), pp. 330–365.

Stokes, M. (1997) Voices and places: History, repetition and the musical imagination, *Journal of the Royal Anthropological Institute*, 3(4), pp. 673–691.

Stone, E. (2004) *Black Sheep and Kissing Cousins: How Our Family Stories Shape Us*, Transaction Publishers.

Stratton, J. (2008) The Beastie Boys: Jews in Whiteface, *Popular Music*, 27(3), pp. 413–432.

Strawson, G. (2004) A fallacy of our age, *Times Literary Supplement* (15th October 2004).

Strawson, G. (2018) *Things That Bother Me: Death, Freedom, the Self, etc.*, New York Review Books.

Street, S. (ed.) (2014) *The Memory of Sound: Preserving the Sonic Past*, Routledge.

Sule, A., & Inkster, B. (2014) A hip-hop state of mind, *The Lancet*, 1(7), pp. 494–495.

Sule, A., & Inkster, B. (2015) Kendrick Lamar, street poet of mental health, *Lancet Psychiatry*, 2(6), pp. 496–497.

Swahn, M.H., & Donovan, J.E. (2005) Predictors of fighting attributed to alcohol use among adolescent drinkers, *Addictive Behaviours*, 30, pp. 1317–1334.

Swart, I. (2013) Overcoming adversity: Trauma in the lives of music performers and composers, *Psychology of Music*, 42(3), pp. 386–402.

Swinney, P., & Williams, M. (2016) The great British brain drain: Where graduates move and why, Centre for Cities. Available online: www.centreforcities.org/wp-content/uploads/2016/11/16-11-18-The-Great-British-Brain-Drain.pdf.

Sykes, O. (2018) Post-geography worlds, new dominions, left behind regions, and 'other' places: Unpacking some spatial imaginaries of the UK's 'Brexit' debate, *Space and Polity*, 22(2), pp. 137–161.

Tahir, I. (2021) The curse of graduating during a recession, *Institute for Fiscal Studies*. Available online: https://ifs.org.uk/publications/curse-graduating-during-recession.

Taraborelli, D., & Ciampaglia, G.L. (2010) Beyond notability: Collective deliberation on content inclusion in Wikipedia, in IEEE (2010) *2010 Fourth IEEE International Conference of Self-Adaptive and Self-Organizing Systems Workshop*, 27th–28th September 2010, IEEE.

Tatar, M. (2009) *Enchanted Hunters: The Power of Stories in Childhood*, W.W. Norton.

Taylor, B., & Rogaly, B. (2007) Welcome to 'Monkey Island': Class, identity and community in three Norwich estates, in Wetherell, M., Lafleche, M., & Berkeley, R. (eds.) *Identity, Ethnic Diversity and Community Cohesion*, SAGE Publications, pp. 61–74.

Teaford, J.C. (2008) *The American Suburb: The Basics*, Routledge.

Theiner, G., & Fogle, N. (2018) The 'ontological complicity' of habitus and field: Bourdieu as an externalist, in Cater, J.A., Clark, A., Kallestrup, J., Palermos, S.O., & Pritchard, D. (eds.) *Socially Extended Epistemology*, Oxford University Press, pp. 220–252.

The Law Pages (2022) Basildon Crown Court (21st January 2022). Available online: www.thelawpages.com/court-cases/Olusogo-Ayodele-Ajewole-34027-1.law.

Thomas, C. (2010) Negotiating the contested terrain of narrative methods in illness contexts, *Sociology of Health & Illness*, 32(4), pp. 647–660.

Thompson, E.P. (1963) *The Making of the English Working Class*, Victor Gollancz.

Thompson, E.P. (1965) The peculiarities of the English, *The Socialist Register*, 2, pp. 311–362.

Thompson, F.M.L. (1982) *The Rise of Suburbia*, Leicester University Press.

Thorn, T. (2020) *Another Planet: A Teenager in Suburbia*, Canongate.

Thorne, A. (2000) Personal memory telling and personality development, *Personality and Social Psychology Review*, 4, pp. 45–56.

Thornton, S. (1995) *Club Cultures: Music, Media and Subcultural Capital*, Polity Press.

Throsby, D. (2008) The concentric circles model of the cultural industries, *Cultural Trends*, 17(3), pp. 147–164.

Tickner, A.B. (2008) Aqui en el Ghetto: Hip-hop in Colombia, Cuba and Mexico, *Latin American Politics and Society*, 50(3), pp. 121–146.

Tillie Allen, N.M. (2005) Exploring hip-hop therapy with high-risk youth, *Praxis*, 5, pp. 30–36.

Toynbee, P. (2023) Polly Toynbee: What my privileged start in life taught me about the British class system, *The Guardian* (20th May 2023). Available online: www.theguardian.com/books/2023/may/20/polly-toynbee-what-my-privileged-start-in-life-taught-me-about-the-british-class-system.

Tripodi, F. (2021) Ms. categorized: Gender, notability, and inequality on Wikipedia, *New Media & Society*. OnlineFirst. doi: 10.1177/14614448211023772.

Tsjeng, Z. (2013) New noise: Context, *Wonderland Magazine*. Available online: www.wonderlandmagazine.com/2013/03/18/new-noise-context/.

Tso, A. (2020) *Literary Psychogeography of London: Otherworlds of Alan Moore, Peter Ackroyd, and Iain Sinclair*, Palgrave Macmillan.

Turner, R. (1947) The Navy disbursing officer as a bureaucrat, *American Sociological Review*, 12, pp. 342–48.

Twenge, J.M., & Campbell, W.K. (2009) *The Narcissism Epidemic: Living in the Age of Entitlement*, Simon & Schuster.

Twenge, J.M., Miller, J.D., & Campbell, W.K. (2014) The narcissism epidemic: Commentary on modernity and narcissistic personality disorder, *Personality Disorders: Theory, Research and Treatment*, 5(2), pp. 227–229.

Twenge, J.M., & Foster, J.D. (2010) Birth cohort increases in narcissistic personality traits among American college students, 1982–2009, *Social Psychological and Personality Science*, 1(1), pp. 99–106.

Tyler, K. (2020) Suburban ethnicities: Home as the site of interethnic conviviality and racism, *The British Journal of Sociology*, 71(2), pp. 221–235.

Tyson, E.H. (2002) Hip-hop therapy: An exploratory study of rap music intervention with at-risk and delinquent youth, *Journal of Poetry Therapy*, 15(3), pp. 131–144.

Tyson, E.H. (2003) Rap music in social work practice, *Journal of Human Behavior in the Social Environment*, 8(4), pp. 1–21.

Unterberger, R. (1999) *Music USA: The Rough Guide*, Penguin Group.

UK Government (2019) National statistics: English indices of deprivation 2019, Ministry of Housing, Communities and Local Government. Available online: www.gov.uk/government/statistics/english-indices-of-deprivation-2019.

Vallat, R., Chatard, B., Blagrove, M., & Ruby, P. (2018) Characteristics of the memory sources of dreams: A new version of the content-matching paradigm to take mundane and remote memories into account, *PlosOne*, 13(2), e0193440.

Vanaken, L., Bijttebier, P., Fivush, R., & Hermans, D. (2022) An investigation of the concurrent and longitudinal associations between narrative coherence and mental health mediated by social support, *Journal of Experimental Psychopathology*, 13(1), pp. 1–15.

Van Klaveren, T. (2016) Fetcham residents defend village over suggestion it is the 'fag end of Leatherhead', *Get Surrey* (19th December 2016). Available online: www.getsurrey.co.uk/news/surrey-news/fetcham-residents-defend-village-over-13647882.

Verstegen, I. (2011) Eminem and the tragedy of the White rapper, *Journal of Popular Culture*, 44(4), pp. 872–889.

Viator, F.A. (2020) *To Live and Defy in LA: How Gangsta Rap Changed America*, Harvard University Press.

Vice (2013) You Need to Hear This: Context 'Small Town Lad Sentiments' (Mike Skinner Remix), *Vice* (23rd July 2013). Available online: www.vice.com/da/article/rmadx8/youneedtohearthis-context-small-town-lad-sentiments-mike-skinner-remix.

Vito, C. (2015) Who said hip-hop was dead? The politics of hip-hop culture in Immortal Technique's lyrics, *International Journal of Cultural Studies*, 18(4), pp. 395–411.

Wacquant, L. (2002) Scrutinizing the street: Poverty, morality and the pitfalls of urban ethnography, *American Journal of Sociology*, 107(6), pp. 1468–1532.

Wade-Benzoni, K.A., & Tost, L.P. (2009) The egoism and altruism of intergenerational behavior, *Personality and Social Psychology Review*, 13(3), pp. 165–193.

Waggoner, B., Bering, J.M., & Halberstadt, J. (2023) The desire to be remembered: A review and analysis of legacy motivations and behaviors, *New Ideas in Psychology*, 69, 101005.

Walkerdine, V. (1984) Dreams from an ordinary childhood, in Heron, L. (ed.) *Truth, Dare or Promise: Girls Growing Up in the Fifties*, Virago Press, pp. 63–77.

Walsh, P. (2022) Man in 20s still in hospital five weeks after serious Norwich attack, *Eastern Daily Press* (26th April 2022). Available online: www.edp24.co.uk/news/crime/20626833.man-20s-still-hospital-five-weeks-serious-norwich-attack/.

Warren, R.P. (1969) *Audubon: A Vision*, Random House.

Waters, T.E.A., & Fivush, R. (2015) Relations between narrative coherence, identity and psychological well-being in emerging adulthood, *Journal of Personality*, 83(4), pp. 441–451.

Watkins, J. (2015) Spatial imaginaries research in geography: Synergies, tensions, and new directions, *Geography Compass*, 9(9), pp. 508–522.

Watson, A. (2008) Global music city: Knowledge and geographical proximity in London's recorded music industry, *Area*, 40(1), pp. 12–23.

Watson, A. (2020) Not all roads lead to London: Insularity, disconnection and the challenge to 'regional' creative industries policy, *Regional Studies*, 54(11), pp. 1574–1584.

Watson, M. (2018) Brexit, the left behind and the let down: The political abstraction of 'the economy' and the UK's EU referendum, *British Politics*, 13, pp. 17–30.

Watson, S. (2008) An extraordinary moment: The healing power of stories, *Canadian Family Physician*, 53(8), pp. 1283–1287.

Watson, S., & Saha, M. (2013) Suburban drifts: Mundane multiculturalism in outer London, *Ethnic and Racial Studies*, 26(12), pp. 2016–2034.

Webber, R. (2007) The metropolitan habitus: Its manifestations, locations, and consumption profiles, *Environment and Planning*, 39, pp. 182–207.

Weller, P. (2007) *Suburban 100*, Century.

Wells, S., Graham, K., Speechley, M., & Koval, J. (2005) Drinking patterns, drinking contexts and alcohol-related aggression among late adolescents and young drinkers, *Addiction*, 100, pp. 933–944.

White, H.L. (1931) The Social Significance of the Industrial Revolution, unpublished MSc thesis (University of Utah). Available online: https://collections.lib.utah.edu/dl_files/de/9c/de9c6ca09de4dd86387d3e35c3ddb9c50b49fb0d.pdf.

White, J. (2017) *Urban Music and Entrepreneurship: Beats, Rhymes and Young People's Enterprise*, Routledge.

White, J. (2020) *Terraformed: Young Black Lives in the Inner City*, Repeater.

White, J. (2021) Growing up under the influence: A sonic genealogy of grime, in Henry, W., & Worley, M. (eds.) *Narratives from beyond the UK Reggae Bassline: The System Is Sound*, Palgrave Macmillan, pp. 249–268.

Whitehand, J.W.R. (1975) Building activity and intensity of development at the urban fringe: The case of a London suburb in the nineteenth century, *Journal of Historical Geography*, 1(2), pp. 211–224.

Williams, B., Woodby, L., & Drentea, P. (2010) Ethical capital: 'What's a poor man got to leave?' *Sociology of Health and Illness*, 32(6), pp. 880–897.

Williams, J.A. (2020) *Brithop: The Politics of UK Rap in the New Century*, Oxford University Press.

Williams, L., Jones, A., & Lee, N. (2006) *Ideopolis: Knowledge City-Regions Enabling Norwich in the Knowledge Economy*, The Work Foundation.

Williams P. (1986) Class constitution through spatial reconstruction? A re-evaluation of gentrification in Australia, Britain and the United States, in Smith, N., & Williams, P. (eds.) *Gentrification of the City*, Allen and Unwin, pp. 56–77.

Williams, R. (2004) The Football Factory: Irresponsible, ill-timed and risible, *The Guardian* (12th May 2004). Available online: www.theguardian.com/football/2004/may/12/sport.comment.

Willig, C. (2008) Grounded theory, in Willig, C. (ed.) *Introducing Qualitative Research in Psychology – Adventures in Theory and Method*, Open University Press, pp. 34–51.

Willis, P. (2000) *The Ethnographic Imagination*, Polity Press.

Willmott, P., & Young, M. (1960) *Family and Class in a London Suburb*, Routledge & Kegan Paul.

Wimsatt, W.U. (1994) *Bomb the Suburbs: Graffiti, Race, Freight-Hopping and the Search of Hip-Hop's Moral Center*, Subway & Elevated Press.

Wimsatt, W.U. (2010) *Please Don't Bomb the Suburbs: A Midterm Report on My Generation and the Future of Our Super Movement*, Akashic Books.

Wines, W.A., & Hamilton, J.B. (2009) On changing organizational cultures by injecting new ideologies: The power of stories, *Journal of Business Ethics*, 89, pp. 433–447.

Wiseman, H., Metzl, E., & Barber, J.P. (2006) Anger, guilt, and intergenerational communication of trauma in the interpersonal narratives of second generation Holocaust survivors, *American Journal of Orthopsychiatry*, 76(2), pp. 176–184.

Wozniak, A. (2010) Are college graduates more responsive to distant labor market opportunities, *The Journal of Human Resources*, 45(4), pp. 944–970.

Wragg, J. (2016) Just don't call it trip hop: Reconciling the Bristol sound style with the trip hop genre, *Organised Sound*, 21(1), pp. 40–50.

Wright, J., & Chung, M.C. (2001) Mastery or mystery? Therapeutic writing: a review of the literature, *British Journal of Guidance & Counselling*, 29(3), pp. 277–291.

Wunsch, J.L. (1995) Review: The suburban cliché, *Journal of Social History*, 28(3), pp. 643–658.

Yalom, I.D. (1980) *Existential Psychotherapy*, Basic Books.

Young, C. (2020) Is this the end for 'urban' music?, *National Public Radio (NPR)* (15th June 2020). Available online: www.npr.org/2020/06/15/877384808/is-this-the-end-for-urban-music.

Zayed, A. (2023) Drill rapped jailed for 7 years after being caught with a gun in his Mercedes, *MyLondon* (5th July 2023). Available online: https://www.mylondon.news/news/west-london-news/drill-rapper-jailed-7-years-27257819.

Zimroth, P.L. (1974) *Perversions of Justice: The Prosecution and Acquittal of the Panther 21*, Viking Press.

Žižek, S. (1989) *The Subline Object of Ideology*, Verso.

Žižek, S. (2002) *Welcome to the Desert of the Real! Five Essays on September 11 and Related Dates*, Verso.

Index

Ackroyd, Peter, 40
Adulthood, 135–137, 149
Aidi, Hisham, 12
Allen, Kim, 125, 126
Ambition, 8–9, 10, 26, 123–128, 142
Ammo (Lamar Skeet), 85
Anthropology, 6, 73, 96, 97, 98
Archer, Graeme, 9
Archer, Louise, 124
Arnett, Jeffrey, 135, 136
Asakaa drill music, 103, 168
Ashon, Will, 22–23
Aspiration, 124, 125, 126
Atkinson, Paul, 82, 83, 84, 96, 99, 122
Authenticity, 14, 17, 82–84, 87, 152–155, 157, 167
Autobiographical memory, 66, 67
Autobiography, 23, 24, 86–88, 157, 164
Autoethnography, 24–25, 26
Autofiction, 23–24, 25, 65, 157, 164

Baker, Tim, 43
Ballard, J.G., *Kingdom Come*, 139
Ballico, Christina, 161–162, 163
Bandura, Albert, 39
Banlieues, 12, 103
Barnsley, 2, *32*
Barron, Lee, 94, 95, 96, 97, 99, 102, 122
Bartleet, Brydie-Leigh, 25
Baudrillard, Jean, 157
Baumeister, Roy, 66
Baumgartner, Mary, 5
BBC
   'Introducing' initiative, 19, 163
   Radio 1, 18, 19, 145
   Radio 1Xtra, 19, 27
Beal, Becky, 147
Beanie Sigel, 87
Beastie Boys, 13
Beauregard, T. Alexandra, 150n1
Beavis, Allana, 90

Becker, Howard, 96
Beer, David, 94, 96, 97, 99
Bender, Kimberley, 91
Bennett, Dawn, 75
Berger, John, 79
Bering, Jesse, 144
Berlant, Lauren, 102
Betjeman, John, 7
Bhattacharya, Kakali, 90
Bilston, Sarah, 8
Birkett, Caroline (née Chapman, sister), 39, 42
Black communities, 12–14, 28n4, 87–88, 93, 95, 137, 154, 165, 167
Blair, Tony, 28n7, 129–130, 150n3
Blues music, 84
Blumenfeld, Simon, *Jew Boy*, 8
Blur, 'Ernold Same', 124
Bochner, Arthur, 25, 65, 82, 83
Bolton, Gillie, 165
Boulton, Jeremy, 6
Bourdieu, Pierre, 4, 56, 72, 73, 74, 75, 125, 168
Bow, East London, 16, 94, 95, 154, 167
Bowers-Brown, Tamsin, 130
Bradley, Adam, 22
Brain, Kevin, 139
Breuer, Joseph, 64
Brexit, 2, 3, 26, 42
Bristol, 21, 51, 93, 94
Bromley, Rosemary D.F., 151n7
Bronfenbrenner, U., 67
Brook, Orian, 71, 72
Brooks, Peter, 81–82, 83, 84, 104n3
Brooks, Sally, 43
Broun, James, 42–43
Brown, Peter, 130
Bruner, Jerome, 66
Burnard, Pamela, 75
Butler, Tim, 125, 126
Byrne, Liam, 139

Campbell, William, 148
Camus, Albert, 150
Carey, Heather, 70
Cave, Nick, 85
Centre for Cities, 133-134
Chapman, Simon (brother), 39, 41
Chapman, Tracy, 43
Chicago, 94, 97, 98
Children and childhood, 64, 76, 136, 149
Ciampaglia, Giovanni Luca, 143
Class
   author family background, 38, 39
   definitions, 83n3
   and identity, 53-59, 74, 76, 150
   life stories as relational stories, 70, 72-73
   narrative and meaning, 150
   possibility and ambition, 128
   rap as music of the city, 13, 15
   representation, 9, 156, 168
   and stories, 63, 81
   writing goals, 26
Coherence, 149-150
Collins, Hattie, 102
Compton, Los Angeles, 16, 154, 159
Context (aka George Musgrave), 30-59
   overview, 4, 30-31
   class and identity, 53-59
   Context as George, George as Context, 23-25
   Context lyrics overview, 105-106
   family, 31-39, 39-53
   images, *18, 20, 32, 35*
   Mike Skinner on, vii
   MistaJam on, vii, 27
   music career overview, 18-20, 80, 103-106
   Sony signing, 19, 105, 128
Context songs. *See also* lyric themes (Context)
   overview, 105-106, 120-121
   'Afghan Letters', 115-116, 123-124, 134, 137, 162
   'Being 21 Goes', 119-120, 132-133, 134, 135-136, 156, 162
   'Choose Lager', 117-118, 135

'Dreams Don't Live Here Anymore', 125
'Drift' (with Phlite), 147
'Drowning', 19
'Frantic', 18, 134, 143
'The Harrier', 18, 145, 157
Hindsight is the Purest Form of Romance (EP), 19, *20*
'I Can't Kickflip Anymore', 112-113, 123, 133, 136, 140, 156
'In the Bag', 19
'Listening to Burial', 18
'Long Way from Nowhere', 110, 123, 131, 135, 137, 138, 146, 156
'Off With Their Heads', 18, 68, 151n9
'1.4 at 12', 111, 140
'Prince of Wales Road' (with Phlite), 139, 141
'Small Town Lad Sentiments', 19, 107, 124, 129, 130, 133, 134
Stealing My Older Brother's Tapes (EP), 19
'Stretch', 114, 127, 129, 137, 142
'This Is Us', 109, 127, 139, 143-144, 147, 161
'20Something', 108, 123, 136, 138, 141, 142, 156, 162
Cook, Jon, 72
Cowan, Jane, 98
Cowley, Jason, 28n10
Crazy Titch (Carl Dobson), 88-89
Creative work, 70-72, 83n1, 91, 125-128, 144, 149, 162-163, 165
Cribs (MTV series), 147
Criminal proceedings, 85-89, 100, 155, 168
Crocker, Frankie, 12
Crunk, 94
Cunningham, Gail, 10, 43

Davis, Fred, 97
Dawes, Robyn, 64
Dennis, Andrea, 85, 86, 104n1
DeNora, Tia, 63, 78, 79
Deprivation, 52, *53*, 125, 127
DeWall, Nathan, 149
Diary keeping, 40, 78, 87
Dickens, Charles, 34, 121n16, 135, 156

Dizzee Rascal, 95, 100, 102, 167
Donoghue, Jane, 28n7
Dorst, John, 5
Dražanová, Lenka, 46
Dreams, 127, 138
Drill, 85, 88, 89, 94, 103
Drinking, 138, 139, 140, 143
Drugs, 37, 86, 88, 90, 129, 143, 147
Durand, Alain-Philippe, 12
Durkheim, Emile, 147

East London, 8, 16, 94, 95, 102, 125, 127, 128, 168
Ebbatson, Roger, 1, 3
Eberhardt, Maeve, 154
Education, 59n3, 68, 74, 129-132, 150n3
8 Mile (film), 17
Ellis, Carolyn, 25
Emerging adulthood, 135-137, 149
Eminem, 13-14, 16, 17
Employment, 70, 72, 73, 128-137
England (overview), 1-28
   defining suburbs and suburbia, 5-17
   English spatial imaginings, 1-5
   knowing by doing, 17-25
   writing goals, 25-27
Englishness, 25, 26
Erikson, Erik Homburger, 67
Ethnography
   characteristics, 98
   defining, 97-100
   ethnographic vignettes, 40
   evocative ethnography, 25
   lyrics, truth and ethnography, 84-104
   rap as ethnography, 94-104, 105, 158
Ewence, Hannah, 8
Existentialism, 121n33, 144, 145, 146, 147, 150, 168
Eyers, Tom, 170n4

Family
   class experience, 72-73, 76
   'family folklore', 56
   intergenerational narrative, 67, 68-69, 80
   and naming, 68-69
   narrative storytelling, 67
   personality types in children, 76
   writing the narrative self, 164, 169-170
Family Narratives Lab, 151n11
Fatsis, Lambros, 88
Feiler, Bruce, 151n12
Fenton, Steve, 2
Fetcham, Surrey, 15, 43-48, 47, 131
Fight Club (film), 145-146, 148, 157
Films, 66-67, 95, 157
Finlayson, Alan, 151n6
Fivush, Robyn, 67, 67, 69, 151n11
Flags, 46
Fogle, Nikolaus, 74
'Folk' music, 84, 85
The Football Factory (film), 141, 157
Foote Whyte, William, *Street Corner Society*, 94
Forman, Murray, 94, 153, 154, 156, 159
Foster, Hal, 96
Foster, Joshua D., 149
Foucault, Michel, 63, 75-76, 77-78, 79, 168
France, 12-13, 24, 103
Frank, Arthur, 82
Franozi, Robert, 73
Freeman, Kara, 154
Freud, Sigmund, 64-65
Friedman, Sam, 69-70, 81
Frith, Simon, 10, 84, 85
Future, and work (as lyric theme), 128-137

Gangsta rap, 14, 86, 94, 137
Garrisi, Diana, 31
Geertz, Clifford, 27
Geographies, 26, 52, 72, 94-95, 153, 153-154, 154, 158
Ghana, 103, 168
Giesen, Carol, 59n1
Gildart, Keith, 10
Ginsburg, Faye, 95-96
Glaser, Barney, 122
Goffman, Erving, 79, 98, 155
Gold, Raymond, 98
Golden, Tasha, 90, 91
Goldie Lookin Chain, 103

Goldsmith, M., 64–65
Gottschall, Jonathan, 64, 82
Gould, Stephen, 64
Graduate employability, 129–132
Grandmaster Flash and the Furious Five, 'The Message', 93
Green, Nick, 10
Greenberg, Jeff, 144
Grime, 11, 16, 21, 88, 94–96, 99–100, 102, 122
Grocke, Denise, 92
Grossmith, George and Weedon, *The Diary of a Nobody*, 9, 10

Habitus, 74–75, 76, 81, 125–127
La Haine (film), 12
Halberstadt, Jamin, 144
Hammersley, Martyn, 59n3, 96, 98, 99
Hammou, Karim, 12
Hancox, Dan, 100
Hanson, Steve, 6
Haralambos, Michael, 84
Harris, John, 8, 10
Harrison, Angus, 17
Harrison, Anthony Kwame, 13, 14
Harvey, Lee, 130
Havoc, 101
Health research, 82
Hegelund, Allan, 46, 170n5
Hemingway, Ernest, 5
Heroin, 37
Hesmondhalgh, David, 83n1
Higher education, 21, 130, 150n3. *See also* universities
Hip hop
  lyrics, truth and ethnography, 94, 95, 96
  performing the 'real', 153–155
  peripherality in Norwich, 163
  rap as music of the city, 11–14, 17
  representation and 'representing', 153–155
  scholarship on, 21–22
  UK hip hop, 17, 21, 102, 163
Hip Hop Psyche, 93

Hjørnevik, Kjetil, 79
Hollingworth, Sumi, 125, 126
Home ownership, 132
Homosexuality, 86, 155
Hunt, Celia, 164
Huq, Rupa, 4, 7–8, 9, 10, 43
Hyperreality, 157, 170n5

Identity
  and class, 53–59, 74, 76, 150
  emerging adulthood, 136
  inclusion and exclusion, 52
  lyrics and truth, 89, 92
  national identity, 46
  places, people and identities, 158–160
  possibility and ambition, 126
  rap and storytelling, 77–80
  recognition and remembrance, 145, 148, 149
  and stories, 63–69
  writing the narrative self, 166, 168, 169
Idol, Billy, 10
Iggy Azalea, 'Fancy', 154
Ilan, Jonathan, 88
Illness narratives, 82
Immortality, symbolic, 144
Immortal Technique, 22
Indices of Deprivation, 52, *53*
Inner cities, 1, 6, 12–13, 93, 165
Intergenerational Commission, 132
Intergenerational narratives, 55, 67, 69, 80, 158, 169
Intergenerational self, 65–69, 73, 75–77, 80, 150, 159
Intergenerational trauma, 69, 73
Ireland, 137, 161

Jæger, Mads, 73
The Jam, 10, 22
Jay-Z, 87, 93, 95, 99, 166
  Decoded, 23, 96
Jones, Simon, 13
Joplin, Janis, 151n10
Joyce, James, *Portrait of the Artist as a Young Man*, 23

Kane, Thomas, 155, 160, 166, 167
Kassovitz, Mathieu, 12
'Keeping it real', 87, 99, 152. *See also* realness; 'realness'
Kekra, 12
Kelley, Robin, 14, 165, 170n3
Key Changes, 93
Keyes, Cheryl L., 88
The Kinks, 'Shangri La', 8
Klokker, Rasmus, 73
Knowles, Caroline, 40
Korea, 154
Kotilainen, S., 68
Kubrin, Charis, 88, 89, 93
Kuhn, Annette, 81
Kulish, Nancy, 64

Labour market, 73, 129, 132, 133
Lacanian Real, 153, 155, 170n4
La Etnnia, 103
Language, 64, 90, 154, 162
Larkin, Philip, 'Going, Going', 1
Latin America, 103
Lawrence, D.H., 62
Legacy, 143, 144, 145, 162
Life stories, 66, 69-77, 79, 158
Lifton, Robert Jay, 144
Lincolnshire, 2, 15, 41-43, 57, 131, 161
Liverpool, 8, 51, 164
Lizardo, Omar, 146
London
    author experience, 2, 15, 48, 105, 128, 137-139, 167
    class and privilege, 70, 72
    defining suburbs, 6-7
    and grime, 16, 21, 94, 95, 102
    lyrics, truth and ethnography, 93, 94, 95
    masculinity and violence, 137-139
    performing the 'real', 153
    peripherality, 161, 163-164
    possibility and ambition, 125-128
    poverty and deprivation, 51, 127
    rap as music of the city, 14, 15
    representation, 153, 161, 163-164
    representations of suburbanites, 8, 10

scholarship on rap, 21
work and the future, 133-134
Los Angeles, 14, 15, 16, 94, 153, 159
Louis, Edouard, *En finir avec Eddy Bellegueule* (*The End of Eddy*), 24, 65
Louth, Lincolnshire, 15, 41-43, 131
Low, Bronwen, 155
Lower Layer Super Output Areas (LSOAs), 52, 125, 126, 158
Lunatic (rap group), 12, 103
Lutz, Frank, 100
Lyrics. *See also* Context songs; lyric themes (Context)
    analysis of rap lyrics, 22-23
    and autofiction, 24
    Context lyrics overview, 4, 20-21, 30, 105-106, 120-121
    function of, 84-85
    lyrics, truth and ethnography, 84-104
    lyrics, truth and ethnography overview, 84-85
    as practice-based research, 20-21
    rap as ethnography, 94-104
    rap lyrics in criminal proceedings, 85-89, 155, 159
    representation of place and personhood, 152-160
    representations of suburbanites, 10
    and revelations, 90-94
    and stories, 62-63
    writing goals, 26-27
    writing the narrative self, 164, 166
Lyric themes (Context), 122-151
    overview of theme coding, 122-123
    masculinity and violence, 137-142
    possibility and ambition, 123-128
    recognition and remembrance, 142-150
    work and the future, 128-137

Mahalik, James R., 138
Mailer, Norman, 'The White Negro', 13
Malik, Kenan, 83n4
Máliková, Lucia, 161
Malinowski, Bronislaw, 97, 99

210 | Index

Manchester, 10, 21, 164
Mann, Robin, 2
Marcus, George E., 43
Margaret, Stacey, 6
Marginalisation, 7, 13–15, 52, 161–163
Martela, Frank, 149
Martin, Clive, 3
Masculinity, 87, 137–142
Massey, Doreen, 158
Masterson, Alice, 151n10
The Matrix (film), 153
Mauss, Marcel, 98
McAdams, Dan, 66
McAndrew, Francis T., 69
McFerran, Katrina, 92
Mckenzie, Lisa, 40, 41, 73, 128, 168
McLean, Kate, 66
McLeod, Kembrew, 11
McNally, Karen, 58
Meaning, 66, 73, 79, 144, 145, 148–150, 159
Measham, Fiona, 139
Media representations, 3–4, 7, 58, 66–67, 96, 157
Melville, Caspar, 16–17, 102
The Members, 'The Sound of the Suburbs', 11
Mental health, 27, 92, 93, 164, 167
Merrill, Natalie, 67, 69
Meyers, Fred R., 43
Miami bass, 94
Middle class, 3, 6, 70, 72, 73, 124
Millennial generation, 148
Miller, Jonathan, 9
Mining, 31–33, 36–37, 39, 59n1, 62, 68, 80, 168
Mishler, Elliot, 82
MistaJam, vii, 27
Mobb Deep, 102, 167
  The Infamous, 100–101
Mohanty, Satya, 83n4
Mortality, 144
Murder, 86, 87, 155, 159
Murger, Henri, *Scènes de la vie de bohème*, 23
Musgrave, Camille (daughter), 170
Musgrave, Charlotte (née Beaumont, wife), 49, 72, 73, 136–137, 165

Musgrave, Edith (née Hallhouse, grandmother), 33, 34, 36, 42
Musgrave, George (grandfather), *20*, 31–35, 36, 57, 62, 68
Musgrave, (George) Glynn (father), 33–39, 43–44, 55–59, 62, 68, 80, 101, 160
Musgrave, George (aka Context). *See also* Context; Context songs
  birth, 38
  childhood, 39–49
  as academic, 19, 21, 105, 167–168, 169
  Context as George, George as Context, 23–25
  family, 31–39, 39–53
  images, *18*, *20*, *32*, *35*, 55
  name, 68
Musgrave, George (son), 170
Musgrave, Jim (brother), 39
Musgrave, Victoria (née Hall, mother), 38–41, 43–44, 54–59, 62, 68, 123, 128, 137, 142, 150
Musgrave, William (brother), 32–34, *35*, 37, 42, 48, 55
Music
  author background, 36–37, 43–44
  as autoethnography, 25
  as ethnography, 96
  mental health and wellbeing, 27, 164–169
  narrative and meaning, 150
  narratives of death, 151n10
  peripheral music scenes, 161–164
  representations of suburbs, 4, 7, 10–11
  as storytelling, 27, 53, 63, 77–80, 83
  for trauma expression, 93
Music industry, 27, 90, 164, 167
Music-making, 53, 63, 77, 78–79, 93, 166
Music therapy, 85, 91–93
MWR, 103

Nairn, Ian, 43, 142
Naming, 68–69
Narcissism, 27, 148–149
Narrative
  function of lyrics, 84
  illness narratives, 82
  intergenerational self, 65–67, 69

life stories as relational stories, 70, 73, 74–77
and meaning, 148–150
narrative psychology, 26, 65, 75, 168
ontological complexity, 74–77
places, people and identities, 158–160
stories and identity, 63–67, 69
stories overview, 62–63, 80–83
writing the narrative self, 164–170
Narrative turn, 65, 82
NaS, 101
Illmatic, 100, 153
National identity, 46
Nayak, Anoop, 76
Negus, Keith, 40
Nelson, Amanda L., 151n7
Nelson, Katherine, 67
New York City, 5, 13, 15, 16, 93, 94, 100–101, 153–154
Nicholson, Graeme, 81
Nicolaides, Becky, 5
Nielson, Erik, 85, 88, 89
Noor, Poppy, 46
Norfolk, 58, 151n6, 158, 161, 162. *See also* Norwich
Norway, 79
Norwich
 author experience, 15, 43, 49–52, 56
 club policies, 120n5
 Context career, 17–18, 21, 105
 graduate employability, 131
 images, *50*, *53*
 masculinity and violence, 138, 139–141
 peripherality, 163–164
 politics of, 151n6
 possibility and ambition, 123–128
 poverty and deprivation, 51–52, *53*
 Prince of Wales Road, 127, 139–141, 146, 154
 representation, 154, 158, 163–164
 work and the future, 129, 131, 132–134
Norwich Union, 50, *50*, 123, 124, 131, 133, 139
Nottingham, 125
Nottinghamshire, 15, 40–43, 54, 62, 128, 131, 161, 165

Objectivity, 46, 170n5
Observation. *See* participant observation
O'Callaghan, Clare, 92
Office for National Statistics, 70, *71*, 132
Office for Students (OfS), 131, 134
O'Kenneth, 103
Olson, Eric, 144
1011, 85
Ontological complexity, 74–77, 80
Orwell, George
 Keep the Aspidistra Flying, 9
 The Lion and the Unicorn, 25
 The Road to Wigan Pier, 32, 83n2, 168
Osei, Reggie, 103
The Ozarks (TV series), 101–102

Paor-Evans, Adam, 22, 163
Pardo-Guerra, Juan Pablo, 167
Paris, 12, 13, 14, 103
Participant observation, 95, 96, 97, 98, 99
Partridge, Andy, 106
Paxman, Jeremy, 26
Pennebaker, James, 165
People Just Do Nothing (TV series), 103
Performance, 155
Peripherality, 5, 15, 160–164
Pet Shop Boys, 'Suburbia', 10
Pevsner, Nikolaus, 43, 142
Phillips, D.C., 170n5
Phlite, 139, 141
Photovoice, 91
Place, 14, 94, 152, 153, 158–160
Playlists, 28n6, 29, 59n2, 59n4, 60, 61
Poetry, 22, 91, 165
Possibility, as lyric theme, 123–128
Poverty, 12, 51, 68, 93, 102, 167
Practice-based research, 20–21
Pratt, Andy, 83n1
Presser, Lois, 91
Prévos, André, 12
Priestley, J.B., 3
 English Journey, 25
Prince of Wales Road, Norwich, 127, 139–141, 146, 154
Privilege, 56, 69–70, 72, 75–76
Prodigy (rapper), 101

Psychoanalysis, 24, 25, 64–65, 155, 168
Psychogeography, 26, 40, 102, 168
Psychology, 4, 7, 26, 62, 65–66, 75, 168
Public health, 85, 90, 92, 168
Punk, 10

Qiu, Lin, 90
Qualitative research, 82, 90, 95, 160, 165
Quarter life crisis, 135, 136
Queensbridge Houses, New York, 16, 100–101, 154
Queer identity, 155

Race, and racism, 11–15, 87–88, 141, 154
Ramsey, Guthrie P., 97
Rap music
  analysis of lyrics, 22
  and autofiction, 23–24
  as ethnography, 85, 94–104, 122, 152, 158, 169
  France, 12–13
  lyrics and revelations, 92–94
  lyrics in criminal proceedings, 85–89
  masculinity and violence, 137
  as music of the city, 11–17
  performing the 'real', 153–157
  places, people and identities, 158–159
  playlists, 28n6, 29
  rap battles, 17
  'realness', 170n1, 170n5
  recognition and remembrance, 142
  representation, 152–159
  scholarship on, 21
  and storytelling, 63, 77–80, 83
  tropes, 157
  White rappers, 13–14, 16
  writing the narrative self, 165–167
Reality, 77, 84, 85, 99, 154, 155, 157
'Realness', 99, 150, 153–157, 158, 159, 166, 167, 170n1, 170n4
Realness, 84, 152–158, 166, 170n1
Reay, Diane, 63, 74, 81
Recognition, as lyric theme, 142–150
Redhead, Steve, 157
Refugees, 69, 92, 137
Reichl, Susanne, 46

Remembrance, as lyric theme, 142–150
Representation
  overview, 152–153
  defining, 153, 170n2
  people, places and identities, 158–160
  performing the 'real', 153–157
  place and personhood, 152–160
  vignette on peripherality, 160–164
  writing the narrative self, 164–170
'Representing', 153, 154, 156, 158, 159, 167, 170n2
Research Excellence Framework (REF), 21, 28n9
Riessman, Catherine Kohler, 73, 73
Robbins, Alexandra, 135
Robinson, Oliver, 136
Robson, Garry, 126
Rock music, 10–11
Rogaly, Ben, 52, 124
Rogers, Jude, 28n6
Roks, Robert A., 170n5
Roots Manuva, 102–103
Ross, Rick, 156
Roy, Donald F., 97
Rukeyser, Muriel, 64
Rza, *The Wu-Tang Manual*, 23

Sandberg, Sveinung, 91
Sanders, Scott, 64
Sartre, Jean-Paul, 147
Saul, Thato, 103
Savage, Jon, 10
Savage, Mike, 6, 58, 83n3
Schmidt, Margarita H., 15, 161
Schmitt, Arnaud, 23, 157
Scott, Martin, 124–125
Self
  and autofiction, 24
  intergenerational self, 65–69, 73, 75–77, 80, 150, 159
  possibility and ambition, 126
  recognition and remembrance, 145
  stories and identity, 63, 65–67, 75, 77, 81

technologies of the self, 63, 77–81, 150
writing the narrative self, 27, 164–170
Self-efficacy, 39, 54, 74, 150
Sexuality, 90
Shakur, Tupac, 147, 155–156, 159–160, 166
   Thug Life, 166
   2Pacalypse Now, 155
Shapiro, Jason, 104n3
Sheeran, Ed, 18
Sheringham, Michael, 99, 168
Shyne, 166
Sibley, David, 52
Silverman, David, 82
Sinclair, Iain, 40
Sioux, Siouxsie, 10
Sitcoms, 8, 9
Skeggs, Beverley, 73, 125
Skepta (Joseph Adenuga), 'Bullet from a Gun', 68–69
Skinner, Mike, vii, 16–17, 19, 102, 139, 156–157
Smalls, Shanté, 155
Smith, Daniel, 26
Smith, Maureen, 147
Smith, Patti
   The Coral Sea, 22
   Patti Smith Complete, 22
Smith, Stevie, 9, 43
The Smiths, 10
Smyth, Hedley, 12
Social sciences, 65, 82, 160, 170n5
Sociology, 4, 6, 40, 56, 59n3, 65, 74, 82, 98, 168
Songs, 67, 85, 144. *See also* Context songs; lyrics
Songwriting, 43, 63, 79, 91–92, 93, 145
Sonke, Jill, 91
Sony Music Publishing, 19, 105, 128
Spatial identity, 158
Spatial imaginings, 3, 5, 101
Spitulnik, Debra, 96
Stahl, Garth, 124
Steger, Michael, 149
Stephens, Huw, 145
Stoia, Nicholas, 87, 89, 157
Stoke on Trent, 125, 126, 139
Stokes, Martin, 95

Stories and storytelling
   overview, 62–63, 80–83
   Context in context, 30–31
   English spatial imaginings, 4–5
   life stories as relational stories, 69–77
   lyric coding, 122
   lyrics, truth and ethnography, 84, 91, 97
   narrative and meaning, 149–150
   places, people and identities, 158–160
   power of stories, 4–5, 27, 73, 150
   problematised role, 81, 82–83
   rap and storytelling, 77–80
   recognition and remembrance, 145, 147–148, 149–150
   stories and identity, 63–69
   what stories do, why stories matter, 62–83
   writing the narrative self, 168, 169–170
Strawson, Galen, 81
Street, Sean, 28n6
The Streets, vii, 16, 19
   'Geezers Need Excitement', 139
   'Has It Come To This?' 16
   Original Pirate Material, 16, 102, 139
   'Streets Score', 157
Subjectivity, 78, 85, 153, 170n5
Suburbia
   analysis of lyrics, 123, 156
   author experience, 43, 44, 45, 49
   defining suburbs and suburbia, 5–17
   definitions, 5–7
   musical representations, 4
   possibility and ambition, 123
   psychology of, 4
   racial diversity, 14
   rejection of, 156, 168
   representations of suburbanites, 7–11
Suburbs
   analysis of lyrics, 22, 124, 139, 143, 148
   author experience, 40, 43
   defining suburbs and suburbia, 5–17
   definitions, 5–7
   English spatial imaginings, 3
   rap in the suburbs, 11–17
   rejection of, 168
   representation of place, 159
   representations of suburbanites, 7–11

Surrey, 15, 43–48, 131, 160–161, 165, 166
Sykes, Oliver, 3
Symbolic immortality, 144

Tahir, Imran, 132
Taraborelli, Dario, 143
Tattoos, 121n39, 147, 151n9
Taylor, Becky, 52
Teaford, Jon, 5
Technologies of the self, 63, 77–81, 150
Terror management theory, 144
Thatcher, Margaret, 9, 36
Theiner, Georg, 74
33 1/3 series, 100
Thomas, Carol, 82, 83
Thompson, E.P., 26
Thompson, Francis M.L., 8
Thorn, Tracey, *Another Planet: A Teenager in Suburbia*, 168
Thorne, Avril, 67
Throsby, David, 83n1
Toynbee, Polly, 72
Trainspotting (film), 135
Trauma, 69, 73, 85, 90, 91, 93
Trip hop, 94
Tripodi, Francesca, 143
Truth
  and autofiction, 23
  lyrics and revelations, 90, 92, 94
  lyrics, truth and ethnography overview, 84–85
  personal truth, 4
  rap as ethnography, 94, 99
  rap lyrics in criminal proceedings, 85–89
  and 'realness', 99, 156, 157
  and stories, 82–83
Tso, Ann, 40
Tupac. *See* Shakur, Tupac
Turner, Ralph, 96
Tuxford, Nottinghamshire, 15, 40–43, 54, 131, 165
Twenge, Jean, 148, 149

UK hip hop, 17, 21, 102, 163. *See also* hip hop
Unemployment, 72, 90, 129, 132

United States, 5, 6, 11, 12
Universities, 129–131, 136, 156
University of Cambridge, 54–56, 58–59, 72, 76, 128, 143, 156, 162
'Urban' music, 11–12, 13

Violence, 86–88, 137–142, 146, 155

Wacquant, Loïc, 99
Waggoner, Brent, 144, 145, 149
Watson, Allan, 163, 164
Webber, Richard, 126, 168
Wellbeing, 27, 149, 164–166
Weller, Paul, *Suburban 100*, 22
White, Harold Leroy, 31
White, Joy, 73, 168
Whitehand, Jeremy, 6
White audience, 13, 14, 165
'White power' music, 87
White rappers, 13–14, 16
Wiese, Andrew, 5
Wilde, Oscar, 86
Wiley, 11, 95
Williams, Beverley, 144
Williams, Justin, 13
Williams, Laura, 124
Williams, Peter, 168
Willig, Carla, 122
Willis, Paul, 95
Willmott, Peter, 6
Wilner, Abby, 135
Wimsatt, William, 11, 28n1
Worcester, 151n7
Work, and the future, 128–137. *See also* employment
Working class, 6, 12, 34, 70, 72–73, 128
Writing, purpose of, 25–27, 164–170
Wu-Tang Clan, 22–23, 166

XTC, 10, 106

Young, Michael, 6
Young Thug, 85

Žižek, Slavoj, 153, 159